FALLOUT

FALLOUT

A Historian Reflects on America's
Half-Century Encounter with Nuclear Weapons

PAUL BOYER

Ohio State University Press
Columbus

Library of Congress Cataloging-in-Publication Data

Boyer, Paul S.
Fallout : a historian reflects on America's half-century encounter
with nuclear weapons / Paul Boyer.
p.   cm.
Includes bibliographical references and index.
ISBN 0-8142-0785-5 (alk. paper). —
ISBN 0-8142-0786-3 (pbk. : alk paper)
1. United States—Civilization—1945–   2. Nuclear weapons—Social
aspects—United States.   3. Cold War—Social aspects—United States.
I. Title.
E169.12.B6845   1998
973.92—dc21   97-47144
CIP

Text and jacket design by Donna Hartwick.
Type set in Adobe Garamond by Graphic Composition, Inc.
Printed by Thomson-Shore, Inc.

The paper used in this publication meets the minimum requirements
of the American National Standard for Information Sciences—Permanence
of Paper for Printed Library Materials. ANSI Z39.48–1992.

9 8 7 6 5 4 3 2 1

CONTENTS

ACKNOWLEDGMENTS

THE AUTHOR WISHES TO THANK the following publishers, who kindly gave permission for the reprint of materials that initially appeared, in somewhat altered form, in newspapers, books, or periodicals:

"The Day You First Heard the News," *The New York Times,* August 4, 1985, Op-Ed. Copyright © 1985 by the New York Times Co. Reprinted by Permission; "The Cloud over the Culture: How Americans Imagined the Bomb They Dropped." *The New Republic,* Aug. 12 and 19, 1985, pp. 26–31. Reprinted by permission of *The New Republic,* Rights and Permissions; "'Some Sort of Peace': President Truman, the American People, and the Atomic Bomb," in Michael J. Lacey (ed.), *The Truman Presidency* (Cambridge: Cambridge University Press, 1989), pp. 174–202. © Woodrow Wilson International Center for Scholars. Reprinted with the permission of Cambridge University Press; "'The Fences Are Gone': American Policymaking in the Dawn of the Nuclear Era," *Reviews in American History,* September 1982, pp. 448–53. Reprinted by permission.

Five articles first appeared in *The Bulletin of the Atomic Scientists:* "A Historical View of Scare Tactics," January 1986, pp. 17–19; review of Fraser Harbutt, *The Iron Curtain,* May 1987; "Arms Race as Sitcom Plot," June 1989, pp. 6–8; "Is War Out of Fashion?" (review of John Mueller, *Retreat From Doomsday: The Obsolescence of Major War*),

October 1989, pp. 38–39; "The Rise and Fall of Project Chariot," May/June 1995, pp. 62–65. Reprinted by permission of *The Bulletin of the Atomic Scientists,* copyright © 1993 by the Educational Foundation for Nuclear Science, 6042 South Kimbark Ave., Chicago, Illinois 60637, USA. A one-year subscription is $30.

"Physicians Confront the Apocalypse: The American Medical Profession and the Threat of Nuclear War," *Journal of the American Medical Association,* vol. 253 (Aug. 2, 1985), pp. 633–43. Copyright 1985, American Medical Association; "Dr. Strangelove" from *Past Imperfect: History According to the Movies,* edited by Mark C. Carnes, 266–69. © 1995 by Mark C. Carnes. Reprinted by permission of Henry Holt & Co., Inc.; "From Activism to Apathy: The American People and Nuclear Weapons, 1963–1980," *Journal of American History* 70, no. 4 (March 1984): 821–44; "The Atomic Bomb and Nuclear War," chap. 4 (pp. 115–51) of *When Time Shall Be No More: Prophecy Belief in Modern American Culture,* by Paul Boyer. Copyright © 1992 by the President and Fellows of Harvard College. Reprinted by permission of Harvard University Press; "Star Wares: How SDI Will Change Our Culture," *The Nation,* January 10, 1987, pp. 1, 16–20. *The Nation* © 1987; "Exotic Resonances: Hiroshima in American Memory," Michael J. Hogan (ed.) *Hiroshima in History and Memory* (Cambridge: Cambridge University Press, 1996), pp. 143–67. © Michael J. Hogan 1996; "Whose History Is It Anyway? Memory, Politics, and Historical Scholarship," in *History Wars: The* Enola Gay *and Other Battles for the American Past,* edited by Edward T. Linenthal and Tom Engelhardt (New York: Metropolitan Books, Henry Holt & Co., 1996), 115–39. Reprinted by permission of the editors; "Variations on a Theme: Nuclear Menace in the Mass Culture of the Late Cold War Era and Beyond," *Journal for the Study of Peace and Conflict,* 1997–98, annual ed. (November 1997): 3–20.

I would like to thank the editors of the periodicals, newspapers, and scholarly journals who first provided a forum for these historical essays and speculative pieces. I am grateful also to the many groups and institutions, including churches, libraries, colleges and universities, activist organizations, and civic bodies, whose speaking invitations in the 1980s gave me opportunities to hone my ideas and profit from the views and perspectives of those in the audience. On several occasions both formal and informal, my colleagues at the University of Wisconsin's Institute for Research in the Humanities have listened patiently to, and commented helpfully upon, the various topics I treat in this book. Eric Idsvoog, my collaborator on chapter 14, also entered much of this manuscript on disk. My thanks go as well to Allan Winkler and James Gilbert for a critical reading of the manuscript, and to Tom Engelhardt for a most helpful reading of chapter 14. The copyeditor, Nancy Woodington, not only improved the manuscript through her careful and perceptive reading, but at several points offered thoughtful comments drawn from her own experiences.

Finally, I am grateful to Barbara Hanrahan, director of the Ohio State University Press, who responded so encouragingly when I proposed the idea for this book. Since my earliest experiences of the nuclear age took place in Dayton, Ohio, the city of my birth and early years, I take particular pleasure in publishing this book under the imprint of the Ohio State University Press.

INTRODUCTION

THE COLD WAR IS OVER; the nuclear arms race, at least in its most sinister form, is rapidly passing into history. Certainly grave nuclear menaces remain: the possibility of terrorist groups or such rogue states as North Korea or Iraq's acquiring nuclear weapons; the danger of regional nuclear exchanges—between India and Pakistan, for example; the future of aging nuclear power plants; the disposal of tons of radioactive wastes that will remain lethal for millennia. Nevertheless, the nuclear arms competition between the United States and the Soviet Union that terrified the world for more than forty years is, blessedly, a thing of the past.

I was forcibly reminded of this in December 1993 when I participated in a Defense Department symposium convened to develop plans for converting nuclear missile silos into national historic landmarks. Silos that once housed nightmarish weapons of mass destruction may soon become tourist stops for family vacationers on their way to Yellowstone, Glacier, or Mount Rushmore.

As the Cold War recedes further into the past, the moment is opportune for those who lived through all or part of that stressful time to begin seriously the process of historical assessment—not just of the diplomacy of the Cold War, but of its social and cultural ramifications as well. It is also a timely moment to remind the rising generation—for many of whom the Cold War and the nuclear arms race are merely words on the pages of history textbooks or grainy images in television documentaries—of the diplomatic, strategic, and technological realities that for decades profoundly shaped Americans' historical experience. This book is one historian's effort to explore one aspect of that vast and complex reality: its intense and continuing impact on American consciousness and culture.

As I sought to conceptualize the cultural effects of the nuclear arms race for this book, I found myself thinking metaphorically. In August 1946, at Bikini atoll in the Marshall Islands, the United States conducted the first of what would prove to be a long series of atmospheric tests of nuclear bombs in the South Pacific. In 1949, the Soviet Union exploded its first atomic bomb, launching its own decades-long cycle of atmospheric tests. By the mid-1950s, with the development of hydrogen bombs a thousand times more powerful than the city-destroying atomic bombs of 1945, the pace and intensity of each nation's testing program quickened. Atmospheric testing by the two superpowers continued until the Limited Nuclear Test Ban Treaty of 1963. (Testing by France and China continued for many years.)

Beginning with the U.S. Bravo test series of 1954, the public gradually awakened to a scary by-product of these tests: Cancer-causing strontium 90 and other radioactive materials released by the explosions were drifting over the globe and filtering back to earth, contaminating pastures, farmlands, lakes, and rivers. Concerned scientists raised the alarm, and despite a disinformation campaign by federal officials pooh-poohing the health hazards of radioactivity, the media publicized the danger, and the public became deeply alarmed. These fears, mobilized by activist organizations, played a crucial role in generating political pressure for a test ban—pressure that culminated in the 1963 treaty by which the signatories (the United States, the Soviet Union, and Great Britain) pledged to confine their tests to underground sites. In a larger sense, the test ban campaign helped lay the groundwork for a broader environmental movement that remained important in the 1990s, forty years after the initial wave of public fear and activism.

The whole episode proved a classic illustration of the phenomenon of unintended consequences. The government agencies, weapons designers, and military strategists who planned and conducted these tests did not deliberately set out to poison the environment or to cause strontium 90 to accumulate in mothers' milk, babies' teeth, or the grass eaten by grazing cows. And they certainly did not intend to stir a hornets' nest of reaction against tests and, to some extent, against the arms race itself. But these consequences followed directly from their actions.

This book is a study of the phenomenon of such unintended consequences. When President Franklin Roosevelt in 1939 authorized the research that led to the successful testing and use of the atomic bomb six years later, he had little awareness (so far as we know) of the far-reaching political and diplomatic ramifications of his decision, or of the social, cultural, and ethical consequences. When President Harry Truman made the fateful determination in 1945 to authorize the dropping of two atomic bombs on Japan, he may well have had larger postwar strategic calculations in mind (historians and the public still debate the question), but he almost surely had little idea that the use of the new weapon would resonate powerfully in American life for half a century and beyond, shaping not only Cold War strategy and diplomacy, but also the nation's art, literature, ethical discourse, religious life, and mass culture.

As journalists of the mid-1950s reported on the deadly by-products of H-bomb tests that were coursing through the atmosphere and settling inexorably back to earth, they popularized a term that atomic scientists had been using at least since 1946: *fallout.* Soon the word, often as part of the phrase "radioactive fallout," became all too familiar to ordinary citizens.

I've chosen this term as the title of this book, for the "fallout" from nuclear weapons was cultural as well as chemical. As early as 1954, *Time* magazine used the word in this metaphorical sense: "The most recent H-bomb test [by the Soviets]," *Time* observed (December 20, 1954), "was made in Siberia about three months ago, but the fallout of fear and worry . . . has by no means died away."

The "fallout" from the nuclear arms race, with its endless rounds of nuclear tests, was clearly not limited to strontium 90 and other deadly substances; it also worked its way into the mental and imaginative world of an entire generation, adults and children alike, producing not only nightmares, worried conversations, and activist campaigns, but also a diverse array of cultural artifacts, ranging from poems, novels, and paintings to popular songs, slang, movies, advertisements, radio shows, and television specials. Without close attention to this larger impact of the nuclear reality, large swaths of American thought and culture in the years after 1945 become opaque and incomprehensible.

This book probes the political, social, psychological, and cultural fallout of the atomic bomb from August 1945 to the mid-1990s. But it is not a conventional work of cultural history, and this invites some explanation and perhaps a bit of autobiography. My training is as a historian, and I have worked on a broad range of topics dealing with American social and cultural history. In 1980, having completed a book on moral reform in the American city, and on the lookout for a new project, I somewhat fortuitously decided to explore the intellectual and cultural impact of the atomic bomb in American life—a topic then very much neglected. As my research proceeded, and I realized the scope of what I had undertaken, I narrowed the time frame of my study to the years from 1945 through 1950. The results appeared as *By the Bomb's Early Light: American Thought and Culture at the Dawn of the Atomic Age,* published by Pantheon in 1985 and reprinted by the University of North Carolina Press in 1994.

Except for an epilogue briefly sketching the rhythms of America's political and cultural responses to the bomb from 1950 to the early 1980s, *By the Bomb's Early Light* was wholly concerned with the immediate postwar period. (An introduction written for the 1994 reissue touches briefly on the eventful decade that began in the early 1980s.) My rationale for limiting that work to the immediate postwar years still remains valid. In that fleeting period, nearly every theme, motif, and fear that would shape America's nuclear discourse for the next half century first emerged, in embryonic but clearly discernible form.

But the publication of *By the Bomb's Early Light* did not end my engagement with nuclear issues. Indeed, the writing of that book appears in retrospect as only a way station in a lifelong encounter that began with my own early nuclear memories, long before I took up the topic as a matter of scholarly interest. Those memories begin with the first news of the atom bomb in August 1945, and my hazy but very real awareness, as a ten year old, of the spike of fear that followed. Among my father's papers is a yellowing 1946 pamphlet entitled "A Statement of Purpose by the Emergency Committee of Atomic Scientists," with passages underlined by my largely apolitical, businessman father.

Then came the nervous talk of atomic confrontation when the Russians exploded their first atomic bomb in 1949 and the Korean War broke out soon after. Even sharper fears of nuclear war in the later 1950s and early 1960s followed, stirred by such movies as *On the Beach,* President John F. Kennedy's sparring with Soviet premier Nikita Khrushchev over Berlin, and the terrifying Cuban Missile Crisis. This, in turn, was succeeded by the uneasy interlude in the later 1960s and 1970s when Vietnam, Watergate, and other crises dominated the headlines without ever fully effacing one's awareness of the superpowers' arsenals of doomsday weaponry—arsenals that seemed to grow in numbers and menace despite periodic "arms control" treaties that were supposed to be reassuring.

My research on *By the Bomb's Early Light* in the early 1980s coincided with the wave of heightened nuclear fear that gripped the nation during President Ronald Reagan's first term. The nuclear-weapons freeze campaign, a grassroots movement calling for a halt in the testing, production, and deployment of nuclear weapons, emerged as the political manifestation of this fear. At the same time, a tidal wave of movies, television programs, rock songs, and science-fiction stories bore witness to the public's renewed obsession with the specter of nuclear holocaust. This outpouring of cultural expression spurred by nuclear fear echoed two earlier cycles, first in the immediate aftermath of Hiroshima and then in the late 1950s and early 1960s, when nuclear alarms and threats had similarly unleashed surges of media commentary, political activism, and cultural attention.

President Ronald Reagan, ever the master of television, undercut the freeze campaign with his dramatic 1983 proposal for a Strategic Defense Initiative, quickly dubbed "Star Wars" by the media and the public. By the end of Reagan's second term and into President George Bush's administration, upheavals in Moscow, the opening of the Berlin Wall, and the collapse of the Soviet Union itself heralded the demise of the Cold War, the end of the superpowers' nuclear arms race, and ushered in nothing less than a new era in world politics.

Curiously, however, the nuclear theme lived on, not only in serious discussion of the real dangers that remained, but also as a motif in pop culture and as a topic of sometimes bitter public debate. In 1995, the

National Air and Space Museum of the Smithsonian Institution announced an exhibit observing the fiftieth anniversary of the atomic
bombing of Japan and featuring the *Enola Gay,* the airplane that carried
the bomb to Hiroshima. A storm of controversy erupted as veterans'
groups, patriotic organizations, and headline-seeking politicians realized
that the exhibit would graphically portray the devastation and human
suffering the bomb had inflicted and, even more provocatively, include
a full range of views by diplomats, military leaders, and historians exploring the murky reasons behind Truman's fateful decision to use the
bomb against a nation already tottering on the brink of defeat. Half
a century on, the events of August 1945 still stirred uneasily in the
nation's memory.

As a historian, citizen, and (intermittent) activist, I observed and, in
small ways, participated in these events. Having chosen a research topic
that in 1980 seemed far from the center of public awareness, I found
myself by 1982 caught up in a sometimes hectic round of public speaking, journalistic writing, and activist strategizing at the local level as the
freeze campaign gained momentum. This book, *Fallout,* thus offers a
somewhat episodic record of America's political and cultural encounter
with nuclear weapons, both as I have written about this encounter as a
scholar and as I have experienced it as someone caught up in the events
of my time.

The essays reprinted here vary widely in character, from newspaper
op-ed columns, book reviews, and journalistic forays to personal reflections and more conventional cultural history that one finds in scholarly
periodicals. For all their diversity, however, these chapters share a common theme: the impact of nuclear weapons in American life from 1945
to the present.

The occasions that called forth these essays are as varied as the pieces
themselves. In part 1, the two opening essays on the earliest reactions to
the atomic bomb (chapters 1 and 2) appeared in August 1985—the fortieth anniversary of the atomic bombing of Japan—as an op-ed piece in
the *New York Times* and an article in the *New Republic.* I wrote the essay
on Truman and the bomb (chapter 3) for a 1984 conference on the centennial of Harry Truman's birth and then expanded it as a chapter in a
1989 book on his presidency. Chapter 4 includes a 1987 review of a book

on early Cold War diplomacy, and a 1982 review essay (my first published work on the nuclear theme) on a book about nuclear-war planning in the late 1940s.

The three essays in part 2 (chapters 5–7) focus on seemingly quite diverse but in fact interwoven aspects of America's nuclear culture during the high tide of the Cold War in the later 1950s and early 1960s: the health professionals and civil-defense experts who insisted that with proper planning, nuclear war would not be so bad; "Project Chariot," Edward Teller's bizarre scheme to use nuclear explosions in a zany "public works" project to convert the outlet of a small stream in Alaska into a major world port; and what many consider the greatest film ever made on a nuclear theme, Stanley Kubrick's *Dr. Strangelove.* Divergent as they seem, these three essays nicely complement each other, since the technocratic mode of thinking revealed in the civil-defense and medical planning for atomic war and in Project Chariot (what C. Wright Mills in another context called "crackpot realism") forms the real-life context for Kubrick's black comedy.

Once again, the nature and the tone of these three chapters reflect the circumstances of their original publication: a 1985 article in the *Journal of the American Medical Association* marking the fortieth anniversary of the Hiroshima-Nagasaki bombings; a 1995 review essay in the *Bulletin of the Atomic Scientists;* and a 1995 contribution to a general-audience book on the way moviemakers have handled historical themes.

Part 3, "Going Underground," offers two perspectives on America's nuclear culture in the years after the 1963 test ban treaty, when the nation's overt political and cultural engagement with the nuclear threat somewhat diminished—but by no means disappeared. Chapter 8, based on an essay first published in the *Journal of American History,* presents a bird's-eye overview of these years, and explores some of the reasons for the "nuclear apathy" that some observers discerned. Qualifying this view of pervasive apathy, chapter 9, drawn from my 1992 book *When Time Shall Be No More: Prophecy Belief in Modern American Culture,* suggests that attention to atomic war continued to flourish in these years in an unlikely source: popular writings on Bible prophecy.

Part 4 (chapters 10–13), on the "Reagan Round" of nuclear fear, activism, and cultural attention in the early 1980s—and its waning later in the decade—reprints some of my late 1980s essays on such topics as the nuclear-freeze campaign, the commercial by-products of Reagan's Star Wars scheme, and the views of college students on nuclear issues as the Cold War wound down. These essays appeared in the *Nation* and, again, the *Bulletin of the Atomic Scientists,* a magazine that has provided a forum for thoughtful commentary on nuclear issues from the very beginning of the atomic age.

Part 5, focusing on the period since the end of the Cold War, documents the "nuclear fallout" that continues to affect American culture and politics. Chapter 14, written with Eric Idsvoog, explores the persistence of nuclear menace in video games, Hollywood movies, and blockbuster novels of the 1990s.

The year 1995, the fiftieth anniversary of both the end of World War II and the atomic bombing of Japan, and especially the angry controversy surrounding the National Air and Space Museum's abortive *Enola Gay* exhibit, provided another occasion for consideration of the cultural resonances of America's half-century encounter with nuclear weapons. With these reflections (chapters 15 and 16), written more than fifteen years after I initially turned my scholarly attention to this topic, the book closes.

The very diversity of these essays and of the publications where they originally appeared is a major reason that the idea of gathering them into a single work originally appealed to me, as the chances of anyone's having read more than three or four of them when they first saw the light of day are surely rather remote! I have arranged these varied essays in a generally chronological order—based on the progression of historical events rather than the dates of composition—moving through the successive stages of the nuclear era, from the dawning of the atomic age in August 1945 to the retrospective moment of 1995 half a century later. Each section and each chapter has a brief introduction relating it to the book's larger contours and themes, and also suggesting something of the circumstances under which it was written. This epoch is not only one that I have studied as a professional historian; I have also lived through it, and its issues and concerns have engaged me as a citizen. *Fallout* is an amalgam of both my scholarly and my personal encounter with the bomb.

The text of the essays as reprinted here is close to that of the original publication. I have, however, made some changes, excisions, and additions to avoid duplication, smooth flow, cut excessive detail, or eliminate material not germane to the purpose of this book, such as paragraphs in book reviews that focused purely on matters of style or organization.

I have made these changes silently, rather than burdening the text with ellipses and brackets that, as someone has said, make the act of reading as laborious as climbing an endless series of picket fences to reach one's destination. Some of the pieces originally included footnotes, but for this book, with its more personal format, the scholarly apparatus has been dropped. The place of first publication of every chapter is clearly indicated, making it easy for anyone to consult the original text or, for those essays originally published in scholarly books or journals, to check a footnote.

Inevitably in a work that draws upon essays and reviews written on a single broad theme over a fifteen-year period, certain events, individuals, and historical developments are alluded to more than once, though in different contexts and from different perspectives. While most repetitions have been quietly edited out, not all could be eliminated without doing violence to the coherence and integrity of specific chapters. Where redundancies still remain, I trust the reader will not find them unduly distracting, and will understand the reason for their presence.

I

EARLY RESPONSES

H. G. Wells predicted atomic bombs as early as 1914, and in the late 1930s some scientists and science-fiction writers wrote of the vast and mysterious power of atomic energy. Nevertheless, President Truman's announcement of the atomic bombing of Hiroshima on August 6, 1945, sent shock waves eddying across America. Suddenly, unexpectedly, the nation and the world were hurled into the atomic age.

The reaction took many forms. Journalists, editorial writers, and religious leaders offered their perspectives. City planners, educators, social scientists, physicians, and other professionals saw opportunities to further their interests. Marketers and mass-culture producers seized on the national obsession with atomic energy. In a curiously symbiotic way, the responses and views of Harry Truman, the man who had made the fateful decision to drop the bomb, initially both mirrored and influenced popular attitudes toward the new reality. Meanwhile, out of public view, statesmen and strategists, too, struggled to adjust their thinking to the atomic bomb. The selections in part 1 explore some of the strands of this earliest phase of America's rendezvous with the atom.

1

THE DAY AMERICA FIRST
HEARD THE NEWS

August 6, 1985, the fortieth anniversary of the atomic bombing of Hiroshima, came at a moment of transition in Americans' perception of nuclear issues. The nuclear-freeze campaign, rhetorically checked by President Reagan's "Star Wars" address of March 1983, was clearly on the wane. But the dramatic changes in the Soviet Union launched by Premier Mikhail Gorbachev, who came to power in March 1985, had barely begun. U.S.-Soviet talks on bilateral nuclear-missile reductions in Europe, sidetracked during Reagan's first term, had at last resumed, but Reagan's November 1985 meeting with Gorbachev in Geneva still lay several months in the future.

Amid much uncertainty, nuclear jitters persisted. The fears roused by the rhetoric and the actions of Reagan's first term, and the resulting surge of antinuclear activism, remained potent cultural forces. In this context, the Hiroshima anniversary attracted much media attention, including a *Time* magazine cover featuring a mushroom cloud. In this setting, I wrote the following, which appeared as an op-ed piece in the *New York Times* on August 4, 1985.

WHERE WERE YOU when you first heard about the atomic bomb? My guess is that most Americans over the age of fifty can answer that question instantly.

August 6, 1945, was one of those days that stick in the brain. The most trivial details of such days can often be recalled decades later, simply because they are associated with the moment one first hears a piece of shocking or frightening news.

I must confess that the radio newscasts of that distant August afternoon have blurred a bit in my mind. But the newspaper memory remains starkly vivid. I can visualize just where the afternoon edition of the *Dayton Daily News* was lying in our kitchen when my eye caught the riveting headline. I can recall reading it aloud to my parents, mispronouncing the strange new word "A-tome" because I had never heard anyone say it before.

Other people, older than I, were also deeply shocked by Truman's announcement. It was a moment that, even then, struck many as a radical turning point in human history, and a surprising number felt impelled to put pen to paper and record their feelings and reactions.

In New York City, Norman Cousins, editor of the *Saturday Review of Literature*, spent the night of August 6 composing an impassioned essay, "Modern Man Is Obsolete." The atomic bomb had made nationalism outmoded and dangerous, he argued, and only a world government could save mankind. In Charlotte, North Carolina, a country-music singer, Fred Kirby, also spent a sleepless night after hearing the news. The next day, he wrote "Atomic Power," a song evoking grim images of divine judgment and apocalyptic destruction. It caught on immediately and, for several weeks early in 1946, was on *Billboard*'s list of top country favorites.

At his summer cottage in Kennebunk, Maine, the Rev. John Haynes Holmes of New York City's Community Church was enjoying the ocean view when he heard the report. "Everything else seemed suddenly to become insignificant," he wrote a few days later. "I seemed to grow cold, as though I had been transported to the waste spaces of the moon. The summer beauty seemed to vanish, and the waves of the sea to be pounding upon the shores of an empty world. . . . For I knew that the final crisis in human history had come. What that atomic bomb had done to Japan, it could do to us."

In Pelham Manor, New York, Patricia E. Munk had just returned from the hospital, having given birth to her second son, when the word arrived. "Since then," she wrote in a letter six days later, "I have hardly been able to smile, the future seems so utterly grim for our two little boys. Most of the time I have been in tears or near tears, and fleeting but torturing regrets that I have brought children into the world to face such a dreadful thing as this have shivered through me. It seems that it will be for them all their lives like living on a keg of dynamite which may go off at any moment."

The atomic bomb announcement elicited very little celebration. A few newspapers published gloating editorials and cartoons; a radio comedian joked about Japan's "atomic ache." Another said the bomb "made Hiroshima look like Ebbetts Field after a game between the Giants and the Dodgers." For most Americans, however, the news brought not joy but profound apprehension.

The *St. Louis Post-Dispatch* warned on August 7 that science may have "signed the mammalian world's death warrant, and deeded an earth in ruins to the ants." The next day, the *Milwaukee Journal* published a map of Milwaukee overlaid with concentric circles showing the pattern of destruction in Hiroshima.

The more highly placed the observer, it seemed, the deeper the uneasiness. Washington, a reporter wrote, was "pervaded by a sense of oppression." "For all we know," intoned the radio announcer H. V. Kaltenborn in his broadcast on the evening of August 6, "we have created a Frankenstein! We must assume that with the passage of only a little time, an improved form of the new weapon we used today can be turned against us."

This primal fear of extinction cut across all political and ideological lines, from the staunchly conservative *Chicago Tribune,* which wrote of an atomic war that would leave the earth "a barren waste, in which the survivors of the race will hide in caves or live among ruins," to the liberal *New Republic,* which on August 20 offered an almost identical vision of a conflict that would "obliterate all the great cities of the belligerents, bring industry and technology to a grinding halt," and leave only "scattered remnants of humanity living on the periphery of civilization."

From our contemporary perspective such cataclysmic imagery may seem so familiar as to be almost trite—if visions of universal destruction can ever become trite. But it is sobering to realize how quickly these dark visions surfaced. Within hours of Truman's announcement, and years before the world's nuclear arsenals made such a holocaust likely or even possible, the prospect of global annihilation already filled the nation's consciousness. In the earliest moments of the nuclear era, the fear that would come to haunt millions of people not yet born in 1945 had already found urgent expression.

In most cases, our memories of even the highest moments of public drama are eventually filed away. They become a reassuring part of our general stock of recollections, to be brought out and nostalgically relived from time to time. But August 6, 1945, is different. After forty years, it still has not receded into that safe and static realm we call "the past."

Kaltenborn's Frankenstein still roams; the *Post-Dispatch*'s kingdom of the ants still waits in the wings. The stab of fear we felt when we read that first newspaper headline or heard that first radio bulletin may not occupy the center of our awareness, but it remains with us still.

2

How Americans Imagined the Bomb They Dropped

This essay, adapted from an article published in the August 12 and 19, 1985, issue of the *New Republic,* further underscores the upsurge of journalistic attention to America's nuclear history elicited by the fortieth anniversary of the first use of the atomic bomb. In this piece, I offered an overview of the nation's earliest, confused responses to the atomic bomb in the immediate postwar period and reflected on Americans' forty-year effort to come to terms with the fact that their nation had used the bomb to destroy two cities in 1945.

"HIROSHIMA." "NAGASAKI." The very words, familiar to the point of banality but restlessly alive, remind us that we have yet to assimilate fully what they represent to our political, cultural, or moral history. "After the passage of nearly four decades and a concomitant growth in our understanding of the ever growing horror of nuclear war," declared the American Catholic bishops in 1983, "we must shape the climate of opinion which will make it possible for our country to express profound sorrow over the atomic bombing of 1945. Without that sorrow, there is no possibility of finding a way to repudiate future use of nuclear weapons."

Catholic bishops choose words with precision. Not remorse, not shame—only sorrow. Yet even that minimal standard seems beyond us. Peace activists will observe the anniversary of the bombing on August 6, but most Americans will ignore it, lapse into banalities about the distant beginnings of the "atomic age," or debate once again the well-worn political questions surrounding the decision to drop the bomb—important questions, to be sure, but so familiar that they have taken on a ritualized quality, in which every response to every point is known in advance.

The bishops are far from alone in concluding that we have failed as a people to come to terms with Hiroshima and Nagasaki. As early as 1946, Mary McCarthy described Hiroshima as "a kind of hole in human history." A few year ago I interviewed Ralph Lapp, the Manhattan Project physicist who later became a vigorous critic of the nuclear arms race. One of his comments was particularly striking: "If the memory of things is to deter, where is that memory? Hiroshima . . . has been taken out of the American conscience, eviscerated, extirpated."

To understand why, we must go back to the beginning. How did Americans first respond to the knowledge that official actions taken by their leaders had resulted in the instantaneous obliteration of two cities and the death of well over 100,000 human beings? In the public-opinion polls, the approval ratings stood at about 85 percent, with what *Fortune* magazine called "a considerable minority of disappointed savagery" wishing that even more Japanese cities had been wiped out. A Wisconsin woman expressed her genocidal impulses in a letter to the *Milwaukee Journal:* "When one sets out to destroy vermin, does one try to leave a few alive in the nest? Certainly not."

At all levels of American culture, there was an almost compulsive post-Hiroshima effort to trivialize the event and avoid its deeper implications. The *New Republic,* ridiculing reports from Japanese sources of contamination by radiation in the destroyed cities, commented on September 24, 1945: "If radioactivity is present in the soil, such plants will be marked by an unusual number of sports and mutations. Here is the ideal job for Emperor Hirohito, an amateur geneticist. . . . Let him go to Hiroshima, sit among the ruins, and watch the mutations grow." By 1947 the Manhattan telephone directory listed forty-five companies that had incorporated the magic word "atomic" in their names, among them the Atomic Undergarment Company. General Mills that year offered kiddies a genuine "Atomic 'Bomb' Ring" for fifteen cents and a Kix cereal box top.

There were exceptions, of course, to this denial of the enormity of the event. From the first, some Americans reacted to Hiroshima and Nagasaki with dismay and anguish. "King Herod's slaughter of the innocents—an atrocity committed in the name of defense—destroyed no more than a few hundred children," a professor at Chicago Theological Seminary wrote in *Christian Century* magazine. "Today, a single atomic bomb slaughters tens of thousands of children and their mothers and fathers. Newspapers and radio acclaim it a great victory. Victory for what?" A somewhat unexpected voice of moral protest was that of David Lawrence, editor of the conservative magazine *United States News.* And in the African American press, such intellectuals and organizational leaders as W. E. B. Du Bois, Langston Hughes, Walter White, and others raised charges of racism in the decision to use the atomic bomb against a darker-skinned people.

Generally speaking, however, the media and the public as a whole approved of the bombing of Japan. This was, after all, wartime. For nearly four years Americans had been subjected to anti-Japanese propaganda, some of an incredibly crude racist character, and this racism spilled over into initial reactions to the bomb. The *Philadelphia Inquirer*'s political cartoonist pictured an apelike creature staring up in gaping incomprehension as the bomb bursts overhead.

President Truman's initial announcement linked Japan's surprise attack at Pearl Harbor to the retribution meted out at Hiroshima, and this moral symmetry appealed to many early postwar commentators on the bomb. In his influential 1946 book *Dawn over Zero,* William L. Laurence of the *New York Times,* the Manhattan Project's official chronicler, described his feelings aboard the plane headed for Nagasaki: "Does one feel any pity or compassion for the poor devils about to die? Not when one thinks of Pearl Harbor and of the Death March on Bataan." Given the intensity of this war spirit, it is hardly surprising that with rare exceptions Hiroshima and Nagasaki figure hardly at all in early postwar American fiction or poetry.

Awareness of the magnitude of the civilian toll at Hiroshima was initially blunted by President Truman's announcement, which declared: "The world will note that the first atomic bomb was dropped on Hiroshima, a military base. That was because we wished in this first attack to avoid, insofar as possible, the killing of civilians." Of course, Americans quickly realized that Hiroshima was not a Japanese Fort Benning, but a major city. Even then, however, they did not respond with the shock that a totally unprecedented innovation in strategic bombing policy might have elicited. By August 1945, Americans were conditioned to accept the slaughter of civilian populations as a legitimate military practice. At Dresden, Hamburg, and other German cities, and then in the Japanese war, the obliteration of cities had become the de facto Allied bombing strategy. More civilians died in the Tokyo firebombing raid of March 10, 1945, than perished at Hiroshima.

The most compelling factor of all in shaping the initial American response to Hiroshima was surely the universal insistence of policymakers and opinion leaders that the only alternative to the atomic bomb would have been a land invasion of Japan costing hundreds of thousands of American lives. A few challenged this assertion. The Manhattan Project scientists who had urgently advocated a demonstration shot prior to all-out military use continued to raise questions after the war's end. Reports of Japanese peace feelers in early August quickly surfaced after V-J Day. In *Fear, War, and the Bomb* (1948), the Nobel Prize-winning British physicist (and political leftist) P. M. S. Blackett suggested that power calculations involving the Soviet Union had figured importantly in Washington's decision.

For the vast majority of Americans, however, the theme that the atomic bomb "saved American lives" took deep root, obviating the need for any further discussion. Blackett's realpolitik argument was angrily denounced by most American reviewers. (Not until the 1960s, in a very different political climate, would this "revisionist" interpretation gain a serious hearing.) Dwight Macdonald was one of the very few to challenge the moral legitimacy of this argument; it could, he said, be used to rationalize "*any* atrocious action, absolutely *any* one." But his was a lonely voice in 1945. Some took the argument even further, claiming that the bomb had saved *Japanese* lives as well by bringing a hopeless struggle to a decisive conclusion. As the *Chicago Tribune* put it in commenting on the American leaders' atomic bomb decision: "Being merciless, they were merciful." A *Tribune* editorial made the point visually, picturing a dove of peace flying over Japan with an atomic bomb in its beak.

Any consideration of the early cultural response to Hiroshima must take into account John Hersey's remarkable work of 1946. Published first in a single issue of the *New Yorker* and then as a book, and now reissued with a new chapter for the fortieth anniversary, Hersey's *Hiroshima,* with its straightforward factual account of the experiences of six ordinary men and women during and after the atomic bombing, helped transform the caricatured "Japs" of wartime propaganda back into Japanese—into fellow human beings. This was unquestionably a significant achievement, and one for which Hersey has been deservedly praised. But it has proven extraordinarily difficult for critics and cultural historians to assess his work's broader impact. For many readers the effect seems to have been at once intensely moving and curiously passive. Hersey's restrained, uninflected *New Yorker* prose offered a kind of expiation and catharsis, a closing of accounts on a troubling episode, rather than a challenge to push on to a deeper, more threatening engagement with it.

That the response of most Americans to Hiroshima and Nagasaki froze immediately at the surface level, never moving to a deeper plane of moral complexity, is surely attributable in large part to the fact that the nation's media and molders of opinion quickly turned to other aspects of the atomic energy story. Within hours of Truman's announcement, newspapers and magazines were offering detailed explanations of nuclear physics, long self-congratulatory histories of the Manhattan Project, and euphoric discussions of an atomic-energy utopia of limitless power, atomic cars and planes, medical wonders, boundless leisure, and revolutions in agriculture. That this latest scientific wonder had burst on the world's consciousness through the obliteration of a city seemed merely a regrettable piece of bad luck—rather as though electricity, with all its benefits, had first become known through the mass electrocution of several hundred thousand people.

Some went further, suggesting that the destruction of Hiroshima and Nagasaki had been an essential step in making atomic energy available for peaceful purposes. Similarly, those who believed that the atomic bomb would assure world peace by making war too horrible to contemplate stressed the symbolic importance of the event. "Never in all the long history of human slaughter have lives been lost to greater purpose," *Reader's Digest* declared reassuringly in November 1945; all mankind was now united by bonds "fused unbreakably in the diabolical heat of those explosions."

Hiroshima and Nagasaki penetrated the postwar American

consciousness in another important symbolic respect as well: as examples of what might lie ahead for American cities. At the moment of victory, the nation suddenly felt itself naked and vulnerable, and Hiroshima became the emblem of that vulnerability. "In that terrible flash 10,000 miles away," wrote Washington correspondent James Reston in the *New York Times,* men and women in the capital had "glimpsed the future of America."

The immense symbolic and polemical value of Hiroshima and Nagasaki was heavily exploited by activist scientists and others who in 1946 sought to arouse public support for the Acheson-Lilienthal international control plan. "Only one tactic is dependable—the preaching of doom," one scientist told the *New Yorker;* anything else was "met with yawns." Without international control of the atom, Americans were endlessly warned, the fate of these two cities would be theirs as well.

Highly effective as propaganda, this shorthand use of "Hiroshima" and "Nagasaki" as abstract cautionary devices further diminished the capacity of Americans to respond directly to the actual fate of two real cities. The emotional thrust of the 1946 fear campaign was directed forward to possible future atomic holocausts, not backward to what had already occurred. Indeed, one international control activist urged the pacifist A. J. Muste to mute his criticism of the atomic bombing of Japan, since it was diverting attention from the important political task at hand. Muste, however, like the Catholic bishops in 1983, was convinced that the nuclear future and the nuclear past were inextricably linked. Without confronting Hiroshima and Nagasaki, he later wrote, "no political or moral appraisal of our age is adequate, no attempt to find an answer to its dilemmas and destiny offers hope."

This brings us to the final, perhaps the underlying, reason why the American people proved so reluctant to grapple with the full implications of Hiroshima and Nagasaki after the war, and why after forty years we still approach with such uncertainty the events of that distant August. The nuclear obliteration of two cities on orders from Washington forced Americans of 1945—and forces us today—to face up to the extent to which the fighting of World War II had descended into wholesale, indiscriminate slaughter. And this recognition, in turn, seems seriously to compromise the moral clarity of what has come to be called "The Good

War." In contrast to the ambiguities of some of America's military involvements since 1945, World War II united the American people in what was seen almost universally as a wholly justifiable struggle against forces that represented the very embodiment of evil. But the nuclear devastation of Hiroshima and Nagasaki, coupled with the destruction of other cities by "conventional" means, adds an unsettlingly discordant note. To contemplate Hiroshima and Nagasaki unblinkingly is to confront our recent moral history in the most radical way imaginable. Few were ready to do that in 1945. Few have been prepared to do it since.

Thus the American cultural and intellectual engagement with Hiroshima has remained episodic and inconclusive. The reasons are clear enough. Hiroshima challenges not only our view of World War II, but also some of our most deep-seated beliefs about the meaning of our national experience. For years, cultural historians have noted the power and the tenacity of the myth of American innocence: the belief that we are somehow set apart from the other nations of the world, our motives higher, our methods purer. This myth has never lacked critics, of course, and as early as the 1920s it came under massive challenge. But it remained potent well after World War II, and is far from dead today. It is very difficult, to say the least, to fit Hiroshima into a moral schema rooted in a national mythology of innocence and exceptionalism.

Hiroshima raises in the starkest imaginable fashion that most troublesome of ethical dilemmas: At what point are good motives corrupted and perverted by the means employed to achieve them? If that point was not reached at Hiroshima—and certainly at Nagasaki—at what conceivable point in the actions of a nation-state would it be reached? These are not questions for which our image of America has prepared us. Consider, for example, Freeman Dyson's reflections, in *Disturbing the Universe,* on the anger of many American atomic scientists when J. Robert Oppenheimer, in a famous comment of 1948, described them having "known sin":

> They lacked the tragic sense of life which was deeply ingrained in every European of my generation [the generation of the First World War]. They had never lived with tragedy and had no feeling for it. Having no sense of tragedy, they also had no sense of guilt. They seemed

very young and innocent although most of them were older than I was. They had come through the war without scars. Los Alamos had been for them a great lark. It left their innocence untouched. That was why they were unable to accept Oppy's statement as expressing a truth about themselves.

Hiroshima challenges another foundation stone of American culture as well: our proud pragmatism, the tradition of William James and John Dewey. Absolutist thinking must be abandoned, James insisted; the best test of truth is its practical usefulness in helping us achieve our purposes. Give up abstract moralizing, Dewey agreed; accept reality as it actually presents itself and concentrate on shaping it toward intelligently formulated social ends. The same experimental method that gave rise to modern science, he said, must now be applied in the social realm. In practice, this philosophy led Dewey to lend enthusiastic support to American intervention in World War I. That conflict, he believed, could be utilized by engaged intellectuals for progressive purposes at home and abroad.

The pragmatic tradition is not conducive to the taking of principled moral stands. (Those like Jane Addams and Randolph Bourne who did take such a stand in 1917–18 found themselves exiled to the margin, if not ostracized.) But if Hiroshima does not demand that one at least most seriously consider such a stand, what situation possibly could? The experimental ethic is serviceable when the results of a failed "experiment" can be corrected with relative ease. It is less satisfactory in helping us formulate a position toward decisions like the one President Truman faced in August 1945—and others may face in the future.

Finally, our national discourse over Hiroshima remains so deeply troubling because it is not merely about a past event, however divisive or traumatic, but also about contemporary public policy issues of the gravest import. Culture and politics are never wholly separable, of course, but in this instance they are interwoven in a particularly complex and volatile way. Our sporadic but continuing effort to come to terms with Hiroshima is part of our larger struggle to clarify, collectively and individually, our view of World War II, our vision of America, our characteristic approach to issues of ethics and value, and is, finally, a way to comprehend the nuclear reality itself.

3

PRESIDENT TRUMAN, THE AMERICAN PEOPLE, AND THE ATOMIC BOMB

Like the essays reprinted in chapters 1 and 2, this one, too, was occasioned by an anniversary: not another A-bomb anniversary this time, but the centennial of Harry Truman's birth (1884). In 1983, I received an invitation to participate in a scholarly conference marking this event, to be held the following year at the Smithsonian Institution's Woodrow Wilson International Center for Scholars. This conference provided an occasion for me to link my research on the responses of the American people to the atomic bomb, a topic in which I was then immersed, with Truman's own public pronouncements and (scanty) private reflections on the bomb.

As I prepared my paper, I was struck by the parallelism of the responses the bomb elicited from the American people and from the American president—responses ranging from giddy euphoria and rigid self-justification to sober second thoughts and uneasy fears. This chapter is adapted from the paper I first presented orally at that 1984 conference, and then expanded for the published volume of conference papers (Michael J. Lacey, ed., *The Truman Presidency* [New York: Cambridge University Press, 1989]). My principal memory from the conference itself is of Truman adviser Clark Clifford commenting emotionally on how many lives the atomic bomb had spared, Japanese as well as American, by rendering unnecessary an invasion of Japan—a faithful echo of an argument Truman himself had often advanced.

FOR MILLIONS OF AMERICANS born before World War II, memories of President Truman are inextricably interwoven with memories of the atomic bomb. To be sure, Franklin D. Roosevelt had launched the Manhattan Project, but that was all in secret. It was Truman who announced the staggering news to the world on August 6, 1945, who was central to the controversies of 1946–47 over both domestic and international control of atomic energy, who announced the first Russian atomic-bomb test in September 1949, and who in January 1950 authorized development of the hydrogen bomb.

For anyone interested in Harry Truman and his presidency, the question of the atomic bomb is clearly central. For the historian concerned with the bomb's effect on American thought and culture, Truman is a key figure. Curiously, however, neither Truman scholars nor historians studying the evolution of popular attitudes toward nuclear weapons have given Truman's comments about the atomic bomb the close attention that one might expect. We have excellent studies of Truman's role in the diplomacy, strategy, and domestic politics of the early postwar period as they related to the atomic bomb, but relatively little attention has been given to a systematic analysis of his views on the atomic bomb per se.

One reason for this is probably the elusive nature of the evidence. Truman had a good deal to say about the atomic bomb, as about most subjects, but much of it was ad hoc and fragmentary. Rarely, if ever, did he offer a comprehensive account of the development of his view of the bomb and its meaning. Adding to the challenge is the fact that Truman commented on the bomb at three quite distinct levels of discourse, two of which have only gradually become accessible to historians. The first level (public pronouncements, formal addresses, messages to Congress, and so on) has, of course, been known for decades, and much of it is so familiar as to be difficult to read with a fresh eye. The second level (oral and written communication that passed between Truman and his advisers) has unfolded only gradually and in piecemeal fashion with the publication of memoirs by participants and the opening of various manuscript and archive collections. Finally, there is the intensely interesting level of Truman's relatively uncensored private reflections, expressed in diary jottings or in personal letters to his wife, Bess, or his daughter, Margaret.

Much of this material, often in striking variance to his public pronouncements, has become available only in the past few years.

This essay draws together some of what we know about Truman's thinking on this subject and relates it to the larger pattern of American attitudes toward the atomic bomb in the early postwar years. Such an effort is revealing in several ways. First, it brings into sharp focus aspects of Truman's character and his mode of dealing with issues. Second, it illustrates how profoundly the advent of this awesome new force could disrupt and disorient even so down-to-earth a man as Truman, producing some quite striking contradictions and inconsistencies. Third, Truman's response to the bomb, in all its ambiguity, mirrors in an uncanny fashion the larger response of the American people. The uncertainties and ambivalences in Truman's own mind on this subject were simultaneously being played out on the larger stage of public discourse and cultural expression in this early post-Hiroshima period. Finally, of course, the views expressed by Truman and top members of his administration on the atomic bomb are important to the cultural historian not only because they mirror the broader national response, but also because they helped shape it.

JUSTIFICATIONS FOR DROPPING THE BOMB

President Truman was lunching with the crew of the USS *Augusta* on August 6, 1945, steaming westward across the Atlantic en route home from the Potsdam conference, when a radio message from Secretary of War Henry L. Stimson informed him that the atomic bombing of Hiroshima had been a "complete success." "This is the greatest thing in history," he spontaneously exclaimed. After breaking the news to the cheering sailors, he rushed to the wardroom to tell the officers, amid more cheers and excitement.

Meanwhile, in Washington, a prearranged news release had been issued that morning by the White House under Truman's name, informing the world that an atomic bomb had been "loosed against those who brought war in the Far East." In this critically important announcement, which shaped Americans' initial perceptions of the bomb, Truman offered only two brief justifications for its use against Japan. First, he cited Tokyo's surprise attack on the United States in 1941: "The Japanese began the war from the air at Pearl Harbor. They have been repaid many-fold." Second, he noted that the Japanese had rejected the Allied surrender ultimatum issued at Potsdam on July 26, 1945—an ultimatum that had warned them of "complete and utter destruction" if they did not surrender unconditionally.

In less formal comments at this time, Truman further justified the atomic bombing on two additional grounds: Japan's wartime atrocities and the racist assertion that the Japanese were subhuman creatures to whom the moral restraint that nations (at least professedly) observed in wartime need not apply. These interwoven themes emerged most clearly in Truman's response to a post-Hiroshima telegram from an official of the Federal Council of Churches, an association of liberal Protestant denominations, urging that no further atomic bombs be dropped. Truman's answer, written on August 9 with the knowledge that a second atomic bomb would in fact be dropped momentarily, declared, "Nobody is more disturbed over the use of the atomic bomb than I am, but I was greatly disturbed over the unwarranted attack by the Japanese on Pearl Harbor and their murder of our prisoners of war. The only language they seem to understand is the one we have been using to bombard them. When you have to deal with a beast you have to treat him as a beast. It is most regrettable but nevertheless true."

As wartime passions subsided after Japan's surrender, another justification emerged. The atomic bomb was the only alternative to an invasion of Japan that would have cost many American lives. The gist of this argument was contained in Truman's message to Congress of October 3, 1945, on the subject of atomic-energy legislation. "We know," the president declared unequivocally, "that [the atomic bomb] saved the lives of untold thousands of American soldiers who would otherwise have been killed in battle." Truman became more specific in his address at the annual Gridiron Dinner in Washington on December 15, 1945. Purporting to describe his thought process at the time he made the atomic-bomb decision, he declared, "It occurred to me, that a quarter of a million of the flower of our young manhood were worth a couple of Japanese cities, and I still think they were and are."

This argument was most fully elaborated in an extremely influential February 1947 *Harper's* magazine article by former secretary of war Henry L. Stimson. Had the atomic bomb not been employed as it was, Stimson contended, a full-scale invasion of Japan, first of Kyushu and then of the main island of Honshu, would have been necessary. This would have extended the war through 1946, he insisted, and entailed horrendous losses: "I was informed that such operations might be expected to cost over a million casualties to American forces alone. Additional large losses might be expected among our allies, and of course, if our campaign was successful and if we could judge by previous experience, enemy casualties would be much larger than our own." Repeating this argument in his 1953 memoirs, Winston Churchill inflated Stimson's projection of a million American *casualties* (i.e., killed, wounded, and missing) into a million American *deaths,* plus a half million British ones.

With the passing years, Truman insisted ever more rigidly that the atomic-bomb decision was totally justified, that he had never had a moment's second thoughts, and that he would unhesitatingly make the same decision again. "I regarded the bomb as a military weapon," he wrote in his 1955 memoirs, "and never had any doubt that it should be used." A fundamental element of Truman's public persona was his cocky self-confidence, with no hint of self-doubt or even of second thoughts about his major decisions. As he wrote in 1957, "I hardly ever look back for the purpose of contemplating 'what might have been.'" Nothing illustrates this trait more clearly than the tone of absolute assurance he adopted in all public comment on the atomic-bomb decision. From August 6, 1945, until his death in 1972, Truman invariably rejected with great vehemence any suggestion that the atomic destruction of two cities might have been unnecessary militarily, tragic in its long-range implications, or problematic on ethical grounds. When J. Robert Oppenheimer, in a White House meeting with Truman shortly after the war, expressed remorse over the dropping of the atomic bomb and alluded to scientists' feelings that they had blood on their hands, Truman contemptuously ridiculed this "crybaby" reaction. (According to one version of the encounter, Truman pulled a handkerchief from his pocket and derisively offered it to Oppenheimer to wipe the blood off his hands.)

So intent was Truman on maintaining his posture of absolute certitude regarding this question that he eventually erected a kind of invisible shield around the subject to ward off any probing by himself or anyone else. In one of his now-famous unmailed letters, he in 1962 unleashed a memorable blast at diplomatic historian Herbert Feis, who was raising troublesome questions as he sought to re-create the strategic considerations underlying the bomb decision. Wrote Truman to Feis:

> It ended the Jap War. That was the objective. Now if you can think of any other . . . egghead contemplations, bring them out. You get the same answer—to end the Jap War and save ¼ of a million of our youngsters and many Japs from death and twice that many on each side from being maimed for life.
>
> It is a great thing that you or any other contemplator "after the fact" didn't have to make the decision. Our boys would all be dead.

The following year, in another unsent letter, this one to *Chicago Sun-Times* columnist Irv Kupcinet, Truman wrote, "I knew what I was doing when I stopped the war that would have killed a half million youngsters on both sides if those bombs had not been dropped. I have no regrets and, under the same circumstances, I would do it again—and this letter is not confidential." Toward the end of his life, when the producers of a television special on his career suggested a trip to Hiroshima in connection with the atomic bomb episode, Truman proclaimed, "I'll go to Japan, if that's what you want, but I won't kiss their ass."

Why did Truman react so violently to even the whisper of doubt about his atomic-bomb decision? Why the insults, ridicule, contempt, and abuse toward those who tried to penetrate his shell of self-righteous certitude? In part, of course, this was simply another manifestation of the cocky self-confidence so central to Truman's public image. Was more involved? Did the strident certainty that eventually reached self-parody perhaps mask a bad conscience? Despite the evidence of Alamogordo, did Truman still not wholly grasp, prior to August 6, the bomb's full destructive magnitude? In his memoirs, he makes clear that he carefully went over the atomic-bomb target list of Japanese cities with his military leaders, and in retrospect he insists that he was fully aware that the bomb "would inflict damage and casualties beyond imagination" and was "potentially capable of wiping out entire cities." Yet on July 5, as the final order for the bomb's use was being drawn up, he wrote in his diary, "I have told the Sec. of War, Mr. Stimson, to use it so that military objectives and soldiers and sailors are the target and not women and children. . . . He and I are in accord. The target will be a purely military one." In the same vein, the August 6 news release described Hiroshima, a city of 350,000, simply as "an important Japanese Army base."

In the days immediately after August 6, before Truman's pronouncements about the bomb decision became so rigid, there are hints that he was shaken and dismayed as the full horror of the civilian toll sank in. On August 7 (in significant contrast to his assertion two days later, "When you deal with a beast you have to treat him as a beast"), Truman rejected Senator Richard B. Russell's demand that the Japanese must be brought "groveling to their knees," commenting: "I can't bring myself to believe that because they are beasts we should ourselves act in the same manner." And, according to Henry Wallace's diary, at the cabinet meeting of August 10, the day after the Nagasaki bombing, "Truman said he had given orders to stop atomic bombing. He said the thought of wiping out another 100,000 people was too horrible. He didn't like the idea of killing, as he said, 'all those kids.'"

Obviously, such sketchy evidence as this does not prove conclusively that Truman felt uneasy about his decision. Yet if the full evidence of the bomb's power to obliterate entire cities did shock and somewhat unnerve him, making a mockery of his earlier insistence on "purely military" targets, the very stridency of his later efforts to place his decision beyond the reach of criticism or even discussion may have been his way of dealing with fugitive doubts that he never openly expressed and perhaps never fully acknowledged even to himself.

How successful were Truman's efforts to explain and justify his atomic-bomb decision? From the first, the president's contention that the atomic bomb was the only alternative to an invasion of Japan aroused skepticism in some quarters. As early as 1946, on the basis of a detailed study of the state of the Japanese war effort by the summer of 1945 and exhaustive interviews with high Japanese officials, the United States Strategic Bombing Survey concluded that Japan would have surrendered "certainly prior to December 31, 1945, and in all probability prior to November 1, 1945, . . . even if the atomic bombs had not been dropped, even if Russia had not entered the war, and even if no invasion had been planned or contemplated."

Beginning with Gar Alperovitz's *Atomic Diplomacy: Hiroshima and Potsdam* (1965) and continuing with such works as Martin J. Sherwin's *A World Destroyed: The Atomic Bomb and the Grand Alliance* (1977), a considerable body of historical scholarship has emerged that reinforces the conclusion of the Strategic Bombing Survey and convincingly shows that calculations involving the Soviet Union were more fundamental to the decision-making process than Truman's or Stimson's version of that process acknowledged. These works have made clear that Japan was almost desperately seeking to end the war by July 1945 and that, thanks to the breaking of the Japanese communications code, these efforts were known to President Truman. Truman's own memoirs acknowledge that as early as the end of May, after the Okinawa campaign, Acting Secretary of State Joseph Grew (the only high administration official with extended experience in Japan) informed Truman of his belief that the Japanese would surrender if they were assured that the emperor could remain on his throne.

The Truman diaries and family letters that have become available to scholars in the past few years further support the revisionist critique of the Truman-Stimson version of the atomic-bomb decision. For example, when Stalin reaffirmed at Potsdam his Yalta pledge to declare war on Japan three months after Germany's surrender, Truman was exultant. "He'll be in Jap War on August 15," Truman wrote in his diary on July 17. "Fini Japs when that comes about." To Bess he wrote: "I've gotten what I came for—Stalin goes to war on August 15. . . . I'll say that we'll end the war a year sooner, now, and think of the kids who won't be killed. That is the important thing." By mid-July, in short, Truman knew that Japan was on the verge of surrender, and he was convinced that the Soviet Union's forthcoming declaration of war would provide the final push. As historian Robert Messer has recently argued, the issue occupying Truman's mind in these critical days was not the nightmare of a costly land invasion of Japan, but the precise means by which Japan's imminent collapse would be achieved.

As the stunning success of the Alamogordo test became apparent, Truman realized that the United States, and not the Soviets, could provide the final blow. "Believe Japs will fold up before Russia comes in," Truman wrote in his diary on July 18. "I am sure they will when Manhattan [the atomic bomb] appears over their homeland." When Stimson flew to Potsdam and gave Truman a full briefing on Alamogordo, the president was (according to Stimson's diary) "tremendously pepped up" and displayed "an entirely new feeling of confidence." Repeatedly Truman thanked Stimson for the report and for "being present to help him in this way." In a 1948 letter to Margaret, Truman regretted that he had worked so hard at Potsdam to get Stalin to reaffirm his pledge to enter the Pacific war: "All of us wanted Russia in the Japanese War. Had we known what the Atomic Bomb would do we'd have never wanted the Bear in the picture."

The precise casualty estimates that Truman cited so authoritatively whenever he discussed the hypothetical invasion that the atomic bomb allegedly prevented have come in for critical scrutiny as well. After an exhaustive study of this aspect of the debate over the atomic-bomb decision, Rufus E. Miles Jr., a former senior fellow of Princeton's Woodrow Wilson Center, argued in the Fall 1985 issue of *International Security* that the figure of a quarter million casualties was "an 'off-the-top-of-the-head' estimate made in the early spring of 1945, before the war and navy departments realized how rapid was the deterioration of Japan's capacity to resist, and then uncritically repeated on various occasions after the situation had radically changed."

Truman's immediate purpose, however, was to persuade not historians but the American electorate that the atomic bombing of Japan had been necessary and praiseworthy, and in this he succeeded brilliantly. Public opinion polls in the autumn of 1945 revealed overwhelming approval ratings; in newspaper editorials, approval was practically unanimous.

Truman's arguments all struck a responsive popular chord. His linking of Pearl Harbor and Hiroshima resonated strongly with Americans, who recalled vividly the treachery of December 7, 1941, and for whom

"Remember Pearl Harbor" had been the most powerful of wartime slogans. Countless post-Hiroshima editorials, cartoons, and letters to the editor enthusiastically endorsed Truman's assertion that the atomic bomb was fair retribution for Japanese atrocities in the Philippines and the brutal island campaigns of the Pacific. Some of this commentary reflected the same racism that underlay Truman's description of the Japanese as beasts. As John Dower argued in *War without Mercy: Race and Power in the Pacific War* (1986), American anti-Japanese propaganda during the war was deeply racist, and it is hardly surprising that racist arguments and images should have been employed in the rush to justify the atomic bomb. Some newspaper letters expressed regret that atomic bombs had not been used to destroy *all* human life in Japan.

Truman's claim that the only alternative to the atomic bomb would have been a protracted land war also went largely unquestioned. But why did most Americans believe so eagerly and uncritically that, if the atomic bomb had not been used, the war would have dragged on for perhaps another eighteen months at a hideous cost in blood and suffering? Why, in the face of the mounting body of historical evidence to the contrary, do many, perhaps most, Americans still remain firmly convinced that the bomb "saved hundreds of thousands of American lives"? The answer, presumably, is that myths of this tenacity serve necessary psychological functions. As Rufus E. Miles Jr. has observed:

> The use of these figures [estimating invasion casualties] by Truman and others can be explained by a subconscious compulsion to persuade themselves and the American public that, horrible as the atomic bombs were, their use was actually humane inasmuch as it saved a huge number of lives. The larger the estimate of deaths averted, the more self-evidently justified the action seemed. Exaggerating these figures avoided, in large part, the awkward alternative of having to rethink and explain a complex set of circumstances and considerations that influenced the decision to drop the bomb.

Not everyone concurred in the government's rationalizations. The nuclear annihilation of well over a hundred thousand men, women, and children of a defeated nation teetering on the brink of surrender was not, for some, so easily dismissed. Even in the pervid emotional climate of the war and its immediate aftermath, a small minority of Americans expressed grave reservations about the official deeds performed in their name. Others who did not categorically condemn Truman's decision were nevertheless unprepared to accept his strident insistence that the action was so obviously justified as not even to merit reflection or debate. These responses, too, constituted a part of the post-Hiroshima cultural and moral landscape, and as such they deserve attention and study. But the fact remains that the overwhelming majority of Americans, as well as the nation's principal media outlets, found little to question in the atomic bombing of Hiroshima and Nagasaki. The pattern of Truman's own response to the bomb—vociferous public justification with an undercurrent of barely acknowledged uneasiness and doubt—accurately reflected and encapsulated the reaction of the larger American public.

THE LARGER MEANING OF ATOMIC ENERGY

What of the atomic future? What were the implications of the unleashing of the atom? And what larger meanings could one extract from this momentous event? Here, too, the responses of President Truman, both public and private, paralleled and helped shape those of the larger public. Again his initial announcement of August 6, 1945, must be the starting point. This eleven-hundred-word message provided no information, even of the sketchiest sort, about the probable human or physical toll at Hiroshima. The Alamogordo test and the scale of destructiveness it had demonstrated were passed over in silence. Radiation was unmentioned.

Rather, the theme of the message was upbeat and positive. The drama and vast scope of the Manhattan Project were vividly evoked, underscoring the supremacy of U.S. industrial might and technological know-how:

> We now have two great plants and many lesser works devoted to the production of atomic power. Employment during peak construction numbered 125,000 and

over 65,000 individuals are even now engaged in op-
erating the plants. Many have worked there for two and
a half years. Few know what they have been producing. They see great quantities of material going in and
they see nothing coming out of these plants, for the physical size of the explosive charge is exceedingly small. We
have spent two billion dollars on the greatest scientific
gamble in history—and won.

Truman's announcement dwelled on the scientific achievement of the
Manhattan Project even more than on its technological wonder. For the
United States in 1945, news of the atomic bomb came embedded in a
glowing hymn of praise to science: "The greatest marvel is not the size
of the enterprise, its secrecy, nor its cost, but the achievement of scientific
brains in putting together infinitely complex pieces of knowledge held
by many men in different fields of science into a workable plan. . . . The
brain child of many minds came forth in physical shape and performed
as it was supposed to do. . . . What has been done is the greatest achievement of organized science in history."

    This dramatic scientific breakthrough, Truman continued, held vast
promise for enlarging human knowledge; it ushered in "a new era in
man's understanding of nature's forces." Truman reiterated the point in
his October 3, 1945, atomic-energy message to Congress. Although the
atom posed "potential danger," it was "at the same time . . . full of promise for the future of man and for the peace of the world."

    As for immediate practical benefits to be expected from this triumph
of science, Truman's August 6 announcement struck a cautious note,
warning that only after "a long period of intensive research" would
atomic energy be available for nonmilitary purposes. But soon the cautionary note faded in a glow of hyperbole. Atomic energy, proclaimed
Truman in his October 3 message, "may someday prove to be more revo-
lutionary in the development of human society than the invention of
the wheel, the use of metals, or steam or internal combustion engines."
Speaking extemporaneously at a county fair in Missouri at about the
same time, he predicted that knowledge of the atom would lead to "the
happiest world that the sun has ever shone upon."

The positive side was also emphasized in several of Truman's State of the Union messages, although the advent of the atomic bomb, surely a major event of 1945, was not even mentioned in Truman's first such message in January 1946. When he first raised the subject of atomic energy in his January 1947 speech, it was in the context of the atom's great promise: "In the vigorous and effective development of peaceful uses of atomic energy," the president declared, "rests our hope that this new force may ultimately be turned into a blessing for all nations." Truman expressed similar bright hopes in the rest of his State of the Union messages.

If Henry Stimson was Truman's principal collaborator in the campaign to justify the decision to drop the atomic bomb, his most effective lieutenant in promulgating the message of the peaceful atom was David E. Lilienthal. As head of the Tennessee Valley Authority in the 1930s, Lilienthal had emerged as a tireless public advocate for large-scale federal development projects. As chairman of the Atomic Energy Commission (AEC) from its creation in 1946 until 1950, Lilienthal brought the same zeal and eloquence to spreading the vision of a world transformed by atomic energy. Often featured in the press as "Mr. Atom," Lilienthal labored mightily to flesh out Truman's message and give a benevolent aura to the new atomic reality. While debunking the more ludicrously exaggerated claims of some popularizers, Lilienthal extolled the atom's peacetime promise in numerous speeches and magazine articles. In a nationally broadcast 1948 high school graduation address delivered at Gettysburg, Pennsylvania, he spoke with almost grating optimism of the vast future benefits of atomic energy, promising "one of the blessed periods of all human history."

Lilienthal frequently described atomic energy as simply a form of solar energy—and potentially as beneficial. As he told another high school graduating class in 1947, the sun was nothing but "a huge atomic-energy factory." Such pronouncements reflected Lilienthal's almost mystical belief in the power of positive thinking—his conviction that merely to turn people's thoughts from the atomic bomb to speculation about possible peacetime applications, whatever the actual reality, was a significant social achievement.

Truman strongly backed Lilienthal's efforts to turn the public mind from atomic weapons to the promise of atomic energy. Dramatizing this theme, at the initiative of the AEC he sent a telegram to an international conference of cancer specialists meeting at St. Louis in 1947, announcing that scientists all over the world would be given access to radioactive isotopes (by-products of the government's nuclear-weapons program) to aid in the fight against cancer. During a February 1950 meeting with Truman, two weeks after the president's hydrogen-bomb decision, Lilienthal noted in his diary Truman's full agreement "that my theme of Atoms for Peace is just what the country needs."

Reflecting Lilienthal's upbeat emphasis, the AEC in the late 1940s initiated the preparation of booklets, films, exhibitions, and curricular materials publicizing the atom's beneficent promise. Prominent in this effort was the Brookhaven National Laboratory, a Long Island facility jointly funded and administered by the AEC and nine large eastern universities. Much of the AEC's limited nonmilitary research was centered at Brookhaven, and members of its staff frequently spoke to public gatherings and the press. Brookhaven's public relations office assembled two traveling exhibits featuring movies, audiovisual displays, and live demonstrations. Exhibitions were mounted in a number of cities and at the American Museum of Natural History in New York. The campaign to counteract the public's atomic phobia crested in the summer of 1948 with "Man and the Atom," a month-long multimedia exhibition in New York's Central Park. This show was jointly sponsored by the AEC, its major corporate contractors for nuclear power development (General Electric and Westinghouse), and the New York Committee on Atomic Information—an umbrella group of various service organizations.

Following the lead of Truman, Lilienthal, and the AEC, the American media in these years heavily promoted the vision of an imminent atomic utopia. Although the "Atoms for Peace" program as a formal U.S. policy initiative dates from President Dwight Eisenhower's United Nations speech of December 1953, the theme was omnipresent in the Truman years as well. In one of its more dramatic expressions, CBS radio in June 1947 broadcast an hour-long documentary, "The Sunny Side of the Atom," designed to publicize the vast promise of radioactive isotopes and, according to a publicist, counteract "the 'scare' approach to atomic education."

Numerous magazine feature articles struck the same note, portraying the enormous promise of the atomic age. The applications of atomic energy to the treatment of cancer and other ills, reported *Collier's* in May 1947, opened the door to a "golden age of atomic medicine." This feature was illustrated with a composite photograph of a former paraplegic, healed by atomic energy, emerging smiling from a mushroom-shaped cloud, his empty wheelchair in the background. Foreseeing cures for cancer, heart disease, and other ailments thanks to atomic energy, *Operation Atomic Vision,* a 1948 high school study unit prepared by the National Education Association, declared: "Many of our generation will reach the century mark. . . . No one will need to work long hours. There will be much leisure, and a network of large recreational areas will cover the country, if not the world."

This government and media blitz had its effect. In a 1948 Gallup poll, 61 percent of college-educated Americans answered yes to the question: "Do you think that, in the long run, atomic energy will do more good than harm?" Other surveys produced similar results. This emphasis on a thrilling—if somewhat amorphous—atomic utopia ahead, tentatively advanced in President Truman's initial atomic-bomb announcement and then massively reinforced by official and media sources in the succeeding months and years, had a profound influence in molding Americans' initial responses to the nuclear reality.

The positive view of science that pervades Truman's August 6 announcement also mirrored and helped shape the broader public response. In the early post-Hiroshima period, newspapers, magazines, and radio were full of glowing accounts of the Manhattan Project as a crowning triumph of the age of science. Photographs of J. Robert Oppenheimer and other leading physicists stared from every page, and the pronouncements of scientists, from Albert Einstein down to the lowliest physics graduate students caught up in the Manhattan Project, received almost reverent attention. In post-Hiroshima editorial cartoons, scientists typically appear as awesome, larger-than-life figures. In one, a scientist, represented as a person so gigantic that only his lower legs are visible, passes the knowledge of atomic energy to a dwarflike figure labeled "The Statesman." Another cartoon portraying a somber scientist offering an atom to the human race (represented as a crawling, diaper-clad infant) was captioned, "Baby Play With Nice Ball?"

But as the mixed messages of such cartoons suggest, the post-

Hiroshima view of science had a darker side, and Truman anticipated this, too. Characteristically, however, he did not reveal his bleaker reflections publicly. On July 16, the day he first learned of the successful test at Alamogordo, he wrote in his diary: "I hope for some sort of peace—but I fear that machines are ahead of morals by some centuries and when morals catch up perhaps there'll be no reason for any of it. I hope not. But we are only termites on a planet and maybe when we bore too deeply into the planet there'll [be] a reckoning—who knows?" On July 25, after Stimson had flown to Potsdam with a detailed account of the Alamogordo blast by eyewitnesses, Truman characterized the report as "startling—to put it mildly." Brooding on this "most terrible bomb in the history of the world . . . , the most terrible thing ever discovered," he expressed his fear of apocalypse in biblical imagery: "It may be the fire destruction prophesied in the Euphrates Valley Era, after Noah and his fabulous Ark."

In these sober reflections on Alamogordo, Truman uncannily reflected a spontaneous popular response to the Hiroshima news that came a few days later—a response of profound apprehension and even terror, often expressed in nightmarish images of universal destruction. Radio newscasters and newspaper articles and editorials compared Hiroshima with U.S. cities of similar size. Photographs of Hiroshima and Nagasaki were transmuted into images of American cities in smoldering ruin.

This fear pervaded all levels of society, from Nobel laureates and government leaders to those who scarcely grasped what had happened but still sensed it as deeply menacing. The "strange disquiet" and "very great apprehension" the atomic bomb had aroused, wrote the theologian Reinhold Niebuhr, were particularly intense among "the more sober and thoughtful sections of our nation." "The 36-Hour War," a November 1945 *Life* magazine article describing the nuclear annihilation of America's cities, featured realistic drawings of a mushroom cloud rising over Washington and of the marble lions of the New York Public Library gazing sightlessly over the rubble of a demolished city.

Truman's diary jottings of July 1945 also reveal a far more ambivalent view of science than he conveyed in his public proclamations—a view not of brilliant researchers unlocking the atom's secrets for the ultimate benefit of mankind but of voracious termites burrowing into the planet with unpredictable but possibly catastrophic consequences. Here again, Truman's response anticipated an important thread in the larger cultural reaction to the atomic bomb. Accompanying the post-Hiroshima praise for the scientific miracle workers who had accomplished this marvel was a strain of nagging apprehension about where science and its hand-maiden technology were leading humankind. If, as Truman was boasting, the atomic bomb was "the greatest achievement of organized science in history," wrote Dwight Macdonald in his journal *politics* a few days after Hiroshima, then "so much the worse for organized science." It was grotesque, he suggested, to present this city-destroying machine as a giant leap forward in the march of science. Macdonald's view of the Manhattan Project was closer to Truman's private apprehensions than to the president's expansive public pronouncements. For Macdonald, the horror of the atomic bomb was immeasurably deepened by the fact that it represented the end product of an elaborately bureaucratized project involving the uncoerced labor of 125,000 people, few of whom had the slightest idea what they were doing.

Macdonald expressed with particular vehemence one extreme of a deeply ambivalent set of public attitudes toward science in the early post-war period. Along with the idea of scientists as technological wonder-workers that Truman (publicly) insisted was the true meaning of Hiroshima, one also finds strong currents of fear, mistrust, and disillusionment. "Grave doubts are in many minds, and science is being regarded both with greater respect and with greater apprehension than ever before," observed *Scientific Monthly* in September 1945.

Much evidence supports such assessments of the public mood. Newspaper editorials and letters to the editor, for example, reflected praise and fear of science in about equal proportions. "Science a Menace" and "Science Moving Too Fast" were the headlines of typical letters. A *St. Louis Post-Dispatch* editorial could simultaneously praise the scientific triumph and worry that it might end in human extinction. The very search for truth that was science's "noblest attribute," observed Raymond B. Fosdick, the president of the Rockefeller Foundation, in a November 1945 radio address, "has brought our civilization to the brink of destruction." Should scientific research be curbed, Fosdick asked, or given free rein, with all the attendant social risks? That dilemma remains with us still, and Harry Truman, in the privacy of his diary, was already struggling with it before the rest of the world had even heard of the atomic bomb.

THE CONTEMPLATED USE OF ATOMIC WEAPONS

What postwar diplomatic and military uses, if any, were envisaged for what Bernard Baruch in 1946 called America's "winning weapon"? On this critical question, too, Truman vacillated in ways that reflected the larger uncertainty of the American people. In his post-Hiroshima public pronouncements, Truman always insisted that a fundamental objective of U.S. policy was to devise a system of international control that would end U.S. atomic supremacy, forestall a dangerous nuclear arms race, and ensure that the bomb would never again be used. The Acheson-Lilienthal plan of March 1946, to which historians have given much attention, was presented to the world as an expression of this high-minded objective.

At the same time, Truman was clearly prepared to gain whatever strategic advantage he could from the American atomic monopoly, which continued until September 1949, and the country's overwhelming atomic superiority, which lasted considerably longer. As he wrote jauntily to Bess from Potsdam on July 31, 1945, using a metaphor drawn from his favorite game: "I rather think Mr. Stalin is stallin' because he is not so happy over the English elections. [Clement Attlee had replaced Winston Churchill as prime minister.] He doesn't know it but I have an ace in the hole and another one showing—so unless he has threes or two pair (and I know he has not) we are sitting all right." As numerous studies have now demonstrated, all Truman's thinking and decision-making about nuclear weapons, from July 1945 through the end of his presidency, invariably reflected his preoccupation with the U.S.-Soviet power nexus.

As the Cold War worsened, did Truman ever envisage the atomic bomb not only as a diplomatic asset in his maneuverings with the Soviets but as something that actually might be used again? In various public pronouncements, as well as in occasional private communications within the government, Truman firmly rejected such an option. When army secretary Kenneth Royall urged a preemptive nuclear strike against the

Soviets during the 1948 Berlin blockade crisis, Truman made plain that he considered such an action not only unthinkable morally but appalling in its strategic and diplomatic shortsightedness: "You have got to understand that this isn't a military weapon. It is used to wipe out women and children and unarmed people, and not for military uses. You have got to understand that I have got to think about the effect of such a thing on international relations. This is no time to be juggling an atom bomb around."

When the Cold War turned hot in Korea, however, Truman himself toyed with the nuclear option. At a news conference on November 30, 1950, after the Chinese had crossed the Yalu River, Truman was asked about the possible use of the atomic bomb. He replied: "There has always been active consideration of its use. I don't want to see it used. It is a terrible weapon and it should not be used on innocent men, women, and children who have nothing whatever to do with this military aggression." When the respected Merriman Smith of the United Press asked the president explicitly to confirm whether dropping the atomic bomb was, indeed, under "active consideration," he answered tersely: "Always has been. It is one of our weapons." When asked whether the targets being considered were civilian or military, he responded that this was a "matter that the military people have to decide. I'm not a military authority that passes on those things. . . . The military commander in the field will have charge of the use of weapons, as he always has."

The newspapers reported the story in banner headlines. A United Press bulletin proclaimed: "PRESIDENT TRUMAN SAID TODAY THE UNITED STATES HAS UNDER ACTIVE CONSIDERATION USE OF THE ATOMIC BOMB IN CONNECTION WITH THE WAR IN KOREA." An alarmed Prime Minister Attlee flew to Washington to dissuade the president from precipitate action.

In her biography of her father, Margaret Truman describes this episode as "all ridiculous, and very disheartening." It was, she writes, a classic example of journalistic distortion and sensationalism. Indeed, she implicitly blames the press's handling of this story for the fatal heart attack suffered a few days later by Truman's old friend and press secretary Charlie Ross. Yet when one reads Truman's clear answers to a series of clear questions, it is difficult to see how the reporters distorted or misrepresented his views. Truman's comments, while perhaps merely propaganda bluster, did clearly indicate that use of the atomic bomb in the Korean War, while deeply deplorable, was indeed under "active consideration" and that targeting decisions would be left to "the military commander in the field"—General Douglas MacArthur, who publicly advocated turning the Korean conflict into a war of destruction against Communist China.

In 1952, with his popularity sagging at home and the armistice talks bogged down at Panmunjom, Truman again considered the nuclear option, this time in the form of two memoranda that came to light years later (*New York Times,* August 3, 1980, p. 20). Evidently written to formulate hypothetical options as a way of clarifying his own thinking, they spell out in specific detail a nuclear ultimatum to the Soviets. The first, dated January 27, 1952, says:

> It seems to me that the proper approach now would be an ultimatum with a 10-day expiration limit, informing Moscow that we intend to blockade the China coast from the Korean border to Indochina by means now in our control—and if there is further interference we shall eliminate any ports or cities necessary to accomplish our purposes.
>
> This means all-out war. It means that Moscow, St. Petersburg, Mukden, Vladivostok, Peking, Shanghai, Port Arthur, Darien, Odessa, Stalingrad, and every manufacturing plant in China and the Soviet Union will be eliminated.

In the second of these two remarkable memos, written in May 1952, Truman actually drafted his ultimatum to "the Commies": "Now do you want an end to hostilities in Korea or do you want China and Siberia destroyed? You may have one or the other; whichever you want, these lies of yours at this conference have gone far enough. You either accept our fair and just proposal or you will be completely destroyed."

It is important to place these documents in context. Apart from the 1950 news conference mentioned above, Truman in his public pronouncements dismissed all talk of employing atomic weapons in the

Korean War. He had even recalled General MacArthur in April 1951 in part over MacArthur's insistent calls for a wider war. And the Truman administration had firmly rejected NSC 100, the 1951 proposal by Stuart Symington (chairman of the National Security Resources Board) to the National Security Council calling for a nuclear attack on China and possibly the Soviet Union. In this context, historian Gregg Herken is probably correct in suggesting that Truman's Rambo-like private musings are best seen as "more an expression of pique than of policy." Yet in a nuclear age, even pique by a U.S. president cannot be dismissed lightly.

Clearly, Truman's feelings about the military and diplomatic utility of the atomic bomb were ambivalent. He could readily state the compelling arguments against using the bomb (except when looking back on Hiroshima and Nagasaki), and he recognized the terrible dangers of nuclear threats and bluster. Yet when his frustration level rose high enough—whether against Stalin at Potsdam or the Communists in Korea—his thinking invariably circled back to the alluring option of resolving his frustrations once and for all with his ace in the hole.

In this respect, too, Truman's ambivalence mirrored the attitudes of the American public: fearful of the bomb, aware of the horror of nuclear war, yet longing to translate the nation's atomic supremacy into a decisive stroke against the new postwar enemy. Here it is important to note that, at least for some Americans, Truman's ringing defense of the use of the atomic bomb against Japan had larger implications. If the bomb was justified against one enemy, they asked, why not against another? As one reader wrote the *New Yorker* after the publication of John Hersey's *Hiroshima* in August 1946, "I read Hersey's report. It was marvelous. Now let us drop a handful on Moscow."

During the Korean War, a strong current of opinion emerged in favor of using the atomic bomb. In August 1950, a few weeks after the war began, 28 percent of Americans endorsed this option. When the Chinese entered the war in November, *U.S. News & World Report* noted a "wave of demand" for a nuclear response. A year later, as the conflict dragged on inconclusively, slightly more than half those polled by the Gallup organization supported dropping atomic bombs on "military targets."

Although periodicals like the *Saturday Evening Post* warned that use of the atomic bomb in Korea would surely trigger World War III, others discussed the matter quite coolly, as a viable option to be carefully weighed. *U.S. News & World Report,* for example, after a narrow tactical discussion that ignored any larger strategic (not to mention ethical) considerations, concluded in December 1950 that U.S. use of the bomb in Korea would probably be "sparing." In "Advice to Joe" (1951), country-music star Roy Acuff warned the Russians that when Moscow lay in ashes they would regret their aggressions. "When the atomic bombs start falling," the song rhetorically asked Stalin, "do you have a place to hide?"

Truman and the American people's parallel patterns of response in their risky flirtation with the atomic bomb during the Korean War were only another manifestation of a congruence of outlook that had been evident for years. From the time he learned of the Alamogordo test in July 1945, Truman's attitude toward the atomic bomb was a bundle of contradictions. He could express awe, fear, caution, bluster, or bravado, depending on his mood, his audience, and the circumstances of the moment. The very diversity and unpredictability of these reactions accurately mirrored the mood of the nation as a whole. Reacting to their political leaders, to the media, and to their own terrors and hopes, the American people displayed wide-ranging and sometimes quite contradictory responses as they struggled to come to terms with the endlessly ramifying implications of the news they had first heard from President Truman on August 6, 1945.

JANUARY 1953

Truman's final and most complete comment on the atomic dilemma as president came in his State of the Union message delivered on January 7, 1953, nine weeks after the United States exploded the world's first hydrogen bomb at Eniwetok atoll in the South Pacific. It was an exceptionally depressing appraisal:

> Now we have entered the atomic age, and war has undergone a technological change which makes it a very different thing from what it used to be. War today between the Soviet Empire and the free nations might dig

the grave not only of our Stalinist opponents but of our own society, our world as well as theirs.

War's new meaning may not yet be grasped by all the peoples who would be its victims; nor, perhaps by all the rulers of the Kremlin. . . . The war of the future would be one in which man could extinguish millions of lives at one blow, demolish the great cities of the world, wipe out the cultural achievements of the past— and destroy the very structure of a civilization that has been slowly and painfully built up through hundreds of generations.

Such a war is not a possible policy for rational man. We know this, but we dare not assume that others would not yield to the temptation science is now placing in their hands.

Truman went on to insist that the United States had done everything in its power to avoid a nuclear arms race; the fault lay entirely with the Soviet Union. But beneath the Cold War rhetoric lay another theme: the inevitability of an upward spiral of nuclear menace rooted in the nature of science itself. "Science and technology have worked so fast" that mere presidents and premiers were helpless in the face of its inexorable advance:

The progress of scientific experiment has outrun our expectations. Atomic science is in the full tide of development; the unfolding of the innermost secrets of matter is uninterrupted and irresistible. Since Alamogordo we have developed atomic weapons with many times the explosive force of the early models, and we have produced them in substantial quantities. And recently in the thermonuclear test at Eniwetok, we have entered another stage in the world-shaking development of atomic energy. From now on, man moves in a new era of destructive power, capable of creating explosions of an order of magnitude dwarfing the mushroom clouds of Hiroshima and Nagasaki.

We have no reason to think that the stage we have now reached in the release of atomic energy will be the last. Indeed, the speed of our scientific and technical progress over the last 7 years shows no sign of abating. We are being hurried forward in our mastery of the atom, from one discovery to another, toward yet unforeseeable peaks of destructive energy. . . . It is no wonder that some people wish that we had never succeeded in splitting the atom.

Truman attempted to summon once more the soothing vision of the peaceful atom as "an instrumentality for human betterment," but his words rang hollow when compared to the bleak panorama of nuclear menace he had conjured up.

Absent from these valedictory passages is the aura of confidence and mastery usually so characteristic of the public Truman; muted is the reassuring image of a beneficent science. Other than stoic fortitude, Truman offered no advice or hints in his farewell message about how the nation might avoid the fate toward which an inexorable science was propelling it. The message was not only bleak but deeply passive and acquiescent in tone, as it described a fearful nuclear future that seemed destined to play itself out beyond human control. Harry Truman—and the American people—had come a long way since that exciting August afternoon aboard the USS *Augusta,* a little more than seven years before.

4

DIPLOMATS AND STRATEGISTS
CONFRONT THE BOMB

The atomic bomb profoundly affected all realms of American life, including postwar U.S. diplomacy and military strategizing. While my own research focused on the bomb's cultural impact, I also quite naturally followed and periodically commented on the scholarly literature relating to these other areas. Beginning in the mid-1960s, a number of diplomatic historians, including Gar Alperovitz, Barton J. Bernstein, and Martin J. Sherwin, had probed the larger diplomatic context of President Truman's A-bomb decision and the bomb's influence on U.S. foreign relations during and after the war. Another historian working in this vein was Fraser J. Harbutt of Emory University, who published his findings in a fascinating 1986 book, *The Iron Curtain: Churchill, America, and the Origins of the Cold War.* My review of Harbutt's work (considerably expanded here) appeared in the *Bulletin of the Atomic Scientists* in May 1987.

Following the review, the second part of this chapter discusses how Defense Department brass and Pentagon strategists incorporated the atomic bomb into their early postwar thinking. As I explored the bomb's cultural effects, and as others studied early atomic-age diplomacy, still other scholars were probing post-Hiroshima developments in military strategy—and reporting scary findings. One who did so, drawing on a rich and largely untapped body of official archival material, was Gregg Herken, whose 1980 book *The Winning Weapon: The Atomic Bomb in the Cold War,*

41

1945–1950 I discuss in the concluding pages of this chapter. Adapted from an essay written in 1981 and published in the September 1982 issue of *Reviews in American History,* this represents my earliest published work on the nuclear theme. I wrote it as my own research in this area was just beginning, and as the early-1980s wave of nuclear fear and activism was taking shape.

While the American people of the early postwar years had responded to the nuclear reality in the various ways described in chapters 1 through 3, and as President Truman, David Lilienthal, and others had offered their upbeat pronouncements about the peacetime uses of atomic energy, military strategists deep in the Pentagon had been devising secret nuclear-war plans. Though "hypothetical," these apocalyptic scenarios, unearthed by Herken and others, make clear that the threat of nuclear holocaust was no mere bugaboo invented by antinuclear alarmists. It was real, and even (or perhaps especially) when clothed in the impersonal, technostrategic language of the war planners, it was nightmarish.

THE BOMB IN POSTWAR DIPLOMACY

How did the Cold War begin? As though trapped in a dull, reiterative dream, we play the tape over and over, straining to decipher the garbled cacophony of voices. If one could only discern precisely when things began to go wrong, we seem to hope, perhaps the tangled skein of U.S.-Soviet relations could be unraveled, and we could start afresh.

Diplomatic historians, sharing this interest not only as citizens but as scholars, have long sought to pinpoint the exact moment at which the Cold War started. In terms of U.S. policy, some have focused on the Truman Doctrine of March 1947, committing U.S. resources to shoring up anti-Communist forces in Greece and Turkey. Others designate George Kennan's famous "long cable" of February 22, 1946, outlining the doctrine of containment.

In *The Iron Curtain: Churchill, America, and the Origins of the Cold War* (New York: Oxford University Press, 1986), Fraser J. Harbutt, a diplomatic historian at Emory University, argues for a still earlier date, which he cites with great exactitude: the evening of February 10, 1946, when President Truman and former Prime Minister Winston Churchill met at the White House to discuss a speech Churchill would soon deliver at Westminster College in Fulton, Missouri. The origins of the speech had seemed innocuous enough. In August 1945, Westminster's president had written a letter inviting Britain's heroic but recently defeated wartime prime minister to deliver a speech. To the letter, President Truman had added a friendly note that said: "This is a fine old college out in my state. If you'll come out and make them a speech I'll take you out and introduce you." Churchill accepted, and the planning that would produce a key Cold War pronouncement proceeded apace. The symbolic importance of Churchill's celebrated "Iron Curtain" speech on March 5, 1946, at Westminster College has, of course, long been recognized. But Harbutt argues for its immediate tactical importance as well, focusing on that fateful February meeting at the White House.

Stated thus baldly, his thesis may suggest sensationalism, but *The Iron Curtain* builds its case painstakingly and, in my view, compellingly. Indeed, the author does not actually get to the Fulton speech until chapter 7. After two introductory chapters tracing Churchill's long-standing visceral hatred of the Soviet Union—"Bolshevism is not a policy, it is a disease"—and his equally long interest in forging a "special relationship" between Britain and the United States, Harbutt devotes the next 230-odd pages to a detailed account of the shifting relations between the United States, the Soviet Union, and Great Britain, from the Tehran Conference of late 1943 through the Iran crisis of early 1946, brought on by Soviet moves in that arena. This account is based on an awesome array of published work and archival material, including the papers of the British cabinet, foreign office, and prime minister.

Building on this solid evidentiary base, Harbutt constructs his careful version of the evolving relationship of the wartime Big Three. If the general contours of the story are familiar, the work's richness of detail and tripartite perspective should assure it a respectful reception as a valuable contribution to historical scholarship.

Toward the end of World War II and in the immediate postwar era, Harbutt argues, Washington distanced itself from imperialist England and sought a bilateral accommodation with Moscow over such matters as the United Nations, sometimes at the expense of British interests. This policy seemed plausible, he notes, since U.S. and Soviet strategic interests did not conflict in any obvious way. British and Soviet interests, by contrast, clashed directly in Poland and in the so-called northern tier of Britain's sphere of influence: Greece, Turkey, and Iran. Between 1943 and 1946, Harbutt contends, prior to the familiar Cold War between the United States and the Soviet Union, came an earlier "Cold War" in which the British and the Soviets struggled to define their postwar spheres, while the United States remained a bystander. Unlike historians who see a consistent anti-Soviet thrust to U.S. policy from Hiroshima onward, Harbutt finds a general pattern of passivity and detachment through the end of 1945.

The heart of Harbutt's book deals with the transformation of this Anglo-Soviet "Cold War" into the U.S.-Soviet Cold War. In this process, Harbutt ascribes a central but complex role to Churchill. By February 1946, he argues, Truman was increasingly uncomfortable with the Roosevelt policy of accommodating the Soviets. Yet reversing that policy posed delicate problems. U.S. public opinion, reflecting the mood of the wartime alliance, remained vaguely pro-Soviet, while those who had been close to Roosevelt, for example, Henry Wallace and Eleanor Roosevelt, staunchly upheld the conciliatory approach. Furthermore, among those urging a harsher policy were some of Truman's bitterest congressional opponents, including Senator Arthur Vandenberg of Michigan. Whatever his personal inclinations, Truman did not wish to be perceived as adopting a get-tough policy merely in response to Republican pressure.

At this point, Truman's and Churchill's interests neatly converged. Churchill had long believed that close Anglo-American ties were essential, not only to fight Bolshevism but also to shore up British geopolitical interests as Great Britain's power waned. Dismayed by the two countries' postwar divergence on Soviet policy (and chafing to resume his accustomed place in the limelight), Churchill early in 1946 undertook a U.S. tour. Disappointed in his hope of addressing Congress, he quickly accepted the invitation to speak at Westminster College on March 5. Truman, recognizing the advantages of having the British leader serve as point man for the policy shift he had already decided to implement, quickly announced plans to attend the speech and introduce Churchill, assuring maximum publicity for the event.

Harbutt presents a careful and illuminating analysis of this seminal address, which Churchill explicitly compared to his speeches of the 1930s warning a complacent England of the Nazi threat. Not only did Churchill invoke (without attribution) the Nazi propagandist Joseph Goebbels's memorable image of an "iron curtain" descending over Europe; he also described a Manichean world divided between the forces of good—variously described as "Christian civilization" and "the English-speaking peoples"—and the forces of evil: the Communist empire centered in Moscow and bent on world domination. Only a closely linked United States and Great Britain, Churchill proclaimed, could resist the menace. Harbutt also notes a key omission: Not once did the British leader invoke the name of Roosevelt, architect of the accommodationist policy Churchill was intent on discrediting.

With persuasive evidence, Harbutt dismisses Truman's subsequent claim that he had not anticipated the impact of the speech and had attended only as a matter of courtesy. Not only did Truman ostentatiously applaud the most militant anti-Soviet passages, but strong circumstantial evidence suggests a high degree of covert advance coordination. Churchill discussed the speech in detail with Truman on February 10, with Secretary of State James F. Byrnes and Bernard Baruch on February 17, and with Byrnes and Admiral William Leahy, Truman's chief of staff, on March 3.

Harbutt also offers strong evidence for a "sudden reorientation" in Washington's Soviet policy immediately after Fulton as accommodationism gave way to "firmness"—the diplomatic buzzword of 1946. This shift included an officially orchestrated anti-Soviet media campaign. Unlike the earlier Anglo-Soviet "Cold War," with its sources in tangible geopolitical rivalries, he argues, the Americanized Cold War was rooted much more in ideological abstractions and generalized conceptions of a global struggle for supremacy.

The new policy was sealed, Harbutt concludes, by a serious Soviet miscalculation that produced the Iranian crisis of February to May 1946, mentioned above. Failing to grasp the rapidity with which an Anglo-American and anti-Soviet front was forming, Stalin sought to extend the Soviet role in Iran, a traditional cockpit of Anglo-Soviet rivalry. He kept Soviet troops in northern Iran beyond the date set by a wartime agreement and fostered separatist movements in the Iranian provinces of Azerbaijan and Kurdistan. In collaboration with London and a some-times reluctant Tehran, Washington utilized the U.N. Security Coun-cil as the forum for a highly public display of the new get-tough policy toward the Soviets, triggering the first of Andrei Gromyko's famous walkouts.

The Iron Curtain is traditional diplomatic history. The focus is over-whelmingly on the maneuvering of statesmen and diplomats, with little attention to the broader political, economic, military, or cultural factors that influence foreign policy. In stressing the aura of cooperation that briefly characterized Washington's Soviet policy during the war, Harbutt underplays the deep strand of anti-Soviet feeling in the United States going back to the Bolshevik Revolution of 1917, expressed in such outbursts of official hysteria as the "Red Raids" of January 1920. As Tru-man knew it would, Churchill's rhetoric at Fulton aroused a powerful answering echo from deep in the American psyche. But if this is tradi-tional history, it is traditional history of a very high order. Harbutt's judi-cious and well-written account of the fateful international realignment of 1946 will surely influence profoundly our understanding of this criti-cal period.

Confirming the conclusions reached by other diplomatic historians, *The Iron Curtain* also underscores the centrality of the atomic bomb in shaping the early postwar relations of erstwhile wartime allies. Allusions to the bomb recur like a Wagnerian leitmotiv throughout Harbutt's ac-count. During the war, the United States had concealed the Manhattan Project from one ally—the Soviet Union—while fully sharing atomic information with another: Great Britain. (Soviet espionage, of course, had circumvented this attempt at secrecy, giving Moscow's leaders at least some knowledge of the bomb project.) In talks with Churchill at Hyde Park, New York, in September 1944, President Franklin Roosevelt had pledged that this full and exclusive sharing of atomic information with the British would continue after the war. One of London's key postwar objectives, then, was to preserve this aspect of a special bilateral relationship with the Americans.

For a time, however, this goal seemed in jeopardy. For a few brief months in late 1945 and early 1946, in a fleeting interlude of internationalist enthusiasm, the Truman administration embraced the so-called Acheson-Lilienthal plan for international control of atomic energy under the monitoring of the United Nations Atomic Energy Committee (UNAEC). A joint U.S.-British-Canadian declaration of November 1945 officially endorsed the international control principle, and Soviet Premier Joseph Stalin embraced this objective at a conference in Moscow in December.

In reality, however, the Truman administration, encouraged by the British, was rapidly backing away from its commitment to international control as 1945 ended. A key signal came in late February 1946, when Truman appointed Bernard Baruch, a vain and pompous anti-Communist hard-liner, as the U.S. delegate to UNAEC, with responsibility to conduct negotiations with the Soviets on the international-control plan. As partisans of the Acheson-Lilienthal plan wrung their hands, the British rejoiced. The Baruch appointment, Churchill wrote his successor, Clement Attlee, "is of the utmost importance to us and . . . in my opinion an effective assurance that these matters will be handled in a way friendly to us." (President Truman's authorization of the 1946 Bikini atomic tests in the midst of negotiations with the Soviets over international control provided further evidence of the new exclusivity and militarization of U.S. atomic policy.)

Churchill's "Iron Curtain" speech, with its multiple goals, must be seen against the backdrop of these rapidly evolving atomic realities. On the one hand, of course, Churchill crafted the speech with an eye to posterity, articulating an overarching spiritual and strategic rationale for a long-term Anglo-American struggle against a godless, anti-Christian Communist power. In Churchill's view, as he would later write in *Triumph and Tragedy*, the final volume of his magisterial history of World War II, postwar America "stood on the scene of victory, master of world fortunes, but without a true and coherent design." Never inhibited by excessive modesty, Churchill saw himself as the person who would provide that design.

But beyond these cosmic objectives, the Fulton speech's immediate goal was to shore up the Anglo-American wartime alliance, and specifically to assure the continuation of a bilateral approach to atomic energy that would freeze out the Soviet Union. As we have seen, Churchill's objective was not so much to *change* U.S. policy as to provide a cover for Truman to signal publicly an already-decided-upon shift from international control to Western exclusiveness in the atomic sphere.

Indeed, from the moment Truman had received news of the successful Alamogordo test while sparring with Stalin at the Potsdam conference, the idealistic vision of international control had clashed with the conviction that the atomic bomb would be America's winning weapon not only in the war with Japan but in the postwar era as well. As Harbutt shrewdly observes, the success of the Manhattan Project had, "perhaps inevitably, created in Truman and [Secretary of State James F.] Byrnes a sense of enhanced confidence if not omnipotence." In this spirit, and despite Washington's official endorsement of international control, Byrnes came to the London Conference of Foreign Ministers in September 1945 with the goal of using America's atomic monopoly to promote U.S. diplomatic objectives. The effort failed, however, as Soviet Foreign Minister Vyacheslav Molotov brazenly joked about the atomic bomb and ridiculed Byrnes's efforts to turn the bomb to Washington's diplomatic advantage.

In this context of a profoundly ambivalent and rapidly shifting U.S. atomic policy, Churchill in his Iron Curtain speech launched a slashing attack on international control of atomic energy as "wrong and imprudent." It would be "criminal madness," he went on, to "cast [the secret of the atom] adrift in this still agitated and ununited world." Truman (who, as we have seen, had carefully reviewed the text of the speech with Churchill) heartily applauded this passage—a fact duly noted by journalists, who were observing his reactions carefully. Although international control ostensibly remained U.S. policy, the shift toward Western exclusiveness had been clearly signaled.

The Soviets, of course, were hardly innocent bystanders as the

Anglo-American hard line on nuclear issues unfolded. Not only did they miscalculate badly in Iran; on February 9, 1946, Joseph Stalin (preparing his people for a harsh new Five-Year Plan) had declared communism and capitalism incompatible. A few days before, on February 3, Washington columnist Drew Pearson had broken the news of a Soviet atomic spy ring in Canada. All this, combined with the earlier failure of the London Conference, fatally weakened the hand of the internationalist group in Washington who sought postwar cooperation with the Soviets on atomic-energy control and other issues, and vastly strengthened the hand of the advocates of firmness.

In late April 1946, with U.S.-Soviet relations deteriorating almost by the day, Truman met with Gromyko in Washington and gave him such a tongue-lashing that (according to Truman) the Soviet diplomat sputtered: "I have never been talked to like that in my life." (To which Truman allegedly replied: "Carry out your agreements and you won't get talked to like that.") The Cold War's temperature quickly plummeted to subzero levels.

By early spring 1946, in short, whatever opportunities might have existed to shape a different postwar atomic history had evaporated, and the stage was set for a decades-long nuclear arms race with the Soviets. Winston Churchill's Iron Curtain speech—certainly one of the most important public utterances of the twentieth century—both marked the moment of transition and helped bring it about.

THE BOMB IN POSTWAR MILITARY STRATEGY

Pincher, Broiler, Grabber, Sizzle. If, like most Americans with a general knowledge of U.S. history, you find these words less familiar than, say, Loco Foco, Mugwump, or Flapper, this fact in itself is a revealing comment on the gingerly way historians have approached the central global reality of our age: the nuclear arms race. For these are the names of a succession of U.S. war plans drawn up between 1945 and 1950. There were others, with equally catchy tags: Fleetwood, Offtackle, Dropshot, Trojan, Charioteer. Each plan assumed that in the event of war the Soviet Union would be obliterated in a massive atomic blitz lasting only a few days. In this ultimate holocaust, death from the skies would rain down on a substantial portion of the earth's population.

In *The Winning Weapon: The Atomic Bomb in the Cold War, 1945–1950* (New York: Knopf, 1980), Gregg Herken sets out to fill in some of the gaps in our knowledge of these matters. The book explores how the United States in the early postwar years handled what statesmen liked to call the nation's "solemn trust"—the burden of being the creators and, as yet, sole possessors of instruments of unprecedented mass destruction.

The book begins with the diplomacy of the immediate post-Hiroshima period. At the London and Moscow conferences of late 1945, Herken suggests, Secretary of State James F. Byrnes tried two diametrically opposed strategies for gaining diplomatic advantage from America's nuclear monopoly, but to no avail; "They don't scare," Byrnes concluded. "We shall have atomic energy and many other things too," declared Soviet Foreign Minister Molotov that November, warning the United States against pushing its temporary strategic advantage. At Moscow, Byrnes substituted the carrot for the stick, holding out the prospect of nuclear cooperation with the Soviets. For a time it seemed possible, but back in Washington, Byrnes's position was eroding. Led by Admiral William Leahy, President Truman's palace guard denounced Byrnes and his "communistically inclined" State Department advisers. The Moscow agreement, charged Senator Arthur Vandenberg, was "one more typical American 'give-away.'" Preoccupied by political problems at home and abroad, Truman turned on his secretary of state; "I'm tired of babying the Soviets," he declared in January 1946. From then until his retirement in 1947, the pliant Byrnes faithfully followed the new "get tough with Russia" policy. The effort to develop atomic policy in collaboration with the Soviets was abandoned, and monopoly and exclusion became the hallmarks of U.S. nuclear strategy.

Turning to the struggle over civilian versus military control of the atom, Herken shows that the 1946 defeat of the May-Johnson bill (providing for military control) and the passage of the McMahon Act (creating the Atomic Energy Commission under a civilian head) was hardly a clear-cut victory for civilian control. In fact, he argues, the military got much of what it wanted in the McMahon Act. Here, as throughout the book, Herken stresses the central role of General Leslie R. Groves, wartime director of the Manhattan Project and a linchpin in postwar nuclear affairs. The national furor over the Soviet spy ring uncovered in Canada in 1946, he suggests, was largely orchestrated by Groves to discredit the supporters of civilian control and international cooperation in managing the atom.

This same period saw the rise and collapse of the move for U.N. control of the atom—a move rooted in Byrnes's desire to clip Groves's wings and bring nuclear policy within the purview of the State Department. In January 1946, Byrnes named a committee under Dean Acheson to draft a plan for international control of the atom. Aided by a board of scientific advisers, chaired by David Lilienthal and including J. Robert Oppenheimer, Acheson's committee drew up its proposals. But then Truman appointed Bernard Baruch to the U.N.'s Atomic Energy Commission and—in the view of the Acheson-Lilienthal-Oppenheimer group—all was lost. Working closely with Groves, Baruch and his coterie of advisers (mainly businessmen and right-wing ideologues obsessed with the Soviet menace) scuttled the Acheson-Lilienthal plan. Abandoning any serious effort for international control, Baruch concentrated on scoring propaganda points against the Soviets and laying the groundwork for a perpetuation of America's nuclear monopoly. Despite the grandiloquence of Baruch's famous June 1946 U.N. speech ("We are here to make a choice between the quick and the dead"), the "Baruch Plan" was from the first, Herken persuasively argues, more propaganda than substance, more a nuclear ultimatum than a genuine bargaining proposal. The collapse of the U.N. negotiations in late 1946 despite last-minute Soviet efforts to keep them going merely confirmed the Truman administration's de facto policy of nuclear monopoly.

The long final section of *The Winning Weapon,* tracing the evolution of American military planning from Hiroshima to about 1950, offers a chilling insight into what passed for strategic thinking a generation ago. Under the various code names mentioned earlier, these plans consisted of little but doomsday scenarios for the obliteration of Russia in a massive nuclear spasm. Some explicitly envisioned the mass killing of civilians as an instrument of psychological warfare; in others, civilian deaths on a scale of millions was simply implicit. (As Herken notes, this was a natural outgrowth of the terror bombing of civilians introduced by the

Germans—and perfected by the British and Americans—in World War II.) Fleetwood (1948) projected eight atomic bombs for Moscow, seven for Leningrad, and so forth. Such an assault, the authors judiciously speculated, "could well lead to Soviet capitulation." In Dropshot (1949), the destruction of Moscow and Leningrad was held off until the beginning of the war's second week, the planners having evidently grasped that if Moscow were wiped out in the first wave of attack, there would be no one around to surrender.

Herken is especially good on the way interservice rivalries, especially the air force's frustrations over its second-class status, shaped nuclear strategy. The annual interservice budget squabbles, he shows, were a crucial propellant of the strategic planning process. The same rivalries also contributed to what little criticism of underlying strategic assumptions was voiced in these years. Increasingly disgruntled over growing air force dominance, the navy began to question the morality of the air-atomic strategy. With some justice, the air force sarcastically retorted that, to the admirals, an immoral weapon was one they couldn't use.

The occasional glimpses of the nuclear-war planner as moral philosopher are diverting. In 1949, for example, the Joint Chiefs of Staff brushed aside all ethical objections to the H-bomb. Since, "in the larger sense, it is war itself which is immoral," they reasoned, it is "folly to argue whether one weapon is more immoral than another." With casual nonchalance, the generals dismissed many centuries of Christian doctrine about the just war that drew precisely such distinctions.

Strategists consistently refused to rule out the unrestrained use of nuclear weapons, the possibility of an American first strike, or even "preventive" nuclear war. The Russians, insisted the authors of NSC 30 (1948), should "never be given the slightest reason to believe the U.S. would even consider not to use atomic weapons against them if necessary." (Along with their readiness to blow up the world, another count against these planners is their atrocious prose style.)

What emerges starkly in these pages is the degradation of the strategic planning process in the years of America's nuclear monopoly. Herken fully documents the Joint Chiefs' "habit of demanding all the traffic would bear from the AEC's bomb factories." As the nuclear arsenal grew, war plans were revised accordingly. In 1946, for example, Pincher projected the obliteration of twenty Soviet cities; by 1948, Fleetwood had upped the ante to seventy-seven cities. In 1950 a demoralized David Lilienthal, retiring as head of AEC, confessed that his agency had become "nothing more than a major contractor to the Department of Defense."

The Soviet nuclear test of September 1949 abruptly ended this first cycle of U.S. nuclear-war planning. But rather than reassessing underlying premises, the administration set off in quest of yet another "winning weapon" that would reestablish U.S. nuclear supremacy: the hydrogen bomb, or "hell bomb," as journalists dubbed it. Herken reviews the H-bomb decision process, including the deeply apprehensive eighty-page memo drafted by George Kennan—a memo Dean Acheson withheld from Truman. With NSC 68 (1950) providing its underlying strategic framework (and with Czechoslovakia and Korea as part of its background), the nuclear arms race entered a new and even more lethal stage. James B. Conant wrote Lilienthal that he had the feeling of watching the same rotten movie a second time.

Herken's most original contribution is clearly the section on military strategy. No other historian has covered this subject so thoroughly or so well. But throughout, Herken deepens our understanding of the inner diplomatic and strategic history of these years, drawing as he does not only on memoirs and the published record, but on interviews and a rich lode of recently declassified government documents, especially in the Modern Military Branch of the National Archives.

The Winning Weapon's compelling power lies in its portrayal of an entire government in the grip of incredible hubris. With rare exceptions, Herken's large cast of characters clings firmly to the delusion that America's nuclear monopoly will continue into the indefinite future. Their confidence on this score reminds one of Herbert Hoover's glowing descriptions of the nation's economic prospects early in 1929. To the moment of his retirement in 1948, General Groves never stopped insisting that a Soviet bomb was fifteen or twenty years in the future. At his last press conference he told reporters he was "not a bit worried" about a Russian bomb. This massive miscalculation in high places did not rest on the vulgar notion that there was a single "atomic secret" locked in a safe somewhere. Rather it reflected the grossly exaggerated belief in the general superiority of American know-how and ability to organize large-scale technical projects—a belief that was rudely shattered in 1949 (and then again in 1957, with *Sputnik*).

It is tempting to read *The Winning Weapon* as a morality play pitting the farsighted and virtuous against the myopic and malevolent. In the rush to exploit the bomb, a few men, like Lilienthal, Kennan, Stimson, and Marshall, do stand out for their moral concern and more reflective cast of mind. For others, like Groves, Leahy, Forrestal, air force secretary Stuart Symington, and army secretary Kenneth Royall, the old propaganda tag "warmonger" seems nothing but the simple truth. The nuclear saber-rattling of these real-life Dr. Strangeloves can still chill the blood, although some of these pronouncements, dating as they do from the era before nuclear-war planners discovered computers and game theory, are almost quaint in their bluster. As for the fatuous Bernard Baruch— FDR's "Great Poohbah"—the less said the better.

But ultimately this is a story less of obtuse or evil individuals than of an entire generation unable to grasp a dramatically changed reality. With few exceptions, these statesmen and strategists tried to force that new reality into comfortably familiar conceptual categories. The atomic bomb was a "weapon"; it could be used to "wage war"; it could help us achieve our "national objectives." Few grasped that the bomb had created its own categories, and that new metaphors were required to comprehend its meaning: a spreading plague, perhaps, or a metastasizing cancer.

What *The Winning Weapon* really portrays is a monumental failure of the imagination. As the seeds of potential world holocaust germinated and took root, it was business as usual in Washington—and no doubt in Moscow as well. The old ideological rivalries among the various military services and government departments all went on as before, with the atomic bomb simply another piece on the chessboard. Most power holders did not notice as we took our first slow, lazy turns around the far outer edges of the maelstrom, simply because their minds were on other matters.

As in so many other ways, President Truman stands as a kind of Everyman for his generation, straining to bend his mind around awesome new realities, yet continually slipping back into old ways of thinking. When Royall blustered that it "doesn't make any sense" not to use the bomb against Russia, Truman (as we saw in chap. 3) shot back: "You have got to understand that this isn't a military weapon." Yet, in other moods, the same man could cockily assure a senator that no one should doubt his readiness to drop the bomb again "if necessary," and—in private notes written for his own purposes—toy with the idea of issuing a nuclear ultimatum to Russia during the frustrating days of the Korean War.

The underlying source of Truman's confused groping is suggested in a terse and anguished entry David Lilienthal made in his diary in 1947: "The fences are gone. And it was we, the civilized, who have pushed standardless conduct to its ultimate."

NUCLEAR CULTURE IN THE COLD WAR'S HIGH TIDE

As the 1940s ended, the raw shock of atomic menace that had burst on the scene in 1945 was wearing off. By the early 1950s, America's preoccupation with the bomb was less blatant, more subterranean. At the same time, however, nuclear weapons production and planning were burgeoning as the Cold War conflict between the United States and the Soviet Union moved into high gear. The Soviet A-bomb test in 1949; the superpowers' race to develop the H-bomb and an arsenal of nuclear weaponry; and the move toward new, highly sophisticated delivery systems—nuclear submarines, high-tech bombers, and intercontinental ballistic missiles—added new levels of complexity and menace to the arms race. Government civil-defense programs proliferated, drawing in educators, urban planners, media specialists, psychologists, physicians, medical researchers, and other professionals. Washington continued to hype the atom's peacetime uses, partly as a means of funding more weapons research and partly as a way of cultivating more positive public attitudes toward atomic energy. Much of the popular culture reflected the Cold War outlook. Such magazines as *Time, Life,* and *U.S. News & World Report* usually echoed official Washington's position on nuclear issues, as did radio commentators and patriotic movies like the stirring *Strategic Air Command* (1955), starring Jimmy Stewart.

But undercurrents of uneasiness persisted, especially as the hazards of radioactive fallout from nuclear testing gripped the public's awareness, and activist organizations campaigned for a test ban—

an idea supported by Democratic presidential candidate Adlai Stevenson in 1956. In the cultural realm, novels, poems, science-fiction stories, the parodies of song-writer Tom Lehrer, and the satirical *Mad Magazine* all in their various ways warned of possible cataclysm ahead.

5

THE AMERICAN MEDICAL PROFESSION AND THE THREAT OF NUCLEAR WAR

Like chapters 1 and 2, this essay was written in 1985, as the fortieth anniversary of the atomic bombing of Japan focused the nation's renewed attention on the nuclear threat. In the spring of that year, the editor of the *Journal of the American Medical Association (JAMA)* asked me to prepare an article dealing historically with U.S. physicians' engagement with nuclear issues. In researching *By the Bomb's Early Light,* I had already observed the way many professional groups, from sociologists to city planners to high school social-studies teachers, had concluded that their particular expertise had become absolutely vital in the new atomic era. (In February 1947, the University of Maine's College of Agriculture published a pamphlet arguing eloquently that the college's agricultural extension workers could play a key role in the quest for peace in the atomic age.) The *JAMA* invitation led me to several weeks of intensive research on a specific professional group whose members became especially involved with the nuclear issue—as radiation specialists, civil-defense advisers, and ultimately as antinuclear activists. Chapter 5 is adapted from the article that resulted. It appeared in the August 1, 1985, issue of *JAMA.* Reprint requests flowed in from many countries, suggesting broad interest in the issues that arise when professional expertise, political involvement, and activist engagement intersect.

IN THE RESURGENCE of nuclear-weapons activism that swept the United States in the early 1980s, physicians figured prominently. The pediatrician Helen Caldicott gained national visibility as president of the thirty-thousand-member organization Physicians for Social Responsibility. Dean Howard Hiatt of the Harvard School of Public Health, psychiatrist John Mack of Harvard Medical School, H. Jack Geiger of the City College of New York School of Biomedical Education, and Yale University psychiatrist Robert Lifton were prominent in the antinuclear cause. In *The Final Epidemic: Physicians and Scientists on Nuclear War* (1981) and *Last Aid: The Medical Dimensions of Nuclear War* (1982), medical leaders spoke out on this issue. The *Journal of the American Medical Association* published articles on aspects of the subject, including the role of the medical profession in preventing nuclear holocaust. This, however, was only the latest chapter in a long and decidedly checkered history.

RADIATION STUDIES AND ISOTOPES: THE INITIAL MEDICAL RESPONSE TO THE BOMB

American medicine's involvement with nuclear weapons began with the establishment of the Manhattan Project in 1942. The project's medical-research division, based at the University of Rochester and directed by Stafford L. Warren, M.D., a professor of radiology, studied means of protecting workers from radiation, tried to establish radiation tolerance levels, and conducted blood studies of more than 100,000 irradiated laboratory animals and genetic studies involving 277,000 mice and 50 million fruit flies.

But this wartime research was secret, and for most physicians, as for other Americans, President Truman's atomic bomb announcement of August 6, 1945, came as a stunning surprise. The *Journal of the American Medical Association* first mentioned the bomb in a brief note on September 22, dismissing "Jap propaganda claims" that people were still dying in Hiroshima and Nagasaki from "delayed radioactivity." Quickly, however, awareness dawned that this new weapon had profound medical implications, not only because it produced blast and burn casualties on an unprecedented scale, but also because of its unique additional property—radioactivity. The biological and physiological hazards of radioactive substances had long been recognized, thanks to the turn-of-the-century studies of the Leipzig clinician Hermann Heineke, but until August 1945, this arcane byway of medical research had received relatively little attention.

All this soon changed. Within days of Japan's surrender, two American medical teams, one representing the military and the other the Manhattan Project, were in Hiroshima and Nagasaki studying the bomb's effects. For the military team, radiological studies were conducted by Dr. Shields Warren, professor of pathology at Harvard Medical School; the Manhattan Project team was led by Stafford Warren of Rochester. In March 1946, Shields Warren reported to the American Association for Cancer Research (of which he was president) on the delayed effects of radiation exposure on some fourteen thousand people in Hiroshima and Nagasaki, including hemorrhage, leukocyte destruction, bone marrow damage, anemia, sterility, and the suppression of menstruation. As for long-range somatic and genetic effects, he cautioned, "It will be necessary to follow the populations of Hiroshima and Nagasaki for many years." In June 1946, *JAMA* published a study of twenty-one Japanese radiation victims admitted to the Osaka University hospital. At the American Medical Association (AMA) convention that July, Dr. George V. LeRoy of Northwestern University Medical School read a detailed report, "The Medical Sequelae of the Atomic Bomb Explosion," which included extensive data on radiation disease. This report, copiously illustrated with clinical photographs, was later published in *JAMA*. The *American Journal of Surgery* published a report on "Trauma Resulting from Atomic Explosions" by the leader of the navy medical team that studied survivors in Nagasaki. (The author described prisoners of war in the city whose "names had been burned onto their chests or backs because the names had been stenciled in black on their white undershirts.")

In November 1946, the National Research Council of the National Academy of Sciences sent five radiologists to Japan to survey possibilities for a long-term research project. In 1947, authorized by a formal directive from President Truman, the council set up the Atomic Bomb Casualty Commission (ABCC) to be funded by and operated under contract with the AEC. Work began in Japan in 1948, with blood surveys and collection of pregnancy data. In the years that followed, the ABCC and its successor, the Radiation Effects Research Foundation, proved an invaluable source of knowledge about the long-term effects of atomic bomb exposure.

In contrast to the medical profession's considerable interest in the clinical aspects of radiation disease in the immediate post-1945 period, one finds little initial attention to the larger medical implications of an atomic bomb attack or to the profession's capacity to cope with such an event. Shields Warren's 1946 report to his fellow cancer researchers noted the "total disorganization" of the Japanese medical service after the bombings, and George LeRoy's address to the 1946 AMA convention mentioned that the bombing of Hiroshima and Nagasaki had presented "the surviving members of the medical profession . . . with an extremely large relief and rescue problem." "From medical and surgical points of view," wrote one early postwar American medical visitor to Hiroshima and Nagasaki in the *American Journal of Surgery* in 1948, "the confusion immediately after the bombing is difficult to imagine." But these passing observations were not elaborated or pursued. LeRoy ended on a cautiously hopeful note, stating, "In the hospitals of the western world where plasma, electrolyte solutions, whole blood and penicillin are available in adequate amounts, a much lower mortality rate could be achieved than was observed in Japan."

The profession's capacity for political activism and engagement with broader social issues in these years seems to have been totally exhausted by its single-minded preoccupation with the evils of "socialized medicine." After the Truman administration proposed a national health insurance plan in 1948, medical attention focused obsessively on this issue. In resisting "the creeping paralysis that is socialism," said *New York Medicine* in 1950, "the medical profession has found it necessary to undertake civic and political action, which a few years ago was remote from the thoughts of most physicians." Even in dealing with the clinical aspects of radiation disease, the AMA's position was sometimes colored by its ideology. In 1947, for example, reporting that British atomic-energy workers were complaining of lassitude, skin eruptions, impotence, and other symptoms, *JAMA* observed: "It has to be remembered that, with a Labour government in control of the country, workers have every opportunity to exploit real or alleged grievances."

It was not the medical profession but a journalist who first brought home to the American public the way an atomic bomb could devastate a city's medical facilities. Two of the six atomic bomb survivors whose stories are told in John Hersey's 1946 best-seller *Hiroshima* are physicians. The first, Masakazu Fujii, regains consciousness after the bombing to find his small private clinic "all around him in a mad assortment of splintered lumber." The other, Terufumi Sasaki, was a surgeon at Hiroshima's large, modern Red Cross hospital. After the blast, glasses lost and vision blurred, he wanders among the maimed and dying who have inundated the partially demolished hospital, "moving aimlessly and dully up and down the stinking corridors with wads of bandage and bottles of mercurochrome, . . . binding up the worst cuts as he came to them. . . . Ceilings and partitions had fallen; plaster, dust, blood and vomit were everywhere. Patients were dying by the hundreds, but there was nobody to carry away the corpses."

There are a few exceptions in these early post-Hiroshima years to the medical profession's general lack of attention to all but the narrowest clinical aspects of the atomic bomb's medical implications. In 1946, *JAMA* published a letter from Dr. Edwin J. Grace, a specialist on radium poisoning, urging the medical profession to launch an educational program "to awaken the public to full realization that they cannot view indifferently this colossal missile of destruction." And after the 1946 Bikini tests, Stafford Warren, the project's radiological safety chief, wrote an article for *Life Magazine* (August 11, 1947), later condensed in *Reader's Digest,* offering in laymen's language a somber and frightening assessment of the test's implications. The radioactive spray of Test Baker (the underwater explosion), he wrote, posed "an entirely new danger of atomic war." It had so penetrated the target ships that scientists and military personnel could visit them only on hurried forays, to avoid radiation sickness. Radioactive algae had been eaten by larger fish, which had died, their decaying bodies then passing the radioactivity back to the algae. Algae-encrusted hulls on the task-force ships had become so radioactive that crew members' bunks had to be shifted. If, under favorable meteorological conditions, a Bikini-type bomb were dropped in the harbor of a great city, he said, the radiological casualties would be ghastly. Warren concluded with a categorical political assertion of a kind exceedingly rare among medical leaders in this period: "The only defense against atomic bombs still lies outside the scope of science. It is the prevention of atomic war."

The physician dealing with the nuclear theme who reached the largest audience in these years was David Bradley, a 1944 graduate of the University of Wisconsin Medical School. A junior member of the radiological team at Bikini, Bradley was much impressed by Stafford Warren's efforts to awaken the public to the hazard of radiation. Having some journalistic experience and an undergraduate degree in English from Dartmouth College, he readily agreed when a friend at *Atlantic Monthly* suggested an article about his experiences. The article turned into the best-selling book *No Place to Hide* (1948), which, condensed in *Reader's Digest* and offered by the Book-of-the-Month Club, sold 250,000 copies by 1950. Reviewers were enthusiastic. E. B. White, in the *New Yorker*, praised Bradley's "casual, personal" tone and added: "His laboratory was a paradise, and the experiment in which he was involved was an experiment in befouling the laboratory itself." Christopher Morley heard in the book "the clock-tick of warning" (*Reader's Digest*, February 1949). Bradley lectured widely, wrote numerous magazine articles, and appeared on the network radio program *Town Meeting of the Air*.

Written in the form of a journal, *No Place to Hide* is structured around the contrast between the edenic setting and Bradley's awakening to the magnitude of the test's radiological aftereffects. This awakening is conveyed through a series of impressions: the coral reefs gradually bleaching white as the algae that gave them color died off, the radioactive fish that took their own pictures when placed on photographic plates, the navy's futile efforts to decontaminate the surviving ships, the pariah fleet of contaminated vessels anchored off Kwajalein atoll, physically unscathed but nevertheless "dying of a malignant disease for which there is no help."

Bradley also reports a September 1946 visit to Rongerik Island, where some 160 Bikini natives had been "temporarily" relocated. (Nuclear testing continued at Bikini until 1958, and in 1985, the atoll was still unsafe for human habitation. In March 1985, confronted by a lawsuit, the Reagan administration agreed to a $42-million cleanup, including the removal and replacement of radioactive topsoil, which would enable the people of Bikini to return.) Emphasizing the lack of any satisfactory protection against atomic radiation or of any effective means of decontamination, and warning of the devastating radiological effect of an atomic bombing attack not only on the immediate victims but on the land itself for centuries afterwards, Bradley insistently called attention to his book's larger implications: "Bikini is not some faraway little atoll pinpointed on an out-of-the-way chart. Bikini is San Francisco Bay, Puget Sound, the East River. It is the Thames, the Adriatic, Hellespont, and misty Baikal."

Despite the impact of *No Place to Hide,* one must emphasize that David Bradley, a young physician not in the top tier of radiological specialists, stood nearly alone among physicians in this period in his efforts to place the medical and environmental hazards of the atomic bomb in a larger social and political context. No medical groups invited him to lecture, he told me in a 1984 interview, and in medical and scientific journals his book was either ignored or dismissed. Austin M. Brues, M.D. (Harvard, 1930), a University of Chicago radiologist with ties to the AEC, responded with an essay in the *Bulletin of the Atomic Scientists* designed to "dispel some of the fear of radiation that is engendered by an unfamiliar natural phenomenon." The genetic risk of radiation exposure, he said, was "overrated," and the whole subject needed a "partial debunking." Certainly radiation could increase the likelihood of cancer—but so could sunlight and tobacco smoking. Radiation sickness was already treatable, and "further means of alleviation" would soon be found. Disposal of radioactive waste was "no cause for anxiety," since "we still have years in which we can settle upon one of a number of feasible methods." "Above all," he concluded, "we should develop a civilian defense organization to the point where we may rely on it to protect the population."

As one might anticipate, given the narrow clinical focus of its response to the advent of the atomic bomb, the medical profession did not play an active role in promoting the Acheson-Lilienthal plan for international control of atomic energy, which won wide public support in 1945–47 (even as the Truman administration distanced itself from the international control principle). Among the most articulate and effective proponents of international control were many scientists of the

Manhattan Project, who became intensely active politically just after the war through their lobbying organization, the Federation of American Scientists. Many religious and professional groups threw their support behind the atomic scientists' cause. For example, the American Psychological Association formed a Society for the Psychological Study of Social Issues, which in June 1946 issued a six-point manifesto that essentially endorsed the political program of the atomic scientists. The international control movement found little answering echo, however, in the leadership of the American medical profession.

PROMOTING THE "PEACEFUL ATOM": THE MEDICAL PROMISE OF RADIOACTIVE ISOTOPES

In somewhat deliberate counterpoint to grim reports about the atomic bomb's clinical effects, the American medical profession in the late 1940s focused much attention on the atom's potential medical benefits, especially the diagnostic and treatment value of radioactive isotopes. In the 1930s, Ernest O. Lawrence had predicted vast therapeutic applications for the isotopes he produced in his cyclotron at the University of California, but not until August 1945 did medicine's interest in isotopes really blossom. As even a casual perusal of the *Index Medicus* for these years makes abundantly clear, the medical journals were full of reports on the use of isotopes of phosphorus, iodine, and cobalt in the diagnosis and treatment of goiter, bone cancer, and other diseases.

These applications were indeed important. In the present context, however, it is noteworthy as well that the widespread publicity given to the medical promise of atomic energy was also culturally significant in shaping public perceptions of the new age that had dawned. Discussions of atomic energy in the early post-Hiroshima period often reflected a stark either-or approach: Either the atomic bomb would destroy civilization, or atomic energy would be harnessed to produce a utopia of unimaginable wonder. If a nuclear holocaust could be avoided, the atom would provide electricity too cheap to meter; fuel automobiles, airplanes, and ships for a lifetime; give mankind mastery of the environment and the weather—and banish disease from the earth. An editorial cartoon published in the *Dallas Morning News* within days of Hiroshima pictured a skeleton labeled "CANCER" fleeing lightning bolts of "Atomic Energy," and this theme loomed large in the early popular writings about atomic energy in such magazines as *Life, Collier's,* and the *Saturday Evening Post.*

The more euphoric of the post-Hiroshima utopian fantasies soon faded, but predictions of the atom's vast medical promise became, if anything, rosier as the decade wore on. Radioactive isotopes were wonder-workers that would transform human existence! Isotope research, proclaimed *Collier's* in May 1947, promised "cures for hitherto incurable diseases" and opened the door to "a golden age of atomic medicine." As soon as hospitals were equipped "to offer atomic medicine to all who need it," this article concluded, "much of the pain and premature death which now face so many of us may prove to be avoidable." Writing in the *American Magazine* in December 1947, Chancellor Robert M. Hutchins of the University of Chicago predicted, "The atomic city will have a central diagnostic laboratory but only a small hospital, if any at all, for most human ailments will be cured as rapidly as they are diagnosed." "The Sunny Side of the Atom," a 1947 CBS radio special, credited isotopes with almost magical powers, artfully blurring the distinction between diagnosis and cure and implying that isotopes had actual healing properties.

Research on the medical applications of atomic energy was strongly encouraged by the U.S. government in these years. Thanks in part to the efforts of Shields Warren, first director of the AEC's division of biology and medicine, the AEC funneled substantial funds to cancer research in medical schools and research institutes, financed construction of the Argonne Cancer Research Hospital at the University of Chicago, and underwrote some 175 pre- and postdoctoral fellowships in the life sciences. With this infusion of federal dollars, research in the field burgeoned. In the six months from January to June 1950, the *Index Medicus* recorded some 250 reports on medical research involving atomic energy.

While the AEC's funding of medical research was legitimate and doubtless praiseworthy, it also had significant public relations value in shaping perceptions of atomic energy—a side benefit the government fully recognized. AEC chairman David E. Lilienthal tirelessly promoted the image of "the peaceful atom," even as the AEC's energies focused heavily on bomb production. As the AEC celebrated the positive side of the atomic story through exhibits, radio programs, magazine articles, and speeches by Lilienthal and others, the atom's medical promise high-lighted the propaganda campaign.

The American medical profession willingly lent itself to this cam-paign. In December 1946, the District of Columbia medical journal published a lengthy article in which a government radiologist deplored the "wild fantastic talk" by "irresponsible" people that was exacerbating public fears of atomic war. Urging a more "common-sense viewpoint," he described the therapeutic possibilities of radiation in cancer treatment and concluded, "The romance which undoubtedly lies ahead for these fortunate investigators who enter this field has probably never been equalled in the past, certainly not in the field of biologic research." In 1947, after glowingly describing the vast medical promise of radioactive isotopes, *Hygeia,* an AMA-sponsored popular health magazine, noted that this dimension of atomic energy development was "not so de-pressing as the thought of an atomic war," and that while the develop-ment of atomic weapons was unquestionably "an unhappy event, . . . the power to learn about better health far outweighs other considerations."

At the 1948 AMA convention, a special session on atomic energy featured a report by Shields Warren on the AEC's medical research pro-gram, a lecture by an AEC scientist on the medical value of isotopes, and a more general discussion of "The Medical Profession and Atomic Energy" by AEC commissioner Lewis L. Strauss. While some peacetime applications of atomic energy were as yet "hidden in the mists of the future," said Warren, its immediate implications for medical research were "as overwhelming as a streamliner rushing down on a grade cross-ing" (an image that may have been less reassuring than he intended). Strauss urged physicians to help in overcoming the unreasoning "preju-dice against work on atomic energy, based on lack of detailed informa-tion" and the "widespread impression that atomic energy is a health hazard of monumental and enduring proportions." "Certainly persons can be injured by loose and restless atomic particles, and chromosomes can be damaged, with resultant mutations," acknowledged Strauss. "But we should remember that these changes can be produced also by any number of agents from sunlight down to the garden crocus. In other words, they are neither very new, nor very startling. It is simply that our attention is focused on them at the moment."

The implicit (and often explicit) message underlying much of this medical discussion of atomic energy—that the therapeutic promise far outweighed and even canceled out the atom's menace—penetrated the profession very deeply. "The effects of the atomic bomb may seem appalling to many persons," Dr. Harold C. Lueth told the West Virginia Medical Association in August 1949, but when the medical benefits of atomic energy were considered, he went on, "a much more hopeful aspect . . . is gained." "Out of the ashes of Hiroshima and Nagasaki," he concluded, "there will come a beneficial atomic energy that will rise phoenix-like to benefit the health and welfare of our nation."

THE FEDERAL MEDICAL BUREAUCRACY AND CIVIL DEFENSE

By the late 1940s, American attitudes toward the atomic bomb were changing rapidly. Hopes for international control had evaporated, the Cold War was under way, and fear of Russia was intensifying. Encouraged by the government and influential voices in the media, many who had earlier viewed the abolition or strict control of atomic weapons as the nation's top priority now concluded that atomic superiority was America's best hope. The Russian atomic-bomb test of September 1949, the arrest of atomic spy Klaus Fuchs in England in January 1950, and President Truman's decision that same month to authorize development of the hydrogen bomb sharply accelerated this profound shift in cultural attitudes. Public-opinion polls overwhelmingly supported the H-bomb decision.

With these developments came a heavy official emphasis on civil defense. In 1948, Defense Secretary James V. Forrestal created an office of civil-defense planning in the Pentagon, and in 1950 President Truman established the Federal Civil Defense Administration. Under its director, Millard Caldwell, the administration moved quickly to draw the medical profession deeply into the process of civil-defense planning and propaganda. A director for health services was appointed, with assistant directors responsible for medical care planning, public health, and the stockpiling of medical and mortuary supplies against the day of atomic attack. State and county medical societies were designated as advisers to local civil-defense offices. Dr. Howard A. Rusk, a professor at the New York University School of Medicine and a national leader in the profession, chaired the medical advisory committee.

Physicians in many branches and agencies of government rallied behind the emerging civil-defense campaign. The Public Health Service established a radiological health division. The Naval Medical Center at Bethesda, Maryland, organized a course on civil defense in atomic war for its reserve medical officers. The director of this program reported in 1950, "At the conclusion of these lectures our Reserve Medical Officers have told me repeatedly, 'Many of us came disheartened and with a helpless attitude on the atomic bomb. The casualties were just too staggering. The course has dispelled this defeatist attitude.'" In "What You Should Know about the Atomic Bomb," the surgeon general of the army, R. W. Bliss, offered an equally optimistic message: Survival was possible; experts had the problem in hand. "Our population need not be defenseless," he declared, "The trained combination of nuclear physicists, engineers, and medical men can operate to protect our Nation if it is ever attacked."

Another government physician to put his expertise at the service of civil-defense planning was the psychiatrist Dale C. Cameron, M.D., assistant director of the National Institute of Mental Health from 1945 to 1950. In "Psychiatric Implications of Civil Defense," read before the American Psychiatric Association in May 1949 and later published in the *American Journal of Psychiatry,* Cameron warned that an atomic attack could have serious psychological effects, ranging from "apathy" to "purposeless hyperactivity." But such undesirable postattack behavior could be minimized, Cameron went on, if citizens were authoritatively assured that atomic attack was survivable, that alarmists were vastly overstating radiation hazards, and that civil-defense planning would protect the nation if atomic war came.

Cameron called for the organization of the population into small groups under psychiatrically trained leaders who would assist groups in "working through . . . fears and apprehensions" and "overcoming attitudes of futility . . . which would be disastrous in the event war should occur." After the bomb fell, these small neighborhood groups could then reassemble and provide mutual support.

Central to the government's civil-defense program was the effort to downplay the danger of radiation in an atomic attack and to emphasize protective measures citizens could take against radiation injury. Radiation was like taxes, wrote one government civil-defense staff member in 1949, not pleasant, perhaps, but you could learn to live with it. This is the central theme, too, of *How to Survive an Atomic Bomb,* a government handbook by Richard Gerstell, holder of a Ph.D. in radiology from the University of Michigan. Don't be taken in by "foolish stories" about radiation causing cancer, sterility, or genetic damage, Gerstell urged, "Learn not to be afraid of those words 'radiation' and 'radioactivity.'" A recurring theme in David Lilienthal's speeches of the late 1940s was that fearmongers were exaggerating the radiation hazard; radiation was like sunlight, Lilienthal insisted—to be treated with respect, but certainly not feared.

Physicians in the government's employ lent their authority to this campaign. In April 1948, clearly seeking to counteract the impact of David Bradley's *No Place to Hide,* the U.S. surgeon general issued a news release deriding the "sensational prophecies" of dire radiological consequences in an atomic war. In 1948, James P. Cooney, M.D., an official of the army medical corps attached to the AEC, told the American Public Health Association that while atomic radiation could indeed cause death and injury, it should be approached with a "practical attitude," not unreasoning fear. Cooney's central concern was not radiation itself, but "the fear reaction of the uninitiated." The potential victims of atomic radiation, he insisted, must be conditioned to think of it as simply another of the many acceptable risks of war. Americans must learn "to live with this piece of ordnance" and if necessary "use it again in the defense of our way of living." Cooney further disseminated his ideas in numerous medical articles of this period, of which "The Physician's Problem in Atomic Warfare" in *JAMA* (March 3, 1951) is representative.

Several physicians with links to the AEC, including Shields Warren and James P. Cooney, contributed to *The Effects of Atomic Weapons,* a technical report issued by the AEC in 1950. The chapter on the bomb's radiological effects offered a detailed summary of current knowledge and cautioned that "the exact magnitude of the risk" of long-term genetic damage was not yet known. But this AEC report was intended as a handbook for civil-defense officials, and its overall theme is the value of informed advance planning in diminishing the bomb's destructive effects. Typical of this action-oriented emphasis is the claim (not in the medical chapter, it should be noted) that lingering radiological contamination from an atomic bomb exploded low in the atmosphere "might be an inconvenience, but it would not, in general, represent a real danger." A simplified AEC booklet based on the longer technical study went much further in downplaying the danger of radiation and stressing the value of preventive measures.

At a news conference introducing this booklet, an AEC spokesman insisted that the radiation danger had been much exaggerated, and concluded: "If an individual can stand up after the bomb goes off and look around and comment 'this place is really beat up' . . . , he has a pretty good chance of surviving." While acknowledging that there was "no specific therapeutic treatment right now" for radiation disease, he insisted vaguely but emphatically, "There is much that we can do about it. We don't have to sit back and say that 60,000 people are going to die because a bomb goes off, because that is not the way to look at it."

THE MEDICAL PROFESSION AS A WHOLE AND CIVIL DEFENSE

The medical profession's role in the early civil-defense campaign was not by any means limited to government physicians. With rare exceptions, all levels of organized medicine actively supported and lent credibility to the government effort to persuade the American people of the urgency and efficacy of civil-defense preparation for atomic war. At a time when American medicine was so vigorously fighting government proposals for national health insurance, enthusiastic support of Washington on the civil-defense issue may have appealed to the medical leadership as a means of demonstrating the profession's patriotism, social consciousness, and civic responsibility.

In these years *JAMA* published frequent and approving reports about the profession's civil-defense role, and it also promoted the expansion of that role. In a 1949 issue of *JAMA*, for example, three veterans of the Manhattan Project's medical-research program, discussing the general question "Physicians in an Atomic War," conceded "the enormity of the medical problem" and even admitted that at the moment American medicine was little better prepared "to cope with an atomic bomb attack on one of our major cities than the Japanese were at Nagasaki." They insisted, however, that with more planning all this could change, and the profession could handle the medical challenge of atomic war, including blood transfusions, intravenous feeding, and pain sedation on a monumental scale. They recommended the construction of backup hospitals in suburban areas and insisted that "an essential part of a physician's training" should be instruction in postattack medical practice, including the principles of triage (the tripartite division of casualties on the basis of survival probability). "The physician must play a role in the investigation of these problems during this period of peace," they concluded bluntly. "That he will play a role in handling casualties in the event of an atomic war is inevitable."

Organizationally, too, the American medical profession cooperated fully with the federal civil-defense program in these years. In 1947, the AMA set up a Committee on National Emergency Medical Service, which met periodically to discuss a variety of post–nuclear attack problems. The AMA also cooperated with a Red Cross program to stockpile blood plasma for use in an atomic attack. At an AMA conference on medical education in 1948, Dr. George E. Armstrong, deputy surgeon general of the U.S. Army, urged medical schools to organize minicourses on radiation disease to "alleviate the worry which pervades the profession." Such courses need take only a few days, he said, since "what every physician should know . . . can be mimeographed on one sheet of paper." Armstrong cautioned, however, that in an atomic attack certain medical procedures customary in disaster situations would have to be delayed, for example, "until trained technicians consider it safe to enter the radio-contaminated areas." Further, vast numbers of victims would be so heavily irradiated that no treatment or transfusions could help them, and "the profession must steel itself to make those persons comfortable and to concentrate every effort to save those who have some chance of survival." Armstrong asked the AMA's "assistance in 'selling' [these] two concepts to the profession—concepts which are contrary to all previous teachings, yet which are vital to the proper handling of casualties in the event of an atomic catastrophe."

Accepting its assigned mission, the AMA cooperated fully in an extensive medical training program that was soon launched by the AEC and the Federal Civil Defense Administration. Under this program, physicians were brought to regional training centers at Rochester, Johns Hopkins, UCLA, and other universities for a brief but intensive course in the medical aspects of an atomic attack, including "the biological, pathologic and genetic effects of radiation" and "psychological factors such as mass hysteria." These trainees were then expected to cooperate with local civil-defense officials in their respective areas in the training of physicians, nurses, and other medical professionals. At a November 1951 conference in Chicago sponsored by the AMA's Council on National Emergency Medical Service, the American Hospital Association, and the Association of State and Territorial Health Officers, 250 delegates from all over the country heard lectures by federal civil-defense officials and discussed all aspects of medical and public-health planning for an atomic attack, from the stockpiling of blood and plasma to latrine policing, the control of hysteria, and the mass burial of radioactive corpses.

Local and state medical societies, too, responded with alacrity to Washington's call for cooperation in civil-defense planning. The Massachusetts Medical Society's "Suggestions for First-Aid Treatment of Casualties from Atomic Bombing," published in the *New England Journal of Medicine* in 1950, was subsequently offered in pamphlet form to the general public. That same year, the Maine medical journal published a three-part series, "What Every Maine Doctor Should Know about the Medical Aspects of Atomic Weapons and Atomic Warfare," which began with a hopeful exhortation by the army's surgeon general, R. W. Bliss, and concluded with a call to every Maine physician to "measure his obligation toward the future," "accept his responsibility for the safety and . . . survival of the great masses of the population if a new conflict should come," and "cooperate wholeheartedly" with civil-defense planning designed to reduce casualties, "should these new atomic or hydrogen bombs ever be dropped . . . over our densely populated civilian centers." In Colorado, Dr. Thad P. Sears, professor at the University of Colorado

Medical School and a member of the state medical society's Disaster Commission, became almost obsessed, according to a colleague, with a "deep-seated conviction . . . that the community in which he lived should be prepared for atomic warfare." Sears gave hundreds of lectures in the Rocky Mountain area, trying to "arouse civilians and his professional colleagues from their unrealistic complacency," and in *The Physician in Atomic Defense* (1953), he reiterated his belief in the medical profession's vital civil-defense role.

Perhaps the most elaborate planning at the state level was by the Pennsylvania medical society's Atomic Energy Medical Steering Committee, set up in 1948 to design a program "to protect the public in event of disaster." Six subcommittees addressed such matters as radiation measurement, postattack epidemic control, and "strengthening public morale." Reviewing these plans at the society's annual meeting in 1949, a speaker reminded his colleagues that the prospect of atomic war "imposed grave responsibilities on the medical profession."

The annual gatherings of the nation's medical associations provided an important forum for government medical officials preaching the civil-defense message. Physicians must "be in a continual state of preparedness," the District of Columbia medical society was told in 1948 by Clarence J. Brown of the navy medical service, since in an atomic attack, responsibility would "rest squarely upon the shoulders of the civilian medical profession, whether or not they are in uniform." The Atlanta medical society was told in 1950 by another navy medical officer that a "sustained and orderly program of education and wise leadership" by physicians was essential to encourage civil-defense preparation and counteract the exaggerated radiation fears that had "captured the popular interest and beclouded the thinking of many imaginative minds."

In the same vein, an alumni-day audience at the Indiana University medical school in May 1950 heard Morton D. Willcutts of the Naval Medical Center denounce exaggerated and misleading reports that had "excited too much respect and fear of the radiation hazards in the wake of an atomic explosion." Willcutts acknowledged that, without advance planning, the casualties in an atomic attack would "swamp normally available facilities," but he insisted that civil-defense preparation could improve the picture dramatically: "There is a defense. We do not need to hide or to become frightened out of our wits into hysteria. Forewarned is to be forearmed." Quoting a navy public-relations officer of his acquaintance, Willcutts ended on a note of aggressive optimism, "We will survive. Our country is young and very, very strong when angered or attacked. . . . 'Through the generations of our existence as a peace-loving democracy, we have formed one excellent habit—we win wars.'"

A number of state medical societies heard the civil-defense message from William W. Wilson, M.D., of the army medical corps. Physicians were understandably feeling "temporary pessimism" as they contemplated the medical consequences of a nuclear war, Wilson told the Florida Medical Association in 1950, but with planning they could enhance their "capabilities for overcoming the hazards attributable to atomic bombing." Such preparation could be relatively simple, he insisted. Pre-1945 civil-defense plans need only be updated to take into account the "vastly increased numbers" of casualties and "the new problems of radiation." Like Willcutts, Wilson ended on an inspirational note: "It has been characteristic of our medical profession . . . to accept no defeats, to know no fears, to withhold no service to victims of disaster." With planning and cooperation, "there could be nothing but triumph if we should ultimately be put to a critical test."

Hospital administrators, too, participated in the officially inspired preoccupation with civil defense. Discussing "Hospitals versus the Atom Bomb" in the December 1950 issue of *Modern Hospital,* an army hospital administrator urged his civilian colleagues to prepare at once for atomic war. "We are not likely to have enough hospital beds for even a limited atomic attack," he warned, "*unless we think now in terms of maximum potentials.*" Administrators, he insisted, should give thought to such matters as tattooing blood type on patients' arms, "emergency morgue facilities," postattack "police and traffic control" at their hospitals, and means of handling hysterical patients. Should beds run short, he noted, "an ordinary house door on a saw horse will suffice in dire need." In an atomic war, he suggested: "Improvisation will be the greatest asset the administrator can have." In the same issue, an architect discussed the need for more blast-resistant hospital design.

The leading civil-defense advocate among hospital administrators was New York City hospital commissioner Marcus D. Kogel, M.D. "The mounting tension in our population makes it imperative that we have a workable plan . . . as quickly as possible," Kogel wrote in *Hospital Management* in 1950, "so that we can get rolling and do something constructive towards its implementation." Recognizing that most urban hospitals would be wiped out in an atomic attack, Kogel advocated the training of mobile paramedical squads, modeled on the army's battalion aid stations, to set up emergency medical centers around the perimeter of the bombed-out area "at intervals as close as a block or two." Kogel's staff even drew up a list of supplies for each emergency medical center, including a lantern, six sheets and pillowcases, a pint of whiskey, and a bottle of sodium bicarbonate. With atomic war looming, he wrote, it was "a matter of plain common sense" to develop "an entirely new concept of a civilian emergency medical service . . . capable of going into high gear the moment the disaster strikes."

Pervading these discussions was the conviction that to sustain civilian morale, the medical profession must cultivate an aura of mastery and total assurance regarding its ability to cope with atomic war. As William Wilson told the Florida Medical Association, it would be "impossible to exaggerate the benefits guaranteed by public confidence that prompt and skilled medical services" would be available in the postattack period. "What the public will believe, as soon as their physicians and health departments tell them at every opportunity," he insisted, was that, with sufficient advance planning, "most of those resisting attack" would survive. Professionally acculturated always to appear hopeful and optimistic in dealing with patients, physicians tried to sustain this manner in their discussion of atomic war. "The task of the medical profession," Dr. Harold C. Lueth told the West Virginia Medical Association, was to "reassure the population that steps can be taken to minimize the effect of the atomic bomb." He acknowledged, however, that this task would become increasingly difficult as atomic war drew closer: "Those persons who have heard only the gruesome results of the bomb will be definitely depressed by the possibility of the threat of immediate death. Anxiety and fear will be kindled in the minds of those who do not understand the bomb. . . . The possibility of lingering illness with no prospect of recovery constitutes a real anxiety."

In this spirit of reassurance, Dr. George F. Lull, secretary of the

AMA, brought a message of both hope and challenge to the public in a 1950 article in *Today's Health.* Physicians were shouldering "the leading role in national preparedness for an atomic war," he wrote, but they needed "the help of every American." To provide that help, he went on, citizens must "treat the problem of possible attack with skill and foresight, and control fear with reason instead of exaggerating it into hysteria." The challenge of preparedness for atomic attack was formidable, said the aptly named Lull, but "the answer lies in a smooth-operating civil-defense setup within every community."

Only in muted, half-acknowledged ways did a few physicians— while ostensibly endorsing civil-defense ideology—hint that the entire approach might be misconceived. In some discussions, for example, the most nightmarish visions of total chaos were followed by the ritualistic insistence that "planning" and "preparation" were nevertheless essential. In *The Physician in Atomic Defense,* for example, Thad P. Sears, estimating (very conservatively) that an atomic attack on a city of half a million would produce 120,000 casualties, of whom 40,000 would die in the first twenty-four hours, wrote: "The remaining case load will therefore be 80,000. . . . Injured persons must be rescued and given first aid. They are then to be passed through a hospital chain and evacuated either to their homes or to off-target convalescent institutions. This service must be rendered in the presence of physical destruction, fire, confusion, rubble-filled streets, poor ambulance transport, disrupted communications, insufficient technical assistance and possibly lingering radioactivity." The disposal of corpses, too, would pose problems "almost bizarre in type and magnitude": "Refrigeration and embalming facilities are entirely inadequate for the care of numbers so great as these. . . . This may mean mass burial in a common grave." Despite these horrifying prospects, Sears insisted that the medical profession must be prepared to cope: "Such a prospect calls for a well-organized plan with careful attention given to every detail, including adequate rehearsal."

Despite its effort at optimism, the Maine medical journal launched its civil-defense series with extensive quotations from Hersey's graphic description of the utter destruction of Hiroshima's medical system—by a single bomb that was already puny by 1950. Every physician should read *Hiroshima,* it said, to learn "what the medical man will . . . face in the event an atomic bomb is detonated over a large industrial area in his vicinity." A number of medical writers recalled how the several hundred burn victims of the 1942 Coconut Grove nightclub fire had swamped the medical resources of Boston. In a 1949 report on AEC-funded research on the effects of flash burns on pigs, two medical researchers at Rochester digressed to reflect on the "staggering" resources necessary to treat the burn victims in an actual atomic attack on a medium-sized city: 170,000 medical professionals; 8,000 tons of oxygen, plasma, drugs, gauze; and so forth.

But such cautionary notes were rare. In the later 1940s, the organized medical profession wholeheartedly lent its prestige and organizational strength to the government's civil-defense program, including the systematic effort to downplay the radiation hazards of atomic war and persuade the public that with sufficient preparation, American society could absorb a large-scale atomic attack with a minimum of disruption. The demands on the medical profession would be enormous, so the litany went, but it would rise to the challenge. As Everett Evans, a professor of surgery at the Medical College of Virginia and consultant to the ABCC, put it in a *JAMA* article, the very fact that the medical situation in an atomic war could easily degenerate into "complete chaos and panic" made it all the more urgent that physicians gird themselves for the eventuality. "Only free men with strong hearts and wills can accomplish the gigantic task of providing by training and discipline the necessary workers." Civil-defense planning must begin at once, said Evans, "lest contemplation of the magnitude of the task only encourage despair." Atomic war would be the ultimate challenge for the American physician, and he must steel himself for it, whatever the odds. Any other response would be unworthy and unpatriotic. Such was the message of America's medical leadership as the 1950s began.

THE ROOTS OF ANTI–NUCLEAR WEAPONS ACTIVISM IN AMERICAN MEDICINE

Beginning in the mid-1950s and increasing through the early 1960s, a few influential medical voices broke the pattern of uncritical support for official government positions on nuclear issues. This development reflected a larger cultural shift in these years—a shift triggered primarily by fear of fallout from the atmospheric testing of thermonuclear weapons. Although the first thermonuclear test was conducted by the United States in 1952, it was the U.S. Bravo test series at Bikini atoll in March 1954, which spread deadly radioactive ash over nearly eight thousand square miles of the Pacific and brought illness and death to the crew of a Japanese fishing vessel, that first alerted the world to the fallout danger.

As American, Russian, and British thermonuclear tests continued, fear of global atmospheric fallout and its possible link to cancer and long-term genetic damage increased, focusing especially on strontium 90, a deadly radioactive isotope with a half-life of twenty-eight years and calcium-like properties. Pumped into the atmosphere by thermonuclear explosions, strontium 90 returned to earth in rain, entered the food chain, and concentrated especially in the bone marrow of infants and children. Geneticists took the lead in sounding the alarm. The Nobel laureate Hermann J. Muller of Indiana University somberly warned of threats to the human gene pool, man's "most valuable irretrievable possession." In a 1956 National Academy of Sciences report, a committee of prominent geneticists concluded that in terms of long-term genetic damage, "the concept of a *safe* rate of radiation simply does not make sense." The University of Wisconsin geneticist James F. Crow declared unequivocally in 1957: "There is no such thing as a safe dose of radiation to the population." Radiologists (including some physicians with AEC ties, such as Shields Warren and Austin Brues) tended to disagree, suggesting that a safe threshold did exist. Warren called the genetic risk from radioactive fallout "so slight in relation to other risks as to be disregarded" and dismissed the entire controversy as "more important as a symbol than it is as an actual health hazard." A 1958 study of irradiated mice at the AEC's Argonne Laboratory in Illinois seemed to confirm the "safe threshold" conclusion, although geneticists sharply challenged its relevance to human beings.

While scientists debated, public alarm mounted. Under growing pressure, the Public Health Service began monitoring the nation's milk supply in 1958. A full-blown fallout scare gripped the nation early in 1959, when tests showed a sharp rise of strontium 90 in St. Louis and other cities. A study of strontium 90 in the bones of children under the age of four, conducted at Columbia University and published in *Science* in May 1959, showed that the level doubled in 1957. The *Saturday Evening Post* in 1959 ran a feature entitled "Fallout: The Silent Killer."

Across the cultural spectrum—from sermons, symposia, poems, and novels to movies, television series, and mass magazines—the fallout scare led to the articulation of more general nuclear fears submerged since the 1945–47 period. Politically, it spawned a campaign to stop nuclear testing. The idea of a test ban, advanced by the Democratic presidential candidate Adlai Stevenson in the 1956 presidential campaign, was broached again by Minnesota senator Hubert Humphrey in the 1960 Democratic primaries. Nearly two thousand scientists signed Linus Pauling's 1957 petition calling for an international test ban agreement. Of the many test ban organizations, the best known, founded in 1957, was SANE, the National Committee for a Sane Nuclear Policy.

Within this sharply altered cultural and political climate, some influential American physicians became politically active on the nuclear issue. Psychiatrist Jerome Frank of Johns Hopkins University, for example, in a November 1958 *Atlantic Monthly* article, drew parallels between society's responses to the nuclear threat and the behavior of mental patients: denial, compulsive repetition, paranoid suspicion, and so on. Frank became a SANE director in 1963 and in 1967 published *Sanity and Survival: Psychological Aspects of War and Peace.*

In St. Louis, meanwhile, Dr. Walter Bauer, a pathologist at the Washington University School of Medicine, joined with physiologist Barry Commoner and others in 1958 to found the Committee for Nuclear Information (CNI) to publicize the fallout danger. The committee's best-known publication, a fictionalized but scientifically accurate account of the effects of a nuclear attack on St. Louis, appeared in the CNI newsletter in 1959 and was reprinted in *Saturday Review* and elsewhere. Another CNI project was the "Baby Tooth Survey" to measure strontium 90 levels. The brainchild of Dr. Alfred Schwartz, a St. Louis pediatrician and CNI vice president, the study accumulated more than eighty thousand teeth by 1962. (Each contributor received a button proclaiming "I Gave My Tooth to Science.") The deans of the Washington University and St. Louis University dental schools sat on the project's scientific advisory board. The results, released in 1962, showed a fourteenfold increase in the level of strontium 90 in the teeth of children born in 1957 compared with those born in 1949.

This first wave of medical involvement in the nuclear issue crested in 1962–63. In 1962, SANE's executive director, Homer Jack, recruited Benjamin Spock to the cause. In a full-page advertisement in the *New York Times,* the famed baby doctor gazed with furrowed brow at a little girl under the headline "Dr Spock Is Worried." In 1963, Spock became SANE's cochairman.

In 1962, an important series of articles in the *New England Journal of Medicine* (which in 1950 had published "Suggestions for First Aid Treatment of Casualties from Atomic Bombing") explored "The Medical Consequences of Thermonuclear War" and "The Physician's Role in the Post-Attack Period." Supplemented by essays by Gerard Piel, publisher of *Scientific American,* and Bentley Glass, professor of biology at Johns Hopkins University, these articles were published in 1963 in a work arrestingly entitled *The Fallen Sky.* In sharp contrast to the earlier exhortations to physicians to prepare for atomic war, these articles insisted that a thermonuclear attack would be a medical catastrophe so enormous and so devastating in its effects on the structure of medical service that physicians should focus their energies on preventing such an event, not preparing for it. "No modern society can survive a full-scale thermonuclear attack," the authors asserted unequivocally, and any civil-defense program that suggested otherwise was "a vast and scientifically unsupportable gamble with human life." A "limited" nuclear attack on metropolitan Boston, the authors concluded, would kill one million of the three million inhabitants outright and another million from injuries and delayed effects. Of the city's 6,560 physicians, 4,850 would die at once, and only 640 would escape unscathed. If each of these 640 worked a sixteen-hour day and spent only fifteen minutes with each casualty, they calculated, it would take about three weeks for all the victims to receive minimal attention.

This influential series, published in one of the nation's most prestigious medical journals, was one of the early projects of a new organization, Physicians for Social Responsibility (PSR). Founded in 1961 by Dr. Bernard Lown, professor of cardiology at the Harvard School of Public Health, PSR served as a rallying point for the growing number of physicians becoming active in the antinuclear cause. "There are situations in which prevention is the only effective therapy," declared PSR's statement of purpose. "The physician . . . must begin to explore a new area of preventive medicine, the prevention of thermonuclear war." Membership increased steadily in the succeeding months, drawing physicians from around the country.

In these years Jerome Frank was not the only psychiatrist to probe the psychological underpinnings of the nuclear arms race and the implications of the civil-defense movement. In the aforementioned 1962 special issue of the *New England Journal of Medicine,* two Harvard Medical School psychiatrists argued that "the psychological and social problems raised in planning a defense-shelter program are of a magnitude and complexity that make it advisable to concentrate massive efforts on *eliminating the need* for such a program." An article reporting the destructive psychological effects of prolonged fallout-shelter confinement appeared in the *Archives of General Psychiatry* in 1963. The following year, the Committee on Social Issues of the Group for the Advancement of Psychiatry (an association of socially engaged psychiatrists founded in 1946) published *Psychiatric Aspects of the Prevention of Nuclear War.*

In these years, too, Robert Jay Lifton discovered his subject—the psychological effects of living with nuclear weapons. Active in the test ban movement at Harvard in the late 1950s, Lifton in 1962, having conducted a two-year study of Japanese youth, spent six months in Hiroshima interviewing atomic-bomb survivors. The first product of this study, a 1963 *Daedalus* article entitled "Psychological Effects of the Atomic Bomb in Hiroshima—The Theme of Death," contained the germ of the ideas Lifton elaborated in numerous books and articles, most memorably in *Death in Life: Survivors of Hiroshima* (1967).

REORIENTATION

The American medical profession's surge of involvement with the issue of nuclear war was not sustained. In common with the rest of the culture, medicine's engagement with this issue diminished sharply after the ratification of the Limited Nuclear Test Ban Treaty in November 1963. This treaty did not stop all nuclear testing, but it did halt atmospheric testing, the source of the dreaded radioactive fallout. This development, plus a series of arms-control agreements, such as the Strategic Arms Limitation Treaty of 1972 (SALT I), an apparent easing of Cold War tensions during the period of détente), and the emergence of the Vietnam War as an issue of compelling urgency all combined to diminish anti–nuclear weapons activism. Groups like SANE and the St. Louis Committee on Nuclear Information, in which physicians had played a prominent role, faded away or turned to other issues. PSR went into eclipse.

Nevertheless, a profound shift had occurred. The narrow clinical focus and uncritical identification with official policy that had characterized American medicine's initial response to the atomic bomb was fundamentally undermined during the period of fallout worry and test ban activism (1954–63). When the cultural and political climate shifted in the late 1970s and early 1980s, bringing the nuclear issue once more to the fore, men and women of the medical profession played a leading role. PSR revived with phoenixlike vitality; old themes were rediscovered; and leaders from the earlier period of activism, reinforced by articulate newcomers, again conveyed the grim tidings to a newly attentive public: If nuclear war comes, organized medicine will be of scant help, for it, too, will be sucked into the all-consuming maelstrom.

6

EDWARD TELLER AND PROJECT CHARIOT

Years after the Cold War ended, Americans continued
to learn more about bizarre byways of the era when
American life was shaped in profound ways not only
by the nuclear arms race itself, but also by the exposure of
military personnel to radioactive fallout from nuclear-
weapons tests, medical experiments that involved giving radioactive substances to the unsuspecting and uninformed
inmates of public institutions, and the erratic if not meretri-
cious official policy toward the release of information about
the hazards of radioactivity from nuclear tests. Only in
1997, for example, forty years or more after the fact, did we
learn that throughout the years of atmospheric nuclear testing, the Atomic Energy Commission had regularly informed
the Kodak Corporation of Rochester, New York, when
atomic tests were scheduled, since as early as the Alamogordo test of 1945, Kodak had experienced problems with
the fogging of X-ray film because of elevated levels of radioactivity in the packaging material in which the film was
shipped. Corporate America thus had privileged access to information about product hazards related to nuclear testing
at a time when the government routinely downplayed or
flatly denied possible human health risks resulting from the
tests. Washington's determined campaign to promote "the
peaceful uses of atomic energy" must be understood in this
climate of deception, misrepresentation, and propaganda
manipulation.

In 1995, the *Bulletin of the Atomic Scientists* invited me
to review a fascinating book by Daniel T. O'Neill, *The Firecracker Boys* (New York: St. Martin's Press, 1994). O'Neill

told of an amazing engineering project conceived by Edward Teller's Lawrence Livermore National Laboratory in the late 1950s, in part as a strategy for circumventing the movement to ban nuclear-weapons testing. This chapter is adapted from that review, published in the May/June 1995 issue of the *Bulletin*.

———

AS THE NUCLEAR ARMS RACE RECEDES, or at least mutates into new forms, we learn more and more about how it polluted and poisoned the streams of our national life—both literally and figuratively. Dan O'Neill's absorbing book *The Firecracker Boys* is a major contribution to this ongoing process of historical excavation. O'Neill, a research associate in the oral history program at the University of Alaska–Fairbanks, re-creates in careful detail the story of Project Chariot, a bizarre plan gestated in the late 1950s at the University of California's Lawrence Livermore National Laboratory. The plan called for the detonation of up to six thermonuclear bombs at a remote point near Cape Thompson on Alaska's coast, where the Ogotoruk Creek flows into the Chukchi Sea.

The initial public rationale offered for the plan was that the explosions could transform the mouth of this small stream into a major international harbor that would stimulate fabulous economic development, dramatically illustrate the peacetime uses of atomic energy, and provide a showpiece for the Eisenhower administration's Project Plowshare, designed to promote the "Atoms for Peace" idea.

But the absurdity of the idea soon became apparent: The region, more than a hundred miles north of the Arctic Circle, is icebound for months at a time, and access to the coalfields of the interior would have required the construction of prohibitively expensive rail facilities. When the hoped-for private investment that was a crucial component of the plan failed to materialize, a more general rationale for Project Chariot emerged: that the "experiment" would advance nuclear knowledge and thus in some vague way promote human happiness and well-being.

O'Neill, an engaging writer as well as a careful researcher, begins his account with a description of Cape Thompson's history and ecology, and of the local Eskimo economy based on fishing and hunting. He then establishes the larger context of Project Chariot's origins. It was the brainchild of the Hungarian émigré physicist Edward Teller, whose fingerprints mark so much of our nuclear history.

A Manhattan Project veteran and "Father of the H-bomb," Teller in 1952 had become head of the Lawrence Livermore nuclear weapons laboratory. In the late 1950s, as the hazards of radioactive fallout became increasingly apparent, and a moratorium on nuclear tests began, Teller avidly embraced Atoms for Peace. If nuclear detonations ostensibly designed to explore the peaceful uses of atomic energy could be exempted from a possible future test ban agreement, covert weapons research could proceed as well.

Teller and his Livermore associates began a quest for monumental engineering projects that could theoretically be undertaken only with the aid of nuclear explosions. Touting the wonders of what he called "geographic engineering," Teller joked at one news conference: "If your mountain is not in the right place, drop us a postcard."

One high-visibility project that quickly surfaced was the idea of rearranging the Panama Canal by a series of blasts to eliminate the many locks, transforming the canal into a sea-level waterway. Another was to bypass the Suez Canal by constructing an alternate canal from the Gulf of Aqaba through the Negev Desert to the Mediterranean. Such a canal would be wholly Israeli territory. Project Chariot initially entered the picture as a preliminary step to lay the groundwork for these visionary undertakings. Despite tensions between the freewheeling Teller and Atomic Energy Commission (AEC) officials in Washington, the AEC under Lewis Strauss generally backed the plans.

The heavily publicized campaign to explore the "peacetime uses" of atomic energy served a broader purpose as well. As the Livermore scientist (and future defense secretary) Harold Brown wrote in a classified 1957 report, dramatic demonstrations of the engineering applications of nuclear explosions would help Americans "gain a more rational viewpoint" about nuclear issues by countering the "phobic public reactions [that] have been built around nuclear bombs."

Thus it was that Edward Teller, the quintessential nuclear-age snake-oil salesman, arrived in Alaska on July 14, 1958, to promote Project Chariot. Initially, he enjoyed remarkable success. O'Neill documents the convergence of interests between Teller and other proponents of nuclear-weapons development on the one hand, and local groups in Alaska on the other. The region's politicians, major newspapers, business groups, and would-be developers quickly fell into line. So, too, did the University of Alaska at Fairbanks and its entrepreneurial president, William Ransom Wood.

When university biologists called for studies of the environmental implications of turning Alaska into a nuclear test site, and the AEC compliantly agreed to fund those studies, dollar signs began to dance in the eyes of university officials. Soon AEC research grants, eventually totaling more than $100,000, were flowing to Fairbanks.

Cementing its profitable link with the AEC, the University of Alaska in 1959 awarded Teller an honorary degree. In his commencement address, Teller spoke enthusiastically of the "industry and progress" that Project Chariot would bring to Alaska, and added grandly (if ungrammatically): "Please God, that by making harbors here in Alaska, perhaps near coal deposits, by exporting this coal cheaper to Japan, the Japanese might become the first beneficiaries of atomic explosions as they have been the first victims."

But tensions quickly arose within the university. On one side were Wood and other administrators eager to maintain a lucrative relationship with the AEC. On the other were the field researchers intent on documenting and publicizing the potentially devastating impact of the proposed detonations on the Cape Thompson ecosystem and on the livelihood of the local Eskimos. O'Neill records in fascinating detail the academic infighting that ensued as university officials first pressured researchers to modify their findings, then censored and rewrote reports, and finally forced out two university staff members who refused to kowtow, William O. Pruitt and Leslie Viereck.

Shabby as it is, the story will hardly shock anyone familiar with academic politics and the ways of university administrators. But unlike many such tales, *The Firecracker Boys* has a qualified happy ending. Pruitt and Viereck, the troublesome researchers who lost their jobs, not only pursued productive careers elsewhere despite attempted blacklisting by the AEC, but in 1993 both returned to the University of Alaska–

Fairbanks to receive honorary degrees. Faculty members with long memories initiated this belated effort to right an old wrong—and they overrode efforts by administrators to substitute bland generalities in the degree citations for an explicit acknowledgment of the events that occurred nearly thirty years before.

On a larger canvas, the happy ending also includes the fact that Project Chariot quietly expired, done in by its own inherent absurdity, by shifting political winds in Washington, and by an increasingly articulate and confident local opposition. Slowly, but with growing effectiveness, some Alaskans began to protest and to mobilize. The Eskimos of Point Hope, a settlement some thirty miles north of the proposed detonation site, displayed a sophistication, worldly knowledge, and media savvy that repeatedly flummoxed patronizing AEC officials. (At one meeting, an AEC spokesman, facing questions far beyond his expertise, made a series of patently false assertions—all captured on tape by Point Hope residents.)

As the environmental researchers, working under rigorous conditions in a frigid arctic setting, painstakingly compiled and publicized their data despite the efforts of University of Alaska administrators to muzzle them, the national media eventually began to pay attention. Stories appeared in the *New York Times, Outdoor Life, Harper's,* the *Christian Science Monitor,* the *Bulletin of the Atomic Scientists* (December 1961), and many other publications.

Advocacy groups from the Sierra Club to the Association on American Indian Affairs also became involved. In St. Louis, Barry Commoner's Committee for Nuclear Information spread word of the danger. And with the election of John F. Kennedy in November 1960, the political climate in Washington became distinctly chilly for Teller and his allies. Interior secretary Stewart Udall forcefully intervened, making clear that, in his view, Project Chariot would violate long-standing Eskimo land rights.

By 1962, the AEC and Livermore officials were looking for ways quietly to scuttle the four-million-dollar project that had become a public-relations albatross. That August, Livermore lamely announced that since other tests had provided the information they had hoped to glean from

the Alaska blasts, Project Chariot would be "held in abeyance." Despite
the qualified nature of the statement, opponents rightly celebrated: The
scheme was dead.

O'Neill's exemplary case study of the politics of nuclear-weapons
testing in the late 1950s and early 1960s illustrates some central features
of this bleak era in America's Cold War history. He amply documents
the duplicity of the AEC and of Livermore officials. In public statements
they insisted that every effort would be made to keep radioactive fallout
from Project Chariot to a minimum, timing detonations so that radioactive debris would drift seaward rather than onto the land. But internal
documents O'Neill uncovered make it clear that one purpose of the test
was to study radiation's effects on the ecosystem of the tundra—implicitly including its human population. When a Livermore study group in
1961 explored the possibility of reducing the yield of the detonations, for
example, one *disadvantage* they listed was that smaller explosions would
reduce radioactive fallout, diminishing the usefulness of the experiment.

O'Neill also documents the way the AEC manipulated research
grants to achieve the results it wanted. When AEC-funded biologists,
botanists, and geographers working on the site produced draft reports
that underscored the environmental dangers and uncertainties of Project
Chariot, the AEC threatened to withhold payments to the University of
Alaska until more "satisfactory" results were forthcoming, rousing con-
sternation in President Wood's office.

Behind the pose of supporting unbiased scientific research on the
project's ecological impact, AEC and Livermore officials from the start
focused mainly on public relations, as they subtly—and not so subtly—
pressured scientists to produce reassuring studies that would allay public
fears and clear the way for the test. O'Neill makes clear how readily university administrators, concerned primarily with maintaining the flow of
research dollars to their campus, collaborated in this process.

The Firecracker Boys also reveals that attempts at public-relations manipulation and cover-up continued long after Project Chariot was all but
forgotten. Edward Teller, the Energizer Bunny of America's nuclear-
weapons program, became so enraged by O'Neill's questions while being
interviewed for the book that, according to O'Neill, he halted the ses-

sion, treated O'Neill to a stream of vituperation, and melodramatically tore up the release form he had earlier signed.

The CIA also stonewalled O'Neill, refusing his Freedom of Information Act request for its file on one of the young scientists who had been most critical of Project Chariot, geographer Don Foote, even though Foote died in 1969 following an automobile accident. (Apparently, as in the Karen Silkwood case, some of Foote's friends found his death suspicious, but O'Neill—invariably balanced and judicious—does not endorse conspiracy theories in the case.)

And his story has a disturbing coda. O'Neill's research in the Livermore records turned up the fact that in August 1962, even as Project Chariot was expiring, government scientists working under contract to the AEC secretly brought to the proposed test site on Ogotoruk Creek 43.5 pounds of highly radioactive sand from a nuclear test conducted in Nevada earlier that summer. They placed this material at various sites along the creek, "to determine the extent to which water passing through irradiated soil would dissolve the fallout radionuclides and transport them to aquifers, streams and ponds."

After the experiment, the scientists gathered some fifteen thousand pounds of contaminated soil into a low mound, bulldozed uncontaminated soil over it, and quietly departed without posting a warning or informing local officials of what they had done. O'Neill's 1992 revelation of this long-suppressed episode led to a wave of fear and anger among the long-suffering Eskimos of Point Hope, some of whom drew a link between the experiment and the high rate of cancer deaths in their community. (Public-health experts believe that diet, cigarette smoking, and other nonradiological factors are the more likely causes—but the people of Point Hope have a well-developed skepticism toward experts.)

Apart from problems with the CIA and Teller, O'Neill faced other roadblocks in getting his story out. He initially planned to produce a program about Project Chariot for Alaska public television, which is based at the University of Alaska–Fairbanks. Although he secured funding from the Alaska Humanities Forum, Alaska public television officials got cold feet and canceled the project. It might jeopardize their funding, they feared, by alienating university bureaucrats, especially ex-president

Wood, still a formidable figure on the local scene. Like the environmental researchers he writes about, O'Neill has shown considerable persistence, ingenuity, and courage in telling a story that influential individuals and institutions would rather keep quiet.

O'Neill documents in illuminating detail the process by which that elusive phenomenon "grassroots protest" actually arises and is mobilized. He re-creates the texture and the feel of tense meetings in the crowded Point Hope town hall, of biologists and geographers slowly coming together to oppose the juggernaut of powerful interests behind Project Chariot, and of the process by which the issue was picked up and publicized by the national media. (An Episcopal priest in Point Hope with good contacts among the East Coast elite played an important role.)

The book also shows how this seemingly isolated episode contributed significantly to the emergence of a larger environmental consciousness in Alaska and beyond, and to a broader awareness among Alaska's Native American population of their legal rights—and the need to stand up for them. When the Alaskan press proved supine and uncritical in its enthusiasm for Project Chariot, for example, the Eskimos of Point Hope took steps to launch their own newspaper, the *Tundra Times*.

The Firecracker Boys is, in short, an important addition to a growing shelf of case studies that present a disturbing picture of the way government authorities, under the justification of defending the nation against "the Soviet threat," seriously damaged the fabric of American democracy. Books like this remind us of the manifold dangers that arise when scientific hubris, ideological compulsions, governmental power, and public-relations manipulation converge behind misconceived "projects" that are profoundly dangerous to the public weal.

Of course, one must guard against the populist fallacy of assuming that "the people" are invariably wiser than those in positions of power and influence. But surveying the half-century history of U.S. nuclear-weapons research and testing, one can hardly avoid the conclusion that time and again it was "the people," or at least local groups of politically attentive citizens, who proved wiser and more responsible than the experts.

7

DR. STRANGELOVE

Stanley Kubrick Presents the Apocalypse

For more than forty years, the nuclear reality penetrated every stratum of American life, including mass culture. This was especially true during three cycles of sharpened public anxiety about the hazards of the nuclear age: (1) the immediate postwar years; (2) the period from 1954 to 1963, when the dangers of radioactive fallout loomed large; and (3) the surge of nuclear fear and activism that erupted during President Ronald Reagan's first term. Stanley Kubrick's celebrated film *Dr. Strangelove* was a product of the second of these periods. When the Society of American Historians in 1994 planned a collection of essays on the way the movies have handled historical events, the opportunity arose for me to take a closer look at Kubrick's masterpiece. This chapter is adapted from my essay in the resulting volume, *Past Imperfect: History according to the Movies* (New York: Henry Holt, 1995).

––––––––––––

AMERICA'S TOP MILITARY AND CIVILIAN LEADERS *gather for an urgent secret session in the nation's capital. An unexpected Cold War crisis threatens to lead to a world-destroying thermonuclear war. A long, rambling message arrives from Moscow, with the Soviet leader alternately blustering indignantly and stammering with fear of what may lie ahead. American strategists solemnly ponder the message: Has the Soviet premier cracked? Is he intoxicated? With humanity's fate hanging in the balance, the hours tick by, and the world edges ever closer to nuclear Armageddon.*

95

This may seem like a scene from Stanley Kubrick's *Dr. Strangelove,* but it really happened. During the October 1962 Cuban Missile Crisis, the White House received a long, almost incoherent message from Nikita Khrushchev, prompting President John F. Kennedy's top decision makers to wonder whether the Soviet leader was drunk. To a greater extent than many might believe, *Dr. Strangelove* faithfully mirrors this historic epoch, in which the world's fate often seemed hostage to accident, miscalculation, and human fallibility.

Of course, *Dr. Strangelove* is not a historical movie in the conventional sense. The precise events it portrays never actually occurred. But this black comedy does have historical resonances. It captures a specific moment and offers a satiric but recognizable portrait of the era's strategic thinking and cultural climate. Its director, Stanley Kubrick, and his cowriters convey all too accurately the weird logic of deterrence theory, the paranoia of the Cold War, and the nuclear jitters of the early 1960s.

Atomic fear, having diminished somewhat from the immediate post-Hiroshima level, increased dramatically after 1954 as hydrogen-bomb tests in the Pacific spread deadly radioactive fallout across parts of North America. While activists demanded a test ban, novelists, magazine editors, science-fiction writers, and moviemakers publicized the threat. Neville Shute's *On the Beach* (1957), made into a bleak 1959 movie by Stanley Kramer, was one product of this apprehension.

Fear intensified during the early 1960s, as President John F. Kennedy, having charged in his 1960 campaign that America faced a "missile gap," approved a nuclear buildup to close it. After sparring with Khrushchev over Berlin in July 1961, Kennedy warned Americans of the dangers of nuclear war and called for an urgent program of fallout-shelter construction. Schoolchildren hid under desks during nuclear drills and, in an animated civil-defense film, learned from Bert the Turtle to "duck and cover." The Cuban Missile Crisis was only the most frightening of a long series of events that made the nuclear threat terrifyingly real. *Dr. Strangelove,* released in January 1964, grew out of this accumulation of nuclear alarms.

Dr. Strangelove, however, does more than just reflect the general nuclear anxiety of the time; it also offers insight into the strategic debates of the day. During the 1950s, U.S. policymakers developed deterrence theory as the surest means of avoiding a nuclear war. The fear of massive retaliation, they argued, offered the most credible deterrent to nuclear attack. But how could such a retaliatory threat remain credible if an attacker could destroy the command-and-control centers responsible for launching the counterattack? This dilemma led to studies of automated response systems requiring no human intervention. In *On Thermonuclear War* (1960) and *Thinking about the Unthinkable* (1962), RAND Corporation strategist Herman Kahn coolly discussed (though ultimately rejected) such a strategy. This arcane debate fascinated Kubrick—in 1963, he wrote that he owned "70 or 80 books" on nuclear strategy—and in *Dr. Strangelove* he translated that fascination into black comedy.

Dr. Strangelove was actually one of two 1964 movies that explored the theme of accidental nuclear devastation. The other, *Fail-Safe,* was based on a best-selling 1962 novel by Harvey Wheeler and Eugene Burdick. While *Dr. Strangelove* presented nuclear holocaust as black comedy, *Fail-Safe* played the story straight. Although directed by Sidney Lumet and starring Henry Fonda as the president of the United States, *Fail-Safe* did not capture the public imagination. Instead, it was Kubrick's sardonic version of Armageddon, not Lumet's earnest treatment, that became a classic.

Kubrick, too, based his movie on a recently published novel of Cold War nuclear crisis, Peter George's *Two Hours to Doom* (1958), issued in the United States as *Red Alert.* Up to a point, *Dr. Strangelove* closely follows the plot of George's novel, in which a demented SAC commander orders the 843rd Bomber Wing to launch a nuclear attack on the Soviet Union, unaware that the Russians have deployed an automated retaliation system. But Kubrick made a crucial change in the ending: In *Two Hours to Doom,* the nuclear bomber crashes, and humankind is spared. In the novel's final paragraph, the U.S. president, shaken by the close brush with disaster, pledges to devote the remainder of his term to the search for peace. Kubrick offered no such pat ending or heavy-handed didactic message. Faithful to his darkly comic vision, he grimly followed the ultimate logic of deterrence theory to its horrifying conclusion.

Kubrick portrays a nuclear holocaust arising from the intersection of contemporary nuclear strategy and human fallibility. The action begins as General Jack D. Ripper (Sterling Hayden), in charge of a Strategic Air

Command unit at Burpelson Air Force Base, launches an unauthorized nuclear attack on Russia. Under the provisions of Wing Attack Plan R, designed as a retaliatory safeguard should Washington be destroyed, only General Ripper has the code necessary to recall the planes. When President Merkin Muffley contacts an inebriated Soviet premier Kissov to warn him of the danger, we learn that the Soviets have built a "doomsday machine." In the event of a U.S. attack, this huge bomb will automatically explode, creating a vast shroud of radioactive fallout that will encircle the earth and kill all life on the planet.

In a brilliant tour de force, the actor Peter Sellers plays a triumvirate of characters: the phlegmatic President Muffley, General Ripper's terrified British aide, Group Captain Lionel Mandrake, and the titular Dr. Strangelove, a former Nazi who changed his name from Unwertigliebe after the war. President Muffley often calls on Strangelove, as the Pentagon's top weapons guru, to explain the intricacies of nuclear strategy. In creating this horribly disabled but ever-smiling character, Kubrick combined parodic elements of Henry Kissinger, the physicist Edward Teller, and the former Nazi rocket scientist Wernher von Braun, each of whom played a central role in U.S. Cold War nuclear policy-making and scientific technology.

Long before he became President Richard Nixon's top foreign-policy adviser, Henry Kissinger had made a reputation for himself as a diplomatic historian and then as a nuclear strategist. His book *A World Restored* (1957) was a scholarly study of Viscount Castlereagh, the conservative statesman who reordered Europe after Napoleon, and it won him a professorship at Harvard. Turning from history to contemporary strategic issues in *Nuclear Weapons and Foreign Policy* (1957), Kissinger urged the United States to deploy a variety of tactical nuclear weapons to provide additional deterrence in the face of the Soviet threat. In *The Necessity for Choice* (1961), picking up on John Kennedy's 1960 campaign theme, he warned darkly of a growing "missile gap" that invited Soviet expansionism and even nuclear blackmail of the United States.

Edward Teller, a Hungarian Jew who, like Kissinger, fled Europe after Hitler's rise to power, was a brilliant physicist who worked during the war on the Manhattan Project. While at Los Alamos, Teller became convinced of the feasibility of a far more powerful thermonuclear weapon. At California's Lawrence Livermore Laboratory, he oversaw the development and 1952 testing of the first hydrogen bomb. An avid Cold Warrior, he used his considerable influence to push for expansion of America's nuclear arsenal, fiercely opposing the 1963 limited test ban treaty. He also promoted such visionary and controversial schemes to use atomic energy for peacetime purposes as the ill-fated marine engineering scheme, Project Chariot (see chapter 6). Teller—whose piercing, deep-set eyes and beetling eyebrows gave him something of the sinister appearance of a stage villain—epitomized the politicized scientists who helped drive the nuclear arms race forward. Antiwar critics recognized his power and in 1970 sardonically presented him with the Dr. Strangelove Award.

Wernher von Braun, blond, blue-eyed, and handsome, was a twenty-one-year-old member of the minor Prussian nobility when Adolf Hitler came to power in 1933. An early rocket enthusiast, the "boy wonder" von Braun became a key technician in the Nazi rocketry program at Peenemünde on the Baltic Sea. Joining the Nazi Party in 1940, he helped persuade Hitler to give the program top priority. In September 1944, the Peenemünde team launched the first V-2 rocket against London. At the war's end, von Braun fled to Bavaria so he could surrender to the Americans rather than to the Russians. Late in 1945 he signed a contract with the U.S. Army. "The next time, I wanted to be on the winning side," he later recalled. By 1950 he was stationed at the army's Redstone Arsenal in Huntsville, Alabama, directing more than a hundred of the German scientists and engineers with whom he had worked in Hitler's day. Von Braun's political flexibility and technocratic approach to missile science inspired a parody by songwriter Tom Lehrer, in which von Braun, in a thick German accent, insists that his job is to launch the missiles, not to worry about where they land: "Dot's not my department, says Wernher von Braun."

Is Dr. Strangelove historically accurate? In some respects, yes. The information on the U.S. nuclear arsenal and the capability of B-52 bombers is factual. The billboard at Burpelson AFB that proclaims "Peace Is Our Profession" actually adorned some SAC bases. The rantings of General Buck Turgidson (George C. Scott) about "doomsday gaps" and "mine-shaft gaps" directly echo Kennedy's 1960s "missile gap" rhetoric, and Turgidson's description of U.S. casualties in a nuclear war as "get[ting] our hair mussed" caught the lingo of such military men as former SAC commander General Curtis LeMay.

As the near-legendary head of the SAC during the 1950s, the cigar-chomping LeMay provided an easily recognizable archetype for both the grimly fanatical General Ripper and (especially) the bombastic and hyperactive General Turgidson. LeMay never met a bombing plan he didn't like. In 1957 he told two members of the Gaither Commission, which had been formed to assess U.S. military policy, that if a Soviet attack ever seemed likely, he planned to "knock the shit out of them before they got off the ground." Reminded that a preemptive first strike was not U.S. policy, LeMay retorted, "No, it's not national policy, but it's my policy." In 1962, as a member of EXCOM, the top-level team that advised President Kennedy during the Cuban Missile Crisis, LeMay urged a preemptive air strike on missile sites in Cuba, to be followed by an invasion of the island. Retiring from the air force, he ran for vice president in 1968 on a ticket headed by the racist, demagogic governor of Alabama, George C. Wallace. Asked what he would do about the war in Vietnam, LeMay said he would "bomb North Vietnam back into the Stone Age."

Yet the air force angrily challenged the movie's basic premise—an attack order that could not be countermanded. Air force crews in such a situation, insisted the Pentagon, would attack *only* if they received explicit additional instructions confirming the original order. To forestall this official criticism, Kubrick included a notice at the beginning of the film that reads: "IT IS THE STATED POSITION OF THE U.S. AIR FORCE THAT THEIR SAFEGUARDS WOULD PREVENT THE OCCURRENCE OF SUCH EVENTS AS ARE DEPICTED IN THIS FILM." (No doubt surmising that filmgoers' thoughts would quickly turn to the likes of Kissinger, Teller, von Braun, and LeMay, Kubrick's deadpan disclaimer continued: "FURTHERMORE IT SHOULD BE NOTED THAT NONE OF THE CHARACTERS PORTRAYED IN THIS FILM ARE MEANT TO REPRESENT ANY REAL PERSONS LIVING OR DEAD.") But even if *Dr. Strangelove* misrepresented U.S. nuclear command policy for dramatic effect, it accurately captured deepening popular uneasiness about science and technology, as well as growing fears of an arms race escalating out of control. As nuclear stockpiles mounted and intercontinental ballistic missles (ICBMs) cut attack times from hours to minutes, the potential for catastrophe soared.

Though an expatriate living in England, Kubrick brilliantly limned U.S. Cold War paranoia. General Ripper, brooding in his claustrophobic office, is a walking embodiment of free-floating cultural fears. Linking his anti-Communist obsessions to his anxieties about the fluoridation of drinking water, Ripper concludes that only a preemptive strike can save America and assure the continued purity of its citizens' "precious bodily fluids." The scenes in which the world's fate hangs on the availability of a dime for a pay phone and President Muffley's ability to reach Omsk Information epitomize both the horror and the absurdity of the nuclear arms race.

Kubrick was also among the first to explore the macho nature of nuclear strategy, a topic much discussed later by psychiatrists and feminists. (See, for example, Helen Caldicott's *Missile Envy: The Arms Race and Nuclear War* [1984] and Carol Cohn's "Sex and Death in the Rational World of Defense Intellectuals" in the Summer 1987 issue of the feminist journal *Signs*.) The movie's title and most of the characters' names suggest a perverse eroticism, and beginning with the celebrated B-52 refueling sequence behind the opening credits (to the tune of "Try a Little Tenderness"), the movie is saturated with sex. General Ripper grips a phallic cigar while pondering his sexual problems. As the holocaust looms, the ever-resourceful Dr. Strangelove describes how the war room elite might survive in deep mine shafts, where it could replenish the human race by copulating nonstop with voluptuous women chosen for their sexual appeal. And in the movie's finale, the B-52 captain played by Slim Pickens mounts a hydrogen bomb as it plummets earthward, waving his cowboy hat in orgiastic ecstasy.

Dr. Strangelove went a long way toward demolishing the traditional war-movie genre. The attack on Burpelson AFB by army troops trying to capture General Ripper is filmed as a grainy newsreel (the entire movie is black-and-white) and staged as a hackneyed combat set piece. Aboard one of the B-52s winging toward Russia, muted drum rolls and the strains of "When Johnny Comes Marching Home Again" echo in the background as Slim Pickens inspires his crew with a cornball homily on the importance of their mission. When the mushroom clouds erupt at last, Vera Lynn croons "We'll Meet Again"—a 1939 song indelibly associated with England's heroic stand during World War II. All of this, of course, is weirdly out of place in the context of global annihilation. It is not only war, suggests Kubrick, but also war movies that will never be the same.

Dr. Strangelove appeared at a transitional moment in America's nuclear history. Nuclear terror, eased by the limited 1963 test ban treaty, diminished still further during the later 1960s and 1970s as arms-control negotiations produced periodic agreements, and as other, temporarily more urgent issues intervened. But as fears revived in the early 1980s, pervasive nuclear anxiety once again produced a cultural fallout of novels, poetry, movies, rock songs, and (something new) television specials that often owed a considerable imaginative debt to Kubrick's pioneering effort. A younger generation rediscovered *Dr. Strangelove* itself.

In the early 1990s, as the nuclear threat eased, the dangers the world had faced in earlier decades loomed even larger in retrospect. Reports of past nuclear accidents and miscalculations surfaced for the first time. Russian and U.S. participants in the 1962 Cuban Missile Crisis gathered to compare notes on their brush with disaster. Simultaneously, revelations from within the former Soviet Union suggested that at one time the Soviets may, in fact, have deployed (or at least developed) an automated retaliatory system—the dreaded "doomsday machine" that is the ultimate deus ex machina of *Dr. Strangelove*. Stanley Kubrick, it now appears, may have cut closer to the truth than even he realized at the time.

GOING UNDERGROUND
Nuclear America, 1963–1980

The first of many lectures I gave in the 1980s discussing the impact of nuclear weapons on American culture took place on a warm summer evening in July 1982 before a small audience at the Madison, Wisconsin, public library. It was sponsored by a new organization, Wisconsin Educators for Social Responsibility, founded to support the nuclear-weapons freeze campaign. Titling the lecture "The Big Sleep," I focused on the years from 1963 through the late 1970s, when the Limited Nuclear Test Ban Treaty that had pushed nuclear testing underground also seemed to have buried Americans' awareness of their nuclear history and of the continuing nuclear threat. It is this period to which we now turn.

8

FROM THE TEST BAN TREATY TO THREE MILE ISLAND

My 1982 talk at the Madison Public Library laid the groundwork for many other lectures in the months and years that followed, as the "Reagan Round" of antinuclear activism and cultural attention to the bomb gained momentum. Much revised and expanded, this talk also provided the framework of an essay published in the May 1984 *Journal of American History* (with full footnote citations) and then condensed in the August/September 1984 issue of the *Bulletin of the Atomic Scientists.* The version reprinted here, adapted from the *Bulletin of the Atomic Scientists* piece, offers an interpretive overview of the years when the nation's level of nuclear awareness appeared—superficially—to be at a low ebb. The essay focuses especially on the complex and troubled relationship between the test ban and nuclear disarmament movements of the 1950s and early 1960s and the New Left leaders and Vietnam War protesters who moved center stage in the later 1960s.

WRITING IN 1981, George F. Kennan described Americans' response to the threat of nuclear war: "We have gone on piling weapon upon weapon, missile upon missile, new levels of destructiveness upon old ones. We have done this helplessly, almost involuntarily, like the victims of some sort of hypnotism, like men in a dream, like lemmings headed for the sea."

Kennan's generalization is not wholly accurate. Americans have *not* always behaved like lemmings in confronting the nuclear danger. Their engagement with this threat has gone through several distinct cycles of activism and apparent passivity. When applied to the years from 1963 to the later 1970s, however, his observations seem chillingly accurate. In these years, public concern with the nuclear-weapons issue sank to a very low level indeed.

In exploring this interval, our starting point is September 24, 1963, when the Senate overwhelmingly approved the Limited Nuclear Test Ban Treaty agreed on earlier in Moscow. The treaty won enthusiastic public and journalistic support. David Lawrence of the conservative *U.S. News & World Report* wrote, "There's a new word in the vocabulary of the day—or at least a more noticeable use of an old word—*euphoria.*" Even I. F. Stone, a skeptical, left-wing Washington journalist not given to flights of easy enthusiasm, wrote, "Peace has broken out, and hope leaps up again." The agreement did not halt all tests; underground nuclear explosions were still permitted. Nevertheless, it was welcomed as the beginning of a process that would ultimately free the world of the nuclear menace. Summing up the prevailing view, the *New York Times* hailed the agreement in a front-page banner headline as a "Major Step toward Easing Tension."

Underlying this collective sigh of relief was the fact that for more than a decade the nation had been gripped by profound nuclear fears. America's atomic monopoly ended in 1949, and in the 1950s the United States and the Soviet Union developed the hydrogen bomb, ICBMs, and sophisticated control systems that raised the specter of a push-button war that could snuff out millions of lives in the blink of an eye.

Feeding the nuclear anxieties of these years was a heavy official emphasis on civil defense. Under the "Operation Alert" program of the Federal Civil Defense Administration, evacuation plans, radio alert systems, warning sirens, school air-raid drills, and films on how to survive a nuclear attack became familiar features of American life.

In May 1961, shortly before the Vienna summit conference, President Kennedy went on television to urge a national shelter program. A few weeks later, during a period of East-West confrontation over Berlin, he delivered an even more alarmist speech on the danger of nuclear war and the urgent necessity for civil-defense preparation. Responding to a deluge of panicky requests, the administration hastily prepared a civil-defense booklet and distributed 35 million copies through schools, post offices, and newspaper supplements. The Cuban Missile Crisis added a grim immediacy to these fears. For a few days in October 1962, Kennedy's warnings seemed about to become reality.

Further, as we saw in chapter 5, these were years shadowed by fears of radioactive fallout, as U.S. and Soviet atmospheric tests of thermonuclear weapons contaminated the atmosphere. Despite soothing words from Washington, the disturbing facts could not be denied. As in the immediate post-Hiroshima period, the mass media once again both articulated and amplified the public's escalating anxieties.

These fears gave rise to a campaign against nuclear testing led by such groups as Leo Szilard's Council for a Livable World, Dr. Bernard Lown's Physicians for Social Responsibility, and the Student Peace Union. Formed in Chicago in 1959, the Student Peace Union's national conventions attracted hundreds of delegates over the next few years.

Above all, there was SANE, the National Committee for a Sane Nuclear Policy, conceived in 1957 by several veteran peace activists who recruited Norman Cousins of the *Saturday Review* and Clarence Pickett of the American Friends Service Committee as cochairmen. With an imposing list of public figures and celebrities as sponsors, SANE announced itself in November 1957 with a large *New York Times* advertisement proclaiming, "We Are Facing a Danger Unlike Any Danger That Has Ever Existed."

A high point of this round of activism came in May 1960, when thousands attended a SANE-sponsored rally in New York's Madison Square Garden to hear speakers ranging from the Republican Alfred M. Landon to the socialist Norman Thomas call for an end to the nuclear arms race. After the rally, five thousand people accompanied Thomas on a march to the United Nations. The organized test ban campaign unquestionably intensified public opposition to testing, though the level of opposition was also influenced by shifting U.S.-Soviet relations. By late 1959, 77 percent of Americans favored a continuation of the temporary moratorium on nuclear testing then in effect.

Nuclear fear became a shaping cultural force. Books, essays, symposia, and conferences explored the medical, psychological, and ethical implications of atomic weapons. Novels like *On the Beach, Fail-Safe,* Dexter

Masters's *The Accident,* and Walter Miller Jr.'s *A Canticle for Leibowitz*
offered visions of nuclear holocaust. The film versions of *On the Beach*
and *Fail-Safe,* as well as Stanley Kubrick's *Dr. Strangelove* (discussed in
chapter 7), attracted large audiences.

The Eisenhower administration was especially concerned about *On
the Beach.* In December 1959, civil-defense director Leo Hoegh criticized
it at a Cabinet meeting as "very harmful because it produced a feeling of
utter hopelessness, thus undermining OCDM's [Office of Civil Defense
Management] efforts to encourage preparedness." An analysis of the film
by the State Department and the U.S. Information Agency warned that
its "strong emotional appeal for banning nuclear weapons could conceivably lead audiences to think in terms of radical solutions . . . rather than
. . . practical safeguarded disarmament measures." Insisting that the
film's ending, in which many doomed Australians choose suicide over
death from radiation poisoning, "grossly misconstrues the basic nature
of man," this analysis declared, "It is inconceivable that even in the event
of a nuclear war, mankind would not have the strength and ingenuity to
take all possible steps toward self-preservation."

The nuclear preoccupation of the years from 1954 through 1963
manifested itself at all cultural levels. Television series like *The Outer
Limits* and Rod Serling's *The Twilight Zone,* when not dealing explicitly
with radioactivity, genetic mutation, and atomic war, conjured up tales
of vague, unseen menaces. A spate of mutant movies—*The H-Man, The
Incredible Shrinking Man, Attack of the Crab Monsters, The Blob, It,
Them!*—had clear psychological roots in fears of genetic damage from
radioactive fallout. In *The Incredible Shrinking Man,* the luckless hero
begins to shrink soon after his pleasure boat passes through a glistening
radioactive cloud generated by a distant nuclear test. In *Them!* twelve-
foot killer ants crawl from the New Mexico A-bomb test site and leave
horrifying carnage in their wake as they head unerringly for the storm
sewers of Los Angeles. (The producer ran out of money and had to stop
filming on location in New Mexico and return to Hollywood.) Small
wonder that the 1963 test ban aroused such euphoria.

It is what happened *next* that is surprising. The sudden fading of
the nuclear-weapons issue after September 1963, whether as an activist
cause, a cultural motif, or a topic of public discourse, is astonishing. Test

ban and nuclear disarmament organizations either collapsed or vanished from public view. When only twenty-five delegates showed up for the convention of the Student Peace Union in spring 1964, the organization disbanded.

One of the first to notice the shift was Eugene Rabinowitch, editor of the *Bulletin of the Atomic Scientists* and a leader of the postwar "scientists' movement" that had campaigned for international atomic control. Writing in the January 1964 *Bulletin,* Rabinowitch observed:

> As the year 1963 drew to its end, it found Americans in a changed mood. A year ago . . . peace movements flourished and disarmament studies proliferated. It looked as if Americans were trying to come to grips with the critical problem of our age.
>
> The acute concern and frantic search for solutions did not last long. . . . The abatement of the Cuban conflict, the test-ban treaty, and vague signs of rapprochement between the Soviet Union and the United States encouraged the public attention to turn in other directions.

Echoing Rabinowitch, the Catholic journal of opinion *Commonweal* in 1965 deplored the lethargy that had enveloped the nuclear-weapons issue. In succeeding years, this lethargy remained a matter of frustrated comment by a few peace activists and social observers.

Of course, the bomb did not totally vanish from the American consciousness. In 1965, a *Pacem in Terris* conference in New York sponsored by Robert M. Hutchins's Center for the Study of Democratic Institutions attracted more than two thousand people, who heard addresses by Linus Pauling and other veterans of the test ban movement. In the later 1960s, considerable journalistic and public attention focused on the Pentagon's proposal to construct an antiballistic missile system in North Dakota—a proposal narrowly approved by the Senate in August 1969. And scattered evidence suggests that the nuclear threat still remained vividly alive, especially among the young, at the subconscious level of nightmares, fantasies, and inarticulate forebodings. Popularizers of Bible prophecy continued through the 1960s and 1970s to search the Scriptures for intimations of atomic war.

What one *does* see, however, is a sharp decline in activism, public discussion, mainstream media attention, and cultural expression focused on the nuclear-weapons issue. Even the ABM debate was confined mainly to strategists, a few columnists, and a small band of arms-control specialists. Jerome Wiesner, provost of the Massachusetts Institute of Technology (MIT), noted in the June 1967 *Bulletin of the Atomic Scientists,* "There seems to be little public concern about the ABM issue, either pro or con."

This climate of apparent obliviousness and unconcern continued well into the 1970s. In 1975, Samuel H. Day Jr., successor to Eugene Rabinowitch as editor of the *Bulletin of the Atomic Scientists,* wrote, "*Public apathy* . . . constitutes perhaps the most ominous of the various forces pulling the world toward a nuclear holocaust." The chorus of lament is striking in its unanimity. "Unless momentarily roused by crisis or threatening alert," asked Richard Rhodes in the November 1975 *Atlantic,* "who among us think of nuclear war anymore?" Reflected Norman Cousins in the *Saturday Review* (April 17, 1976), "Hardly anyone talks anymore about nuclear stockpiles as the world's No. 1 problem. . . . The anti-testing clamor of the Sixties now seems far off and almost unreal." Political journalist Peter Ognibene, in the same issue of the *Saturday Review,* agreed. "Any politician who would now speak, as President Kennedy once did, about 'the nuclear sword of Damocles' poised above our collective head would be dismissed out of hand as an anachronism. The fear of nuclear war, once so great, has steadily receded."

Why did the era from 1963 through the 1970s see such quiescence on issues related to nuclear war and the nuclear arms race? The most reassuring answer would be that the complacency was justified—that the nuclear threat did diminish in these years. And, indeed, by 1975, 106 nations had signed the test ban treaty; 99 had signed the 1968 Nuclear Non-Proliferation Treaty; and the nuclear powers had agreed not to place atomic weapons in space, on the moon, or on the ocean floor. In 1967 a number of Latin American states pledged by treaty to forswear nuclear weapons. In 1972 the Strategic Arms Limitation Talks, begun in 1969, produced the SALT I and Anti-Ballistic Missile (ABM) treaties, restricting the United States and the Soviet Union to two ABM systems each and pledging each nation to limit for five years its missile capability to launchers already operational or under construction.

But when one turns from the realm of treaty making to the real world of nuclear weaponry, a different and bleaker picture emerges. In both the United States and the Soviet Union, nuclear-weapons research, construction, and deployment went forward rapidly after 1963. Taking advantage of the test ban treaty's gaping loophole, both sides developed sophisticated techniques of underground testing. The United States conducted more tests in the five years *after* 1963 than in the five years before, some involving weapons fifty times the size of the Hiroshima bomb. The physicist Bernard Feld of MIT concluded in the January 1975 *Bulletin of the Atomic Scientists* that the test ban treaty, while perhaps an "ecological blessing," was "an arms-control disaster." For one thing, the treaty's signatories did not include the nations most likely to develop nuclear weapons. Moreover, as Milton Leitenberg noted in the January 1972 *Bulletin,* "No one believes it will long remain as a viable treaty unless the two major powers begin substantial disarmament."

As for the SALT I agreement, it sidestepped what had by 1972 emerged as the most volatile feature of the nuclear arms race: missiles' growing destructive power and technical sophistication. While the Soviet Union opted for larger ICBMs and warheads, America moved toward diversification and technical refinements such as MIRV (Multiple Independently Targetable Re-entry Vehicles), by which each missile could carry up to sixteen highly accurate and separately targeted warheads.

What Robert McNamara in 1967 called the "mad momentum" of the nuclear arms race steadily accelerated in these years. The SALT process had "institutionalized" the competition, observed Swedish arms-control specialist Alva Myrdal in 1976, but "by no stretch of the imagination can this be called arms limitation." In the December 1967 *Bulletin of the Atomic Scientists,* Milton Leitenberg noted that in the flurry of nuclear treaty making, not a single weapons system had been reduced or dismantled—except to be replaced by a more modern one.

With so little objective basis for this decade and a half of comparative nuclear complacency, why did it occur? Many have attributed it to the influence of the Department of Defense and the major military contractors. Writing in 1970, one arms-control advocate blamed nuclear passivity on the Pentagon's "in-house steam roller" that "forges ahead over all objections." Few would deny the existence of the military-industrial complex. For the principal military contractors and their hundreds of subsidiaries, as indeed for entire regions of the country, nuclear-weapons research, development, and construction represented economic interests of vast proportions. But simply because the military-industrial complex has powerful economic incentives for shaping public attitudes in certain ways, does this mean it has the power to do so?

Certainly the military services and corporate interests engaged in planning and producing nuclear weapons have their media outlets, and their influence on public perceptions is formidable. But this does not seem a sufficient explanation for the public's unconcern. For one thing, this explanation is not time specific; it cannot account for *variations* in public responses to the nuclear threat. Nuclear-weapons research and development have constantly loomed large since the early 1950s. Yet there have been dramatic shifts in the level of activism and cultural expression directed to the nuclear issue. The question, then, remains: Why did nuclear awareness and activism decline so precipitously in the period we are examining? Several reasons suggest themselves.

The perception of reduced danger. Although the various treaties of these years failed to slow the nuclear arms race, they did convey the *appearance* of progress. For those already inclining toward psychic denial, this appearance provided a plausible rationalization. To nuclear activists, this situation was intensely frustrating: "The elaborate staging of arms control negotiations," wrote Samuel H. Day Jr. in the September 1975 *Bulletin of the Atomic Scientists,* "doubtless persuaded many that the threat is diminishing."

Nor, perhaps, was this perception entirely illusory. The intensity of nuclear fear at any given moment is presumably influenced by two distinct though connected realities: the quantity and nature of the world's nuclear arsenals, and judgments about the likelihood of their use. In the 1950s and continuing through the Cuban Missile Crisis, the fear that nuclear war might actually break out received periodic reenforcement from political pronouncements and international crises. With the Cold

War thaw that began in 1963 and continued episodically through the détente of the early 1970s, the diminution of nuclear-war fear had a certain rational basis, despite the superpowers' growing nuclear arsenals.

The growing remoteness of the nuclear reality. Memories of Hiroshima and Nagasaki were dimming. Civil defense was played down. And with atomic tests and radioactive fallout no longer dominating the media, the world's nuclear stockpile seemed increasingly unreal.

"Familiarity takes the sting out of practically anything, even Armageddon," noted the journalist P. E. Schneider in the *New York Times Magazine* (August 14, 1966). "Nuclear weapons constitute a danger so theoretical, so remote, as to be almost non-existent." The psychiatrist Jerome Frank made this point in 1967: "Nuclear missiles poised to kill cannot be seen, felt, tested, or smelled, and so we scarcely think of them." With the end of aboveground testing, observed the *New York Times* in 1969, nuclear fear had become "diffuse and inchoate." "Our capacity for . . . response is dulled," agreed the MIT physicist and arms-control advocate Kosta Tsipis in 1972, "because the danger is not present to our daily experience; it is a mental image . . . inconceivable to the large majority."

The muting of the sense of urgency was furthered by the abstract vocabulary of nuclear strategies and weapons technicians. These years brought an array of acronyms confusing enough to make even a New Dealer blush: ABM, AWACS, ELF, FOBS, MIRV, MARV, SLBM, GLCM, MX, TNW, and so on. Even the names given the various missile systems evoked not their actual doomsday potential but reassuring associations with the heavens, classical mythology, American history, and even popular slang: Polaris, Nike-Zeus, Poseidon, Tomahawk, Minuteman, Pershing, Davy Crockett, Hound Dog.

The sense of the issue's remoteness was self-reenforcing. As nuclear weapons literally went underground after 1963, the torrent of novels, movies, and television programs that had both fed and reflected nuclear fears slowed to a trickle. This in turn facilitated the numbing process. Remote and largely invisible, nuclear weapons proved particularly ill-suited to the insatiable visual demands of television.

Some tried to restore the lost sense of immediacy. In the 1970s, the

Catholic activists Daniel and Philip Berrigan took hammers to missiles on the production line, as in 1968 they had poured blood on draft records. In 1970, two University of Missouri sociologists showed their students the documentary film *Hiroshima/Nagasaki,* which portrays the victims' sufferings in horrifying detail. Predictably, when tested immediately afterward, students showed a heightened resistance to the idea of nuclear war. But for how long? Was it like the well-known phenomenon of drivers creeping along for a few miles after passing a terrible highway accident—only to speed up again as the memory fades?

The tranquilizing effect of the "peaceful atom." President Eisenhower launched the international "Atoms for Peace" program as early as 1953, and the first domestic nuclear power plant opened in 1957, but in the mid-1960s the program really gained momentum. By 1973, thirty-seven plants were in operation in the United States, with many more planned. Concurrently, the atom's peacetime potential was given enormous publicity.

The most indefatigable cheerleader after David Lilienthal's retirement from public life was the chemist and Nobel laureate Glenn T. Seaborg, chairman of the Atomic Energy Commission from 1961 to 1970. In speeches, articles, and interviews, Seaborg described the nuclear utopia ahead: cheap power, medical wonders, agricultural abundance, a "junkless society" through the nuclear processing of waste materials, "international understanding and peace" thanks to nuclear-powered communications satellites. "Designed to blend into the natural landscape, low in profile . . . with all the distribution lines underground," and nestled in "park-like settings," Seaborg declared, future nuclear power plants would be "as close to an extension of nature as any human enterprise." The expansive Texan in the White House echoed Seaborg's enthusiasm. In 1967, Lyndon Johnson delivered a speech entitled "Nuclear Power: Key to a Golden Age of Mankind."

In the nation's collective unconscious (to use that Jungian term loosely), a kind of psychological trade-off seems to have occurred, with glowing images of the benevolent atom obscuring and to a degree neutralizing dark images of the destroying atom. Support nuclear power and other peacetime uses of the atom, the tacit argument went, and the threat of nuclear war will diminish correspondingly. As *U.S. News & World Report* put it in December 1967, the world had wandered far down the nuclear-weapons path, but was now at least crossing "the threshold into the era of the peaceful atom, with its promise of better things for all mankind." In reality, of course, there were not two separate worlds of atomic energy but only one, whose various aspects were deeply intertwined. Still, for a time, the allure of the peaceful atom played its part in muting fears of nuclear weapons.

The arcane reassurance of nuclear strategy. From 1945 to 1950, and continuing into John Foster Dulles's term as secretary of state, atomic strategy as practiced in Washington was a fairly simple (if often unnerving) matter. By the 1960s, however, it had become a highly specialized pursuit dominated by a small group of civilian experts under contract to the military and based at semiautonomous research institutes at larger universities or at such "think tanks" as the Institute for Defense Analysis, the System Development Corporation, the Center for Naval Analysis, the Research Analysis Corporation, and the RAND Corporation.

Using computer simulations, John von Neumann's game theory, and other analytical tools, these "defense intellectuals" transformed nuclear strategy into a rarefied, quasi-scientific discipline. Conveying "the impression of holding membership in a closed club" (as the *New Yorker* put it in 1971), they increasingly moved in their own intellectual and even social orbit.

The physicist Ralph Lapp, in a 1965 book, called them "the new priesthood," noting that even in academia, with its tradition of scholarly openness, "they enjoy a privileged area of argument and can always retreat to a sanctuary of secret dataland." Of the key strategists—Herman Kahn, Thomas Schelling, Henry Kissinger, Donald Brennan, Bernard Brodie, William Kintner, Fred Iklé, Oskar Morgenstern, Robert Strausz-Hupé, William Kaufmann, Albert Wohlstetter, Glenn Snyder—the names of only one or two would have been recognizable even to politically attentive citizens.

As for the strategic theories they debated, only the dimmest awareness—analogous, perhaps, to a medieval peasant's grasp of the theological concepts with which monastic scholars like St. Thomas Aquinas wrestled—filtered beyond the walls of the institutes and think tanks. This had a profoundly discouraging effect not only on potential activists, but also on those seeking to remain informed on nuclear issues. As early as 1959, Robert M. Hutchins questioned whether democratic theory retained much relevance in the new era of strategic planning, and similar questions gained force in succeeding years. In the mid-1960s, the political scientist Hans Morgenthau stated: "The great issues of nuclear strategy . . . cannot even be the object of meaningful debate . . . because there can be no competent judgments without meaningful knowledge. Thus the great national decisions of life or death are rendered by technological elites, and both the Congress and the people retain little more than the illusion of making the decisions which the theory of democracy supposes them to make."

The substance as well as the process of nuclear strategy changed in these years. As the Soviets moved toward parity with the United States in nuclear warheads and ICBMs, American atomic saber-rattling gave way to a new strategic emphasis: deterrence. The essential elements of deterrence theory had been developed by the Yale political scientist Bernard Brodie in a seminal 1946 work *The Absolute Weapon: Atomic Power and World Order* and elaborated by Albert Wohlstetter in a 1954 RAND study published as "The Delicate Balance of Terror" in the January 1959 issue of *Foreign Affairs*.

It was in the 1960s, however, particularly toward the end of Robert McNamara's tenure as secretary of defense, that deterrence theory was officially endorsed and given extensive public visibility as the cornerstone of U.S. nuclear strategy. As elaborated by McNamara in 1967, deterrence theory held that the point of stockpiling nuclear weapons was not the anticipation of ever *using* them, but of *preventing* their use by the other side.

Specifically, the Soviets had to be convinced that a nuclear first strike by them would trigger a retaliatory "second strike" that would devastate their country. In McNamara's memorable phrase (which of course soon gave rise to the acronym MAD), nuclear security lay in "mutual assured destruction," that is, "the certainty of suicide to the aggressor—not merely to his military forces, but to his society as a whole." By challenging the common-sense assumption that the vast buildup of nuclear weapons increased the likelihood of their eventual use, deterrence theory helped dull nuclear fears and activist impulses. To march and demonstrate for nuclear disarmament, deterrence theorists suggested, was to advocate a destabilization of the "balance of terror" that could in fact increase the risk of nuclear war.

Not all Americans found deterrence theory and its seemingly perverse corollaries persuasive. To traditional pacifists, disarmament advocates, and others who believed that the reduction and eventual elimination of nuclear weapons must be a fundamental objective of U.S. policy, the abandonment of this goal, implicit in deterrence theory, was dismaying. In the 1950s and early 1960s, deterrence came under heavy criticism on these grounds. Criticism diminished after 1963, reflecting the larger cultural shift we have been examining, but it never disappeared entirely.

Many who approached the nuclear dilemma from a religious or ethical perspective were appalled by the moral implications of a strategy predicated on threatening to wipe out an entire society. The elaborate edifice of deterrence theory rested on the threat of retaliation, and that threat had to be credible for the theory to make any sense at all. McNamara insisted on the government's "unwavering will" should the awful moment of decision ever come. In the *New York Times Magazine* of June 7, 1964, Walt W. Rostow, chairman of the State Department's policy planning council, assented: "The heart of a credible deterrent in a nuclear age lies in being prepared to face the consequences, should deterrence fail." American security, Rostow went on, demanded an unflinching readiness to match any Soviet escalation "up to and including all-out nuclear war."

The moral dilemma lay precisely here, giving rise to considerable soul-searching in religious circles, not only in the historically pacifist denominations—Quaker, Mennonite, Church of the Brethren—but also in the mainstream Protestant denominations and even in the Roman Catholic hierarchy, traditionally a bastion of support for a policy of military strength. In 1965, drawing on the church's traditional just-war doctrine, Vatican Council II declared: "Any act of war aimed indiscriminately at the destruction of entire cities and of extensive areas along with their population is a crime against God and man himself. It merits unequivocal and unhesitating condemnation."

What, then, was the church to say of a strategy whose avowed aim was to avoid nuclear war, but which depended on an "unwavering will" to destroy an entire people? "Surely there is something obscene," said the Catholic journal *Commonweal* in 1971, about a policy predicated on such a threat. What if human error, technological malfunction, or some unforeseeable combination of circumstances triggered an attack, or led to the mistaken impression that one was under way (the *Dr. Strangelove* scenario)? The consequences if deterrence failed through mischance did not bear contemplating.

At the other end of the spectrum, many strategists, Pentagon planners, and weapons researchers never fully accepted the operational implications of deterrence theory. New weapons proposals continued to proliferate, beyond any rational function. And even after McNamara publicly endorsed deterrence theory, the Pentagon's computerized war plan, SIOP (Single Integrated Operational Plan), continued to give targeting preference to Soviet military sites and missile bases, reflecting not only the deterrence principle but also the desire to maintain an actual nuclear war fighting capability.

Despite these qualifications, deterrence theory, as publicized in the later 1960s, clearly helped calm the nuclear anxieties of many Americans. It offered hope that ultimately the nuclear arms race would reach a point of equilibrium. Once each side had achieved a credible second-strike capability (McNamara's "mutual assured destruction"), the "race" would end in a tie. Nuclear warheads would remain, but they would simply rest in their silos and submarine bays forever, endlessly deterring. Thanks in part to this theory, editorialized *Business Week* on July 13, 1968, "living with the atomic bomb has turned out to be less frightening than it once seemed."

Other issues and concerns. The nuclear-weapons issue did not exist in a vacuum in these years; it was but one element of a complex cultural and political reality. Even as Americans hailed the test ban treaty, the war in Vietnam was becoming more threatening. With Lyndon Johnson's postelection escalation of forces in February 1965, the Vietnam conflict began to rule the media, dominating public discourse and drawing ever greater waves of protest. From the first tentative campus protests in March 1965 to the final outburst on campuses and in Washington in the spring of 1970, the war in Southeast Asia absorbed nearly all the available protest energy of peace activists, religious leaders, and college students facing the draft.

Always present on the nation's television screens, the war and the domestic turmoil it engendered had an immediacy that the more abstract nuclear-weapons issue could not begin to approximate. Missile tests were out of sight, deep underground, and the missiles themselves were similarly hidden in subterranean silos, in B-52 bomb bays on remote, heavily guarded air force bases, or in nuclear submarines patrolling the world's seas. The war and the protest demonstrations, by contrast, conveyed in urgent, often shocking visual images, appeared constantly on television news programs, in radio bulletins, and on the pages of newspapers and news magazines. In this situation, there was little question which would dominate public debate and the outlets of cultural expression. A new cycle of arms-control talks had begun, the *Wall Street Journal* reported on January 11, 1973. But, it predicted, few would notice "amid the distractions of Vietnam hopes and fears."

When a 1969 Gallup poll asked subjects to list the "two or three most important problems" facing the nation, 63 percent mentioned Vietnam and only 2 percent the danger of nuclear war. The shift of attention to Vietnam, according to Roy E. Licklider in his 1971 book, *Private Nuclear Strategists,* removed "much of the public pressure on the American government to alter its nuclear policies."

The impact of Vietnam on the nuclear disarmament movement is vividly illustrated in the history of SANE. While Benjamin Spock and other SANE leaders turned completely to the Vietnam issue, still others urged continued attention to nuclear weapons. At a 1966 SANE board meeting, issues related to the nuclear arms race were relegated to near the bottom of a long agenda dominated by the Vietnam War.

When Spock and other leaders of SANE increasingly linked the organization to the most militant wing of the antiwar movement, particularly at the National Conference for a New Politics held in Chicago in September 1967, these deepening differences in the organization exploded openly. The executive director, Donald Keys, and Norman Cousins resigned; Spock himself soon departed. A shadow of its former self, SANE in 1969 eliminated the word *nuclear* from its name.

Similar seismic shifts were occurring throughout the nuclear disarmament movement. At the University of Wisconsin, Students for Peace and Disarmament, founded in 1962 to oppose nuclear testing and the arms race, dropped the nuclear issue abruptly in the fall of 1963 to organize a rally protesting America's deepening involvement in Vietnam. Understandable and even inevitable as it seems in retrospect, this process was distressing to the dwindling band of older activists who continued to focus on the nuclear threat. "From the long-range . . . point of view," wrote the physicist and Manhattan Project veteran David Inglis in the May 1967 *Bulletin of the Atomic Scientists,* "the most tragic feature of the war in Vietnam . . . is that preoccupation with this struggle is being allowed to stand in the way of the urgent business of making a far more devastating nuclear war less likely."

A closely related influence on post-1963 American nuclear attitudes was the emergence of the New Left, particularly the campus-based radical organization Students for a Democratic Society (SDS). Founded in 1960 as an offshoot of the socialist League for Industrial Democracy, SDS at its peak in 1968 had some seven thousand members, with upwards of forty thousand more affiliated with local campus branches. It would be foolhardy to treat SDS, or even a more loosely defined "New Left," as synonymous with the large and diverse 1960s antiwar movement. Even the New Left itself was notoriously amorphous; John Diggins, in *The American Left in the Twentieth Century* (1973), called it "a mood in search of a movement." Nevertheless, New Left ideology was one important force shaping 1960s activism. At the rhetorical level, the New Left talked a lot about nuclear weapons. In their 1962 Port Huron statement, SDS founders proclaimed themselves seared by atomic fears "when we were kids" and "guided by the sense that we may be the last generation in the experiment with living." "Our hopes for the future have been corroded by the Bomb," added the 1963 SDS manifesto *America and the New Era.*

Adult sympathizers helped spread the idea that the activists' lifelong association with nuclear weapons was crucial to their political orientation and gave them a unique moral sensitivity. "The bomb has had a wide, corrosive, and depressing effect upon the young," wrote the novelist Fletcher Knebel in the December 1968 issue of *Popular Science.* "They sing their sad laments over guitars while the girls' long hair weeps for the coming suicide of humanity."

But when one moves beyond the rhetoric, it is striking both how little serious attention the New Left gave to the nuclear issue and how little effort it made to sustain the momentum of the pre-1963 nuclear disarmament movement. "It's just a cliché," was the succinct comment of one Harvard activist on the claim that the New Left's outlook was profoundly shaped by the bomb.

Nuclear disarmament was doubtless implicit in the New Left's vision, but one finds few specifics in the literature. When nuclear weapons are mentioned, it is usually as part of an exposé of the universities' role in military research, or a more general indictment of capitalist society. In his 1969 book *The Making of a Counter Culture,* Theodore Roszak argued that the central issue was not nuclear weapons but "the total *ethos* of the bomb"—an ethos that also pervaded "our culture, our public morality, our economic life, our intellectual endeavors." The central significance of "the shadow of thermonuclear annihilation beneath which we cower," said Roszak, was as "the prime symptom" of morbidity in a society that was "fatally and contagiously diseased."

The vague and general talk about "the Bomb" in New Left circles sometimes suggests an effort to establish at least a rhetorical link with the earlier anti–nuclear weapons campaign. What in fact emerges, however, is the sharp discontinuity between the two movements. The explanation suggested above—that the Vietnam War in all its urgent emotional intensity preempted all other concerns—certainly has validity; but the discontinuity is rooted as well in the inner history of the test ban movement in the early 1960s and in the effect of this history on the New Left in its formative stages.

From the first, relations between the test ban and nuclear disarmament organizations, on the one hand, and student activists, on the other, had been strained at best. Organizations like SANE sought to shape public policy through speeches, sober pronouncements and advertisements featuring famous names, and access to sympathetic politicians. SANE's

1960 Madison Square Garden rally notwithstanding, its members were not oriented toward demonstrations, marches, and mass action. SANE's campus branch, Students for a Sane Nuclear Policy, enjoyed little autonomy. "On arms control, we weren't looking for help from the youthful *polloi*," one SANE leader has candidly acknowledged. The campus-based Student Peace Union emerged in 1959 partially out of frustration with SANE's rigidity, exclusivity, and general stodginess.

These latent stresses were vastly exacerbated early in 1960 when Senator Thomas Dodd of Connecticut charged that SANE was infiltrated by Communists. An alarmed Norman Cousins privately assured Dodd that SANE was determined to rid itself of any taint of disloyalty. SANE's national board excluded Communists from membership, revoked the charter of the Greater New York Committee (a major target of Dodd's charges), and pointedly announced that SANE was a "deliberately autocratic organization" whose membership could be closely monitored.

All this caused an upheaval in SANE and in the peace movement. Several directors resigned, and SANE's student branch broke away from the parent organization. Campus groups committed to a test ban and nuclear disarmament, but independent of SANE, proliferated: Tocsin at Harvard, Students for Peace and Disarmament at Wisconsin, and so on. The pace of activism—marches, demonstrations, petitions—quickened markedly: A San Francisco peace march in October 1960 drew two thousand participants. Women's Strike for Peace, a grassroots movement started in the Washington area in 1961, quickly organized demonstrations in sixty cities, involving fifty thousand women. Discontent with SANE and similar narrowly based, top-down groups intensified. The *Nation,* in its March 3, 1962, issue, saw in the ferment of 1960–62 not just a new phase of the peace movement, but "the birth of a new" movement.

The volatility of the situation emerged clearly in February 1962 when a coalition of campus peace groups led by Todd Gitlin and Peter Goldmark of Tocsin organized the Washington Project, which drew five thousand students to the nation's capital. Some, attired in suits and ties, met with senators, congressmen, and State Department officials. But others—the wave of the future—organized a mass meeting and took to the streets, marching, chanting, and waving placards for nuclear disarmament.

By 1962, then, thousands of students had abandoned SANE's approach in favor of direct-action strategies aimed at fomenting a mass movement against nuclear testing and the nuclear arms race. With the test ban treaty of 1963, the urgency drained from the nuclear issue, but the activist zeal and spirit of tactical innovation remained. Waiting in the wings was SDS. For many students, the "new" peace movement of 1960–62 provided a bridge to the New Left.

The early New Left was determined to avoid what it saw as the failings of SANE and the 1950s peace movement. Unlike SANE, SDS adopted a "non-exclusionist" membership policy, prized face-to-face relations and the spirit of community, and was casually organized and decentralized to the point of chaos.

Tactical differences were no less pronounced than were those of structure and style. SANE relied on its access to Washington powerbrokers and its ability to influence the educated middle class through the prestige of its sponsors and the impact of its psychologically manipulative (if factually sound) advertisements. The early SDS, by contrast, focused on the poor, prided itself on its nonmanipulative, nonexploitative approach, and adopted an ideological stance of radical opposition to the "Establishment."

With a grant from the United Auto Workers, the SDS Economic Research and Action Project in 1963–64 sent organizers into ghettos and slums to discuss the residents' grievances, help them plan protest actions, and (so it was hoped) gradually lead them to an awareness of the larger realities and class inequities that shaped their lives. In gradual stages, the poor would be radicalized and become a part of the force contributing to the emergence of a new social order. "Only in this way," wrote SDS president Tom Hayden in *Dissent* (January/February 1966), "can a movement be built which the Establishment can neither buy off nor manage." The group's Port Huron statement gave a name to this strategy: participatory democracy. An article of faith for the early New Left, this concept was both its most significant contribution to the radical tradition and its most explicit repudiation of SANE and much of the 1950s peace movement.

SDS community organizers quickly found that the nuclear arms race ranked well below such matters as garbage collection on the list of slum dwellers' concerns. As one activist later wrote, the poor were often openly

hostile to "large, organization-funded, top-down peace propaganda programs." This realization made the New Left retreat still further from the
issue of nuclear disarmament.

If SANE was the negative role model for the early New Left, the
civil-rights movement was the positive one. The tactics of black activist
groups like SNCC (Student Non-violent Coordinating Committee),
with its sit-ins and marches, seemed eminently more promising—and
exciting—than the staid, desk-bound approach of organizations like
SANE. Black activists understandably gave other issues priority over the
nuclear arms race, reenforcing the inclination of their white emulators
in the New Left to do the same.

Ideological as well as tactical considerations underlay the early New
Left's downgrading of the nuclear-weapons issue. Assuming that the
Washington technocrats understood the irrationality of nuclear war and
an out-of-control nuclear arms race, SDS further believed that they
would devise ways to avoid nuclear catastrophe. This assumption
emerges most clearly in the 1963 manifesto *America and the New Era,*
written soon after the test ban treaty was announced. Citing this
agreement as well as "other first-step efforts at curtailing the arms race,"
this analysis concluded, "A deep desire to avoid general nuclear war is
fundamental to the Administration's 'rational military policies.'. . . The
Administration recognizes that some forms of agreement with the Soviet
Union are necessary if nuclear war is to be prevented." But while the
technocratic managers in Washington could be counted on to avoid nuclear war and a spiraling nuclear arms race, SDS went on, they would
not hesitate to engage in subversion, counterinsurgency wars, and other
nonnuclear power tactics to protect corporate America's global political
and economic interests.

The radicals' assumption that the technocrats' rational calculations
and managerial skills would prevent nuclear war despite the continued
existence of vast nuclear arsenals (a belief they shared with the deterrence
theorists) was a remarkable gesture of faith in human reason and technocratic expertise. As such, it represented a sharp break with the activist
perspective and cultural ethos of the 1950s and early 1960s, which
viewed the nuclear arms race as a fundamentally irrational, unstable, and
highly dangerous process that might at any time escape from control

through accident, technical breakdown, or some sudden escalation of local conflict. The early New Left, for all its talk of "the looming shadow of the bomb," did not share such fears—or at least did not systematically explore them in its theoretical work or embody them in its operational planning.

The relationship between the radical movement of the 1960s and the nuclear-weapons issue, then, was a complex and subtle one. After 1965, anti–Vietnam War activism played a paramount role in pushing the nuclear issue to the background. But even earlier, the ideological and tactical thrust of the New Left had led it to break decisively with the organized test ban and nuclear disarmament activism of the 1950s. Convinced of the superiority of its tactics and the greater sophistication of its political analysis, the New Left downplayed its roots in the antinuclear and test ban movements. The earlier campaign was significant, New Left ideologues suggested, primarily because its limitations had propelled some of its youthful adherents beyond liberal reformism to a larger radical consciousness.

Even qualified efforts at rapprochement soon faded. In *The Making of a Counter Culture,* Theodore Roszak, himself a veteran of the earlier peace movement, wrote: "Precisely what do groups like SANE . . . tell us about adult America even when we are dealing with politically conscious elements? Looking back, one is struck by their absurd shallowness and conformism, their total unwillingness to raise fundamental issues about the quality of American life, their fastidious anti-communism, and above all their incapacity to sustain any significant initiative on the political landscape." Roszak's analysis is insightful, but its dismissive, contemptuous tone also indicates the depth of the chasm between the radicals of the New Left and the earlier nuclear-weapons protest movement.

The New Left's hostility toward the older generation of nuclear activists was in many instances fully reciprocated. Eugene Rabinowitch, editor of the *Bulletin of the Atomic Scientists,* was deeply critical of the 1960s activists, expressing his dismay in editorials with titles like "Student Rebellion: The Aimless Revolution?" (September 1968) and "The Stoning of America" (November 1971), a bitter attack on Charles Reich's *The Greening of America* (1970), a paean to the political potential of the counterculture.

One of the bitterest denunciations came from Donald Keys, SANE's executive director. The differences between the New Left and older organizations like SANE, he said, were fundamental. SANE believed in democracy and in the "common sense and goodwill" of the American people, and placed "communication and dialogue with the public and the power structure at the center of its approach." SANE believed in working through the system for its broad-ranging, though limited, goals. New Left radicals, by contrast, "reject the democratic process, encourage violence, and offer only protest and opposition." Young people, "becoming conscious of social issues for the first time," Keys went on, had reacted "in a total way against the hypocrisy, gross materialism, and dehumanization of their society." They seemed unable or unwilling to "compartmentalize or fragment their response." Two such dissimilar approaches, concluded Keys, shared no common ground. As he put it in a November 13, 1967, memorandum to SANE, "The two major trends in the peace movement are by their nature incompatible and mutually divergent." The breakdown of communication and even civility between the New Left and the activists who for years had worked against the menace of nuclear war could hardly have been more complete.

As the 1970s ended, with the Vietnam War over at last and the Watergate crisis resolved, the combination of circumstances that for more than a decade had mired the American public in nuclear apathy was rapidly breaking up, giving way to the early stirrings of renewed political activism and cultural attention. The issue of nuclear proliferation, highlighted by India's test of a nuclear device in 1974, demonstrations in Europe against NATO's deployment of Pershing and cruise missiles, and a grassroots campaign against nuclear power plants all helped revive activist energies.

But much time had been lost. From the early 1960s to the late 1970s, most Americans had seemed oblivious to a danger that many in earlier years, and many others in the years to follow, considered the most urgent ever to confront the nation, and indeed the entire human race.

9

NUCLEAR WAR IN THE WRITINGS OF BIBLE-PROPHECY POPULARIZERS

I n the early 1980s, as I researched the cultural impact of the atomic bomb, I encountered a vast and neglected lode of source material: scores of popular paperbacks that purported to interpret Revelation and other apocalyptic portions of the Bible. After August 1945, these pious popularizers, long accustomed to finding current events foretold in the Bible, lost no time in incorporating images of atomic destruction into their scenarios, where they remained firmly implanted for half a century.

I was able to include only a few brief references to this material in *By the Bomb's Early Light,* but in 1987, after the publication of that book, I decided to explore this specific part of the nuclear culture more fully. My research quickly expanded, however, to include not only the nuclear-war-in-prophecy theme, but the much larger panorama of apocalyptic belief in contemporary America. My 1992 book, *When Time Shall Be No More: Prophecy Belief in Modern American Culture,* was the result. This chapter is based on a fully documented chapter in that book that explores prophecy popularizers' view of the atomic bomb and the nuclear threat.

Bible popularizers seem to have been immune to the cycle of America's nuclear awareness discussed in chapter 8. Even during the "Big Sleep"—the period of diminished attention to nuclear issues that extended from 1963 to the later 1970s—the topic of nuclear war remained vividly alive for the nation's millions of Bible-prophecy believers.

Instructed by television evangelists and by paperback popularizers, these millions remained convinced, despite arms-control treaties, diminished antinuclear activism, and the secular media's neglect of the topic, not only that the Bible foretells a world-destroying thermonuclear holocaust, but that the holocaust would probably erupt in their lifetimes. Despite the end of the Cold War, many still believe this today.

FROM CHRISTIANITY'S EARLIEST DAYS, biblical images of the earth's convulsive final cataclysm both awed and challenged prophetic interpreters. "This our city will be burned with fire from heaven," Christian warns his family in John Bunyan's *Pilgrim's Progress* (1678). A nineteenth-century American prophecy work, D. T. Taylor's *The Coming Earthquake* (1870), vividly pictured a planet trembling on the brink of disintegration:

> Modern science . . . teaches that this globe is an enormous "terrestrial bombshell" . . . , its hidden interior . . . an intensely heated mass in a condition of molten fluidity, agitated, restless, and rolling its fiery waves hither and thither age after age, incessantly seeking with a terrible expressive power an outlet to diffuse its igneous elements over the surface and into the atmosphere. On this thin, rocky film, or outer surface, dwells a fallen, sinful, and dying race of mortals. . . . Is it any wonder that thinking, sober people have from the earliest ages looked for a final, awful convulsion and burning day?

Down to 1945, interpreters of prophecy typically envisioned this "burning day" in naturalistic terms—earthquakes, comets, volcanic eruptions—or as an eschatological event beyond human understanding. One writer, for example, simply attributed the destruction at Armageddon to "the all-consuming 'breath of God'" and did not speculate further.

With the coming of the atomic bomb, all this changed. Man himself, it now seemed, had in the throes of war stumbled on the very means of his own prophesied doom. Beginning in autumn 1945, a chorus of preachers, Bible scholars, and paperback writers insisted that the Scriptures not only foretold atomic weapons, but also their eventual cataclysmic use.

FIRST ASSESSMENTS

President Truman's August 1945 announcements of the atomic destruction of Hiroshima and Nagasaki triggered a torrent of apocalyptic pronouncements, many of them explicitly biblical. "Atomic Energy for War: New Beast of Apocalypse," headlined the *Philadelphia Inquirer.* William Laurence of the *New York Times* titled the final section of his history of the Manhattan Project "Armageddon." Countless commentators quoted 2 Peter 3:10: "The heavens shall pass away with a great noise, and the elements shall melt with fervent heat, the earth also and the works that are therein shall be burned up."

A popular culture steeped in prophecy quickly enveloped the bomb in an aura of biblical imagery. Fred Kirby's 1945 country-music hit "Atomic Power," which imagined brimstone fire raining down from heaven and described atomic energy as "given by the mighty hand of God," tapped directly into this reservoir of grassroots end-time belief. In the privacy of his diary, even President Truman, as we have seen, responded in biblical terms to the first A-bomb test in New Mexico as possibly the means of "the fire destruction prophesied in the Euphrates Valley Era, after Noah and his fabulous Ark." Truman, who knew his Bible, doubtless had in mind such Old Testament passages as Deuteronomy 32:22: "For a fire is kindled in mine anger, and shall burn unto the lowest hell, and shall consume the earth with her increase, and set on fire the foundations of the mountains."

At the level of popular religious belief, the bomb's impact was immediate and dramatic. In contrast to the secular press, where relief at its apparent role in ending the war counterbalanced fears about the future, prophecy writers from the first adopted an unrelievedly somber tone. "It is the devil who caused man to devote his highest and most successful potencies to the discovery of those things by which man destroys his fellows," commented E. Schuyler English, associate editor of *Our Hope,* a magazine of prophecy exposition, late in 1945, "and no greater weapon has ever been devised than this one, the A-bomb." The ultimate cataclysm foretold in the Bible, English went on, sounded "singularly similar in its effects to those of the atom bomb." *Moody Monthly*, the publication of Chicago's Moody Bible Institute, agreed: "The Bible is ahead of science again," it said; an atomic blast offered an "exact picture" of the burning and melting of 2 Peter 3:10.

Philadelphia's Donald Grey Barnhouse, prophecy writer and radio preacher, explored the bomb's prophetic significance in his *Eternity* magazine in December 1945. Commenting on those who were expressing hope that global holocaust might yet be avoided, Barnhouse declared somberly: "It is already too late. The threads of inevitability have been caught in the mesh of the hidden gears of history and the divine plan moves toward the inexorable fulfillment." Weighing the prospects of atomic war, Barnhouse diverged sharply from the self-congratulatory mood of a nation flushed with victory. The bomb, he said, had given fresh plausibility to a speculation he had long entertained: that New York City was the Babylon whose obliteration in one hour is foretold in Revelation. With atomic power, not only New York but all the nation's great cities could be instantly wiped out. "The destruction of the United States . . . is certainly consistent with the nature of God," Barnhouse declared implacably: The nation had sinned and faced "terrible judgment." Barnhouse's calm in contemplating mass slaughter reflected his conviction that believers faced a happier destiny. "If atomic bombs fall upon our cities," he wrote a few weeks into the nuclear age, "we shall be in heaven the next second."

Of postwar prophecy writers who combed not only the Bible but also the interpretive literature of the past for anticipations of the atomic bomb, the most indefatigable was surely Wilbur M. Smith (1894–1976). The son of a prosperous Midwest apple grower, Smith in 1913 enrolled at Moody Bible Institute, where his father served on the board. A 1914 prophecy conference awakened Smith's lifelong interest in this subject. In 1938, after service as a Presbyterian minister, Smith returned to Moody to teach. In 1947, he joined the newly founded Fuller Theological Seminary in Pasadena. A prolific writer and conference speaker,

Smith was America's best-known and most erudite prophecy expounder of the early postwar era.

The atomic bomb immediately riveted Smith's attention. Like many others, he preached on 2 Peter 3:10—"the passage that was in everyone's mind"—after Hiroshima, and in November 1945 produced a booklet, "This Atomic Age and the Word of God," that sold fifty thousand copies and was condensed in the January 1946 *Reader's Digest*. His much expanded book of the same title appeared in 1948.

God may have destroyed Sodom and Gomorrah with nuclear power, Smith speculated, foreshadowing the judgment now confronting all humanity. Smith scoured the press for doomsday pronouncements by scientists. "The very phrases [foretelling the earth's destruction] that were formerly . . . laughed at by the world," he observed, "are now being used by our outstanding thinkers without any reference to the Scriptures and without any knowledge of prophetic truth." He cited the clock of the *Bulletin of the Atomic Scientists,* poised a few minutes before midnight, and Harold Urey's *Collier's* article, "I'm a Frightened Man." Never in history, asserted Smith, had Jesus' prophecy of men's hearts failing them for fear been more clearly fulfilled.

While activist scientists evoked the horrors of atomic war to rally support for world government or the Acheson-Lilienthal plan, prophecy writers like Smith marshaled the rhetoric of terror to underscore the hopelessness of humanity's situation as the end approached. The bomb, said Smith, forced unbelievers to consider the truth claims of Bible prophecy seriously. The fear aroused by the prospect of atomic annihilation, he asserted, had focused attention on teachings about the Second Coming and end-time events. Like Barnhouse, Smith rejected the idea of world government as a solution. Without God's blessing, he warned, world government would lead only to global tyranny under the Antichrist. The international atomic-energy control agency envisioned by the Acheson-Lilienthal plan would be the perfect vehicle for the rise of the demonic end-time ruler.

Smith gleefully quoted numerous fatuous comments by pre-1914 liberal theologians hailing the imminent advent of the Kingdom of God through human effort. The atomic bomb, he said, should finally quash all such "foolish dreams." Far more on target, he suggested, was Bishop John Ryle, the Anglican evangelical, who as early as 1883 had written: "The last days of the earth shall be its worst days. The last war shall be the most fearful and terrible war that ever desolated the earth." Smith reflected on the contrast between the world of 1948 and the "bright, warm, unclouded days" of his youth, when "a sort of general conviction [prevailed] that we were on the verge of a millennium," and "the idea of atoms was only a theory in our textbook of physics." The bomb, he insisted, radically challenged not only the notion of inevitable progress, but also the cyclical theories of history in which renewal follows degeneration and collapse. History's "great, awful climax" was at hand, he proclaimed, "and every act and plan and invention of godless men can only hasten that day."

One of the more interesting early efforts to link the atomic bomb to the tradition of prophetic interpretation came not from the evangelical ranks, but from Harvard's Perry Miller, the intellectual historian of American Puritanism. In his 1950 essay "The End of the World," Miller noted the similarities between post-Hiroshima doomsday rhetoric and the work of late seventeenth-century prophecy writers whose end-time scenarios had incorporated current scientific thinking. But the intimations of doom in contemporary secular discourse, Miller suggested, differed radically from those of earlier writers, for whom the coming cataclysm had profound eschatological meaning. The nuclear end that seemed all too possible after 1945 lacked such a framework. In an era when "the very concept of a future becomes meaningless," Miller suggested, the sense that history had meaning—and that America had a special role in history—might finally atrophy and die.

Miller's distinction between a theologically rooted apocalypticism and a merely rhetorical one grafted on an essentially secular worldview was important, but for many evangelical ministers, revivalists, and prophecy popularizers, not to mention millions of believers, the intellectual distance between 1650 and 1950 was narrower than Miller might have imagined. Numerous early postwar prophecy writers viewed atomic war as apocalyptic not in a metaphorical but in a literal sense. For them, the bomb and the global holocaust it portended brought infinitely closer the fulfillment of a divine plan formulated before the dawn of time.

Many writers echoed Smith in dismissing proposals for the international control of atomic energy, and indeed all efforts to reduce the risk of atomic war, as further manifestations of the vain hope that humanity could avoid catastrophe through its own efforts. All plans for controlling the atom would fail, one proclaimed in November 1945, "and the nations will be destroyed, because God's word declares it." The United Nations was "doomed to failure," asserted Barnhouse in 1951. The stark marble monolith rising in New York might well serve as the smoldering city's tombstone.

Even those who deplored the post-Hiroshima surge of interest in prophecy could not ignore its intensity. In 1949, Henry Sloan Coffin of Union Theological Seminary (a bastion of liberalism) lamented that mainstream Protestantism's neglect of eschatology had left the field to "sensational propagandists" and "mushrooming cultists" who found blueprints of the future in Daniel and Revelation and promised their followers easy escape from the coming cataclysm. The liberal *Baptist Courier* lashed out at "cults that preach the doom of the present evil order by a sudden intervention of God." Like Communism, the *Courier* said, "This doctrine thrives on darkness and distress."

In response, the Fundamentalist *Sunday School Times* pointed out that the heightened receptivity of the "plain people" to an eschatology that taught a convulsive end to human history ought not be surprising, since the experience of recent decades had so utterly discredited "the dream of a better world" long preached by theological liberals. In a world shadowed by nuclear fear, premillennialism (belief in the Christ's imminent return to earth after a terrible interval of wickedness, violence, and war) had taken a vigorous new lease on life.

THE 1950S AND 1960S: PROPHECY WRITING AND THE NUCLEAR ARMS RACE

Reflecting a broader trend in U.S. culture, prophecy writers devoted somewhat less attention to the bomb in these years. But this lull was relative. Wilbur Smith commented in 1953 on the prophecy books "pouring from the presses," and many of them dealt with the atomic bomb. Despite Washington's efforts to allay nuclear fear, prophecy writers could find no silver lining to the mushroom cloud. "Today the whole world lives in fear of annihilation," declared the manifesto of a 1952 prophecy conference in New York City, and several speakers elaborated the point. Implicitly dismissing government propaganda touting the atom's peacetime uses, one speaker insisted on "the dreadful implications of modern atomic science." Another cited the environmental damage inflicted by U.S. atomic tests in the Pacific, described in David Bradley's *No Place to Hide*, as a sign of the approaching end.

From the mid-1950s to 1963, as we have seen, fears of radioactive fallout triggered a second wave of nuclear fear and political activism. Mirroring this trend, prophecy writers' attention to the bomb picked up sharply. "At no time in past history has the universal situation of the human race been so desperate as it is today," wrote the author of a 1955 prophecy work. "Dread of a third world war hangs heavily on the hearts of men." A 1960 *Moody Monthly* article cited "the piling up of nuclear weapons" as a major contributor to a climate of terror comparable to the biblical accounts of the last days. Given the world situation, wrote J. Dwight Pentecost of Dallas Theological Seminary in 1961, the cataclysmic war prophesied in Ezekiel could break out at any time.

These authors interlaced their discussions of the nuclear threat with a stock set of proof texts: the vision of a melting earth in 2 Peter; the crescendo of catastrophes in John's Apocalypse; the all-consuming conflagration and terrifying astronomical events woven through the Book of Joel's three short chapters ("O Lord, to thee will I cry; for the fire hath devoured the pastures of the wilderness, and the flame hath burned all the trees of the field" [1:19]. "The sun shall be turned into darkness, and the moon into blood, before the great and the terrible day of the Lord comes" [2:31]); and the prophet Zechariah's terrifying description of Jehovah's judgment on Israel's enemies—a description strikingly similar to John Hersey's account of Japanese atomic-bomb victims in *Hiroshima:* "And this shall be the plague wherewith the Lord will smite all the people that have fought against Jerusalem; their flesh shall consume away while they stand upon their feet, and their eyes shall consume away in their holes, and their tongue shall consume away in their mouth" (14:12).

One of the most influential prophecy interpreters of this period was M. R. DeHaan of Grand Rapids, whose "Radio Bible Class" aired on five hundred stations, including the Mutual and ABC networks. In broadcasts and books of the early 1960s, DeHaan often discussed the nuclear threat. "Hanging over the heads of the nations," he wrote in 1962, "is the dire, horrible fear that at any moment some trigger-happy despot will . . . drop a missile that would set the world on fire." Demonstrating the skill of prophecy writers at incorporating new developments into their scenarios, DeHaan discussed the neutron bomb, "technology's deadliest weapon," designed to destroy life without harming physical structures. Elaborating a passage from Jesus' "Little Apocalypse," recorded in the Gospel of Mark, DeHaan proclaimed: "This present age will close with a time of peril and war and destruction so great, what with our atomic weapons and supersonic missiles, that God must halt the holocaust, or man would utterly destroy himself."

Prophecy conferences helped believers place the deepening nuclear threat in biblical context. A speaker at a 1956 gathering in New York City quoted Zechariah's account of human flesh "consum[ing] away," and asked: "Did you ever wonder how it could be fulfilled? Well, the atomic bomb, the hydrogen bomb, and the cobalt bomb have made real this passage of Scripture." The arms race, he went on, was "the training ground for Armageddon." Added John Walvoord, a prophecy writer based at the Dallas Theological Seminary, at a 1961 Los Angeles prophecy conference: "The Bible plainly forecasts the coming of yet another great war . . . eclips[ing] anything that the world has ever seen before."

Given this conviction, prophecy writers dismissed Washington's message of peace through strength, survival through civil defense, and utopia through peacetime uses of atomic energy. Whatever the soothing rhetoric, they insisted, the nuclear arms race obviously represented a giant step toward Armageddon. "No shelter . . . can protect us from the bombs being perfected today," declared DeHaan in 1962. "The only way *out* is *up.*" The rosy talk of "converting atomic energy into useful industrial purposes," he went on, "is completely overshadowed . . . by the threat of wholesale annihilation."

As they updated the premillennial scenario with images of nuclear war, prophecy writers maintained a tone of calm assurance. All is foretold; if the prophetic plan is understood, one need feel no alarm. As one interpreter wrote in 1957, amid deepening anxiety about radioactive fallout: "Wars and disasters may come and go; atom bombs may pose their threat of universal annihilation. . . . But these things are recognized as part of the great design of the God of Israel."

The narratives of horror ended formulaically: The Christian would escape it all. One writer, after a particularly gruesome recital of the disasters facing humankind, went on, "But let us turn our face from that dreadful scene, and be reminded that the redeemed of God . . . shall not be on the earth at that time." Despite the ubiquitous fear of nuclear war, observed Dwight Pentecost in 1961, "the child of God who is acquainted with the prophetic Scriptures rests in assurance because he has before him God's own blueprint." And what did this blueprint tell the believer? Before the final crisis, "You and I . . . will have been translated into the presence of our Lord and Savior Jesus Christ." DeHaan agreed: "One of these days [the Rapture] is really, actually going to happen. . . . The darker the days become, the more glorious this blessed hope shines in our lives."

The world's doom was sealed, but individuals might still be snatched as brands from the burning. After describing the grim nuclear prospect and the Christian's blessed hope, the prophecy writers always concluded with the ancient, yet ever urgent theme: Accept Christ today, and escape the horror that could engulf the earth at any moment. As one reminded his readers, updating Jonathan Edwards's spider dangling over a flame: "Only the touch of a button stands between you and eternity at every moment of every day."

THE 1970S AND BEYOND: HAL LINDSEY AND HIS SUCCESSORS

In 1970, a newcomer among Bible-prophecy popularizers, a young campus evangelist named Hal Lindsey Jr., published what became a multi-million-copy best-seller: *The Late Great Planet Earth*. The phenomenal success of this book (it sold more copies than any other nonfiction work of the 1970s) makes plain that despite reduced attention in the mass media and the reassurance offered by the test ban treaty and the ongoing arms-control process, nuclear fear lurked just below the surface of the American consciousness. In this paperback and a stream of sequels, all of which offered a colloquial and highly accessible version of the premillennialist prophetic system, Lindsey skillfully wove the biblical apocalypses into a narrative of the coming holocaust, which he labeled "World War III" and explicitly portrayed as a global thermonuclear war.

Assuming that all scriptural allusions to fiery destruction and mass suffering foreshadowed nuclear war, Lindsey (usually with qualifying phrases like "quite possibly" or "may very well be") relentlessly turned the Bible into a manual of atomic-age combat. Zechariah's image of human flesh consuming away portrays "exactly what happens to those who are in a thermonuclear blast"; "fire and brimstone" means tactical nuclear weapons; the falling stars and stinging locusts of Revelation are warheads fired from space platforms and Cobra helicopters spraying nerve gas; the scorching heat and awful sores mentioned in Revelation describe the effects of radiation as observed at Hiroshima and Nagasaki. For page after mind-numbing page, Lindsey systematically enumerated the apocalyptic scriptures, mechanically transcribing every phrase and image into the vocabulary of Pentagon strategists.

Biblical writers, said Lindsey patronizingly, had been unable to decipher their own visions. "After all," he wrote, "how could God transmit the thought of a nuclear catastrophe to someone living in the year A.D. 90!" The "hail and fire mingled with blood" of Revelation 8, he says, are clearly missiles as they appeared "to John's eyes, unsophisticated as to ICBM's." Similarly, John's image of horses with lionlike heads and fire pouring from their mouths was his feeble effort to describe "some kind of mobilized ballistic missile launcher."

Lindsey paraded his insider's knowledge of current events and scientific developments. "Recently as I was studying about nuclear weapons," begins a typical passage, "I discovered that science has perfected a cobalt bomb—one of the most lethal weapons known to man. . . . By placing a shield of cobalt 59 metal around a hydrogen bomb . . . the destructive capacity . . . is doubled. More significantly, however, the radioactive contamination . . . is tremendous. Scientists have dubbed it "the dirty bomb" because of its fallout. This is what I believe may be pictured in Revelation 6:12."

Lindsey described the end-time holocaust with unholy zest, hypnotically piling catastrophe on catastrophe: "Multiplied millions" of soldiers are incinerated; civilian casualties mount into the billions amid nuclear

horrors including a "quadrillion megaton explosion"; mass poisoning results as water turns to blood ("There's going to be a big run on Coca-
Cola, but even this will give out after a while!"). Reflecting on all this,
the political scientist Michael Barkun has perceptively observed: "As the
exclamation points march forward, it becomes clear that Lindsey finds
these prospects enormously attractive. His prose pants on with scarcely
a word of sympathy for the hundreds of millions killed or maimed. For
him, the tribulation is grand, cosmic theatre, the ultimate Hollywood
spectacle."

Not only secular critics, but many from the religious world, even
evangelicals, dealt harshly with Lindsey's imaginative flights. One dismissed his "science fiction fantasy" as "a farrago of nonsense." A seminary
student called him "the Geraldo Rivera of the Christian world." Nevertheless, in embedding nuclear war in a framework of foreordained meaning, Lindsey struck a note that resonated with millions of Americans.

A torrent of prophecy books in the 1970s and 1980s imitated Lindsey in making nuclear war a centerpiece of their scenarios. "Billions will
perish in the coming cataclysm," wrote Merrill Unger of Dallas Theological Seminary in *Beyond the Crystal Ball* (1973), adding that while the
approaching judgment would ultimately be God's doing, "on the natural
plane, H-bombs and the latest thermonuclear weapons will play a large
part." John Phillips, in *Only the Bible Can Foretell the Future* (1975), after
describing the effects of a thermonuclear attack on the eastern United
States ("The entire East Coast, from Portland, Maine, to Norfolk, Virginia, and up to 150 miles inland, would become a lake of fire"), concluded somberly: "Truly, the dawning of the atomic age is of great
prophetic significance."

Among the post-1970 prophecy popularizers who proclaimed a
coming nuclear war, few reached a larger audience than evangelist Jack
Van Impe of Royal Oak, Michigan, whose weekly broadcasts appeared
on more than ninety television channels, the Trinity Broadcasting religious network, forty-three U.S. radio stations, and internationally on
Trans-World Radio. Van Impe also promulgated his end-time interpretations in short, easy-to-read paperbacks with titles like *The Signs of the
Times, The Coming War with Russia,* and *11:59 and Counting.* Describing
a visit to Hiroshima, he foresaw much worse in "the near future" as "a

holocaust of fire" unleashed "atomic devastation beyond comprehension." Biblical quotations studded Van Impe's apocalyptic predictions, including not only the familiar ones from Revelation, Zechariah, and 2 Peter ("as clear a definition of atomic warfare as is contained in any library"), but also more obscure selections from Joel, Zephaniah, Malachi, and this from Ezekiel: "The flaming flame shall not be quenched, and all faces from the south to the north shall be burned therein. And all flesh shall see that I the Lord have kindled it: it shall not be quenched" (20:47–48).

Striving to outdo one another, the post-Lindsey popularizers produced ever more sensational prose and tortuous interpretations. Jeremiah's phrase "make bright the arrows" (51:11), suggested one, described the launching of a nuclear missile. Another triumphantly unearthed a cryptic phrase from Habakkuk—"for they shall heap dust and take it" (1:10)—as an obvious prophecy of radioactive fallout. Expounding Ezekiel 39, in which the armies of a northern kingdom called Gog are wiped out after invading the land of Israel, another popularizer hypothesized that the seven-months' delay in burying the dead would be a "cooling off period" because of the corpses' radioactive contamination.

To keep their apocalyptic scenarios timely (and perhaps gain an edge in a highly competitive field), these writers also followed Lindsey in citing the latest developments in nuclear technology. "An entire country's targets could be hit simultaneously by releasing a SWARM of . . . cruise missiles," wrote a breathless Leon Bates; "This is a major development in modern warfare, *just in time for the TRIBULATION!*" A writer of the 1980s, discussing Antichrist's feat of calling down fire from the skies (Rev. 13:13), described a satellite device allegedly under development by the Soviets that could "at any given moment . . . trigger the release of a laser beam flame which could descend in an apocalyptic flash on a predetermined target."

This decades-long effort to find prophetic intimations of mankind's nuclear fate helps one understand the excitement set off by Edgar Whisenant's two-million-copy best-seller, *Eighty-Eight Reasons Why the Rapture Will Be in 1988*. Marshaling elaborate and highly ingenious prophetic evidence, Whisenant foresaw a final global cataclysm that would begin with Russia's invasion of Israel at sunset on October 3, 1988, and

end one hour later with Russia's annihilation. This divinely ordained holocaust, he predicted, echoing many other prophecy writers, would produce nuclear winter, mass starvation, radioactive water, and mountains
of unburied bodies.

Few prophecy writers followed Whisenant's venture into precise
date-setting, but many did go beyond general predictions of global thermonuclear war to speculate about the form it would take and the nations
that would be involved in it.

SCENARIOS OF NUCLEAR WAR

As prophecy writers reflected on the end-time cataclysm foretold in the
Scriptures, some tried to work out the precise details. Although, as two
1974 authors admitted in a rare confession of uncertainty, it is often "not
quite clear who fights with whom about what," innumerable writers' attempts at interpretation, while puzzling to the uninitiated, illuminate
the complex ways in which prophetic belief influenced perceptions of
humankind's nuclear future.

One troublesome issue was whether the cataclysm prophesied in the
Bible would in fact be a nuclear war as conventionally understood, or a
divine intervention in which God punishes mankind, possibly by nuclear
means. In contrast to Lindsey's detailed nuclear scenarios for World War
III, other writers stressed the transcendence of eschatological fulfillment.
Merrill Unger, for example, while not excluding nuclear conflict from
his end-time scheme, emphasized that the devastation portrayed in Revelation might well be a direct "outpouring of God's wrath" on humanity.
Even Jack Van Impe, ever ready to find atomic war foretold in biblical
prophecy, conceded that "God does not need man's modern inventions"
to achieve His purposes.

Some resolved the dilemma by positing *two* nuclear-related end-time
events: first World War III, and *then* God's destruction of the earth. In
11:59 and Counting (1983), for example, Van Impe hypothesized a thermonuclear conflict during the seven-year interval known as the Great
Tribulation, followed, after the Millennium, by God's nuclear annihilation of the world in preparation for the new heaven and the new earth
foretold in the Book of Revelation. Proponents stressed this theory's

hopeful aspect: Although World War III will be devastating, many will survive. Even if a billion people die, one writer pointed out, "there would be a couple billion others left."

Those who sought nuclear allusions in the prophecies faced another problem. Biblical writers' visions involved weapons of their own day—spears, bows and arrows, mounted warriors, and the like. Some prophecy writers, faithful in their literalism, argued that precisely these weapons would be used in the final battle. But most, for all their insistence on scriptural inerrancy, freely followed Hal Lindsey in transmuting swords and chariots into modern-day nuclear weaponry. As S. Maxwell Coder explained in *The Final Chapter* (1984), elucidating a passage from Ezekiel:

> Hebrew is a language of word pictures. . . . The word for "arrow" means a piercing missile, and the word for "bow" means a launching device for such a missile. . . . If we use the word pictures instead of what was meant in ancient times, the verse [Ezek. 39:3] translates, "And I will smite thy launcher out of thy left hand, and will cause thy missiles to fall out of thy right hand." . . . The word pictures can describe modern weapons just as accurately as they described those in use twenty-five hundred years ago.

What nations would be involved in the coming holocaust? While many Cold War prophecy writers, drawing on the allusions to a mysterious northern foe in Ezekiel 38–39, tied their nuclear-war predictions to forecasts of Russia's destruction following an invasion of Israel, most proceeded cautiously in discussing the precise nature and source of that destruction. Writing of the Ezekiel passage in *What's This World Coming To?* (1970), Ray Stedman said: "It is apparent from this description that God himself will assume the prerogative in dealing with the Russian threat. Whether it will involve nuclear warfare, or be purely a natural disaster, is difficult to determine." Doug Clark, in *Shockwaves of Armageddon* (1982), perhaps came closest to identifying the fire that incinerates the invading nation in Ezekiel: "Could this . . . be European and

American nuclear power destroying the Soviet Union? Certainly it could. God uses earthly as well as heavenly powers to do his will."

But nuclear war did not figure in these prophecy popularizations solely in an anti-Soviet context. Whatever its specific cause, the final conflict would soon engulf the globe. As a speaker at a 1970 prophecy conference put it, "The very idea of a coming cataclysmic judgment that will destroy the nations seems preposterous; yet for those . . . acquainted with the prophetic word, there resides the conviction that the dissolution of the present world order must be near." James Boice, a Philadelphia Presbyterian minister and leader of a popular religious radio program called the *Bible Study Hour,* explicating Ezekiel 38–39 in 1984, foresaw "a general exchange of nuclear missiles" in a "horribly destructive war" overcoming every nation, including "the United States, Great Britain, Japan, China, and other world powers."

The most precise list of the nations facing nuclear destruction appeared in Jack Van Impe's *Signs of the Times* (1979). Noting the prophecy in Revelation that a third of the world would be consumed by fire, Van Impe, citing *Life's Pictorial Atlas of the World,* calculated one-third of the earth's land mass as 18,963,194 square miles. He next listed the area of the nations he believed destined for annihilation: Israel, the "Persian Empire (including West Pakistan)," Ethiopia, Libya, the Soviet Union, the Warsaw Pact nations, the ten nations of Western Europe ruled by Antichrist, and the United States. The total? *Precisely* 18,963,194 square miles! "How much more proof is needed . . . that Christ's return is very near?" he concluded triumphantly.

As Van Impe's calculations suggest, the United States fared poorly in most narratives of nuclear destruction. Late twentieth-century prophecy writers, after chronicling America's decline into wickedness and apostasy, usually concluded that it would share the judgment foretold for the nations as a whole. For many, this meant nuclear destruction. The United States will either ally with Antichrist, declared Thomas S. McCall and Zola Levitt in *The Coming Russian Invasion of Israel* (1974), and face direct annihilation, or be a "helpless casualty of global thermonuclear effects." A 1985 author expressed the prevailing view with particular starkness. America, the latter-day Babylon whose doom is foretold in Revelation, "is going to be destroyed by fire! Sudden destruction is coming and few will escape. . . . [A] hydrogen holocaust will engulf America—and this nation will be no more." Some popularizers foresaw America's nuclear judgment coming directly from God, others from human intermediaries—usually the Soviet Union. "Russia possesses enough hydrogen bombs . . . to devastate America," wrote Roy Hicks, a Pentecostal prophecy writer and speaker, in 1982. "Of course, this must be in the knowledge and timing of the Lord, but her threats to bury us cannot be ignored."

These prophetic visions of nuclear war share certain common themes. First is the pervasive sense of inevitability. God's plan for mankind, established before the world began, is unalterable. As a chapter title in one book put it, the drift toward nuclear Armageddon is "A TREND THAT CANNOT BE REVERSED." These works abound with fatalistic pronouncements: "It is only a matter of time . . . [a] nuclear holocaust is coming"; "Our world is in a death-dive. We have peaked and now we're plunging rapidly to the end"; and so on and on.

Second, nuclear war, while horrendous, will also be the means to a beneficent and even glorious outcome. "If God permits men to use atomic warfare," Merrill Unger wrote, "it will be to accomplish His purpose and to glorify His name." Robert Gromacki, an Idaho Baptist minister and church-college professor, observed in 1970: "Although Armageddon will be an awesome and terrifying experience for the world, it should be welcomed by the child of God as the day of vindication of our holy and sovereign Creator. Many beneficial results will be produced by this great battle. . . . What then should be the believer's attitude to the destruction of the world by fire? First of all, he should welcome it and pray for its nearness."

David Wilkerson, an Assemblies of God minister and Pentecostal leader, elaborated the point in *Set the Trumpet to Thy Mouth* (1985):

> Are we so blind, so earthbound, that we want God to keep us alive physically, only to live in a contaminated, hostile environment? Why can't we see that a holocaust can only dissolve this earthly body; but that very dissolving brings us into a celestial one. It will be instant glory. How can we who are already dead to the world be

adversely affected by a holocaust? As for me, I died to
the world—its pleasures, its pains, its destruction—so
that a meltdown simply brings me into the fullness of
an inheritance I already possess in measure. . . . To me,
going home to Jesus in a sudden fiery holocaust *is* an
escape from God's wrath. How can it be wrath when He
takes me by the hand and leads me to paradise? God's
chosen can look at every disaster right in its fury and
declare: "Nothing can move me; I am safe in the palm
of his hand."

Finally, as we have seen, this hopefulness found further grounding
in the assurance that Christians will escape earth's ultimate crisis by way
of the Rapture. (Citing a passage in 2 Thessalonians, Rapture believers
hold that before the Great Tribulation, all true believers will be bodily
taken from the earth to join Jesus Christ in the air, whence they will
return at the Battle of Armageddon to share in Christ's millennial reign.)
As the Fundamentalist leader Carl McIntire put it exuberantly in 1965:
"Thank God, I will get a view of the Battle of Armageddon from the
grandstand seats of the heavens. All who are born again will see the Battle
of Armageddon, but it will be from the skies." Added the California
prophecy expositor Chuck Smith in *What the World Is Coming To* (1977):
"The world has one great war yet to endure. . . . The slaughter that will
take place is too frightening to imagine. Just be thankful that you're not
going to be around!"

Clearly, then, prophecy writers viewed nuclear holocaust from a
unique vantage point. They described its horror as graphically as any
antinuclear activist, but did not see it as a possible historical outcome to
be avoided at all costs, but as the probable form of earth's divinely ordained end. For these authors, *escape* had an individual meaning, not
a corporate, social meaning. Hope lay only in accepting Christ and
holding oneself in readiness for the Rapture. In the secular world, the
possibility of thermonuclear war tended to be either psychologically
numbing or politically energizing, as people transformed anxiety into
action. For prophecy writers, it served different functions: spurring

missionary effort, promising future judgment, and validating the premillennial belief system and the Bible itself.

FALWELL, ROBERTSON, GRAHAM: THREE NUCLEAR-AGE PROPHECY INTERPRETERS

Politics penetrated even the hermetically sealed world of prophecy popularizers, causing subtle shifts in the treatment of nuclear war. Such shifts occurred in particularly interesting ways in the pronouncements of three politically active late twentieth-century evangelical leaders: Jerry Falwell, Pat Robertson, and Billy Graham.

Falwell, prince of the electronic church, New Right leader, and confidant of President Reagan, offered a succession of prophetic pronouncements on nuclear war in the 1970s and 1980s. Most of these echoed the familiar post-1945 premillennialist theme: Nuclear destruction is prophesied and inevitable. In a 1980 pamphlet, "Armageddon and the Coming War with Russia," complete with mushroom-cloud cover, Falwell described the "final holocaust" to follow Russia's invasion of Israel. "All hell will break out" at this time, he told an interviewer in 1981, paraphrasing Ezekiel 39; "blood shall flow in the streets up to the bridles of the horses." "The Tribulation will result in such bloodshed and destruction that any war up to that time will seem insignificant," he told his *Old-Time Gospel Hour* audience in 1983. Falwell's grim descriptions of Armageddon took on special resonance when, on tours of Israel, he preached from the actual prophesied site of the battle at Megiddo, near Haifa. "God only knows how many human beings will be wiped out in that battle," he reiterated in his *Fundamentalist Journal* in 1988, "but they *will* be wiped out." Believers, however, will escape the approaching horror: "If you are saved, you will never go through one hour, not one moment of the Tribulation."

But with Falwell's growing political involvement, he periodically qualified the view that nuclear war was inevitable and (for most human beings) inescapable. In 1983, for example, he endorsed the position that the final holocaust will come only *after* the Millennium, as God uses nuclear power "to destroy the present universe" and make way for the

new heaven and the new earth. Therefore, he said reassuringly, "We don't
need to go to bed at night wondering if someone's going to push the
button and destroy the planet between now and sunrise." The 1983 Falwell even suggested that Americans could influence their nuclear destiny,
not only individually through conversion, but collectively through diplomacy. Washington had a duty "to negotiate for peace with the Soviet
Union and other nations." "We have a human responsibility to do all we
can to seek sensible arms controls." In finding earth's nuclear annihilation foretold in the Bible while simultaneously hinting that the end
might be long delayed—and even that politics could make a differ-
ence—Falwell hewed to a central post-Hiroshima premillennial theme
while at the same time preserving the role in Reagan-era conservative
politics that he so clearly valued.

The words of Pat Robertson, a U.S. senator's son who experienced a
religious conversion in 1956 and went on to found the Christian Broadcasting Network, reveal a similar tension between the stark premillennial
view of nuclear war and the lure of politics. In the late 1970s and early
1980s he, like Falwell, often foretold a nuclear war triggered by Russia's
invasion of Israel. Israel's 1967 capture of Jerusalem's Old City, he wrote
in 1980, had set the stage for Antichrist's reign and Armageddon. Ven-
turing into date-setting, he predicted the ultimate holocaust by 1982 and
became increasingly apocalyptic as that year wore on. "The onrush of
events toward the end of the year may see the world in flames," he wrote
in February. "I guarantee you by the fall of 1982 there is going to be a
judgment on the world," he added in a May broadcast.

But when 1982 passed—and as presidential hopes beckoned—Robertson backpedaled from his doomsday predictions. In 1985 he told the
Wall Street Journal that he no longer anticipated nuclear war or history's
end in the near future. "There is no way I feel I'm going to help the Lord
bring the world to an end," he added elsewhere; "God doesn't want to
incinerate the world. . . . [Armageddon] is an act of God Almighty that
has nothing to do with human abilities whatsoever." In fact, already in
his book *The Secret Kingdom* (1982), deep fissures had emerged in Robertson's eschatology, as he both embraced the standard premillennial
position and espoused a breathtakingly optimistic postmillennialism,
which holds that conditions on earth will grow progressively better

through human effort. Through Christ, he proclaimed, we can enjoy the Millennium here and now: "There *can* be peace; there *can* be plenty; there *can* be freedom." Citing God's grant of dominion to his human creations in Genesis, Robertson urged Christians to "assume the authority, power, and dominion that God intends for men to exercise over the rest of creation." Although this "dominion theology" eased Robertson's transition to a more politically viable stance, his 1988 presidential campaign collapsed, as voters remained leery. He returned for a time to the more comfortable precincts of television evangelism only to re-emerge on the national scene as founder of the Christian Coalition, a conservative force in Republican Party politics in the 1990s.

Even more interesting, because less obviously motivated by political ambition, was the eschatological evolution of Billy Graham, who burst on the revivalist scene in 1949 and remained influential into the 1990s. While his sermons and books did not heavily emphasize prophecy, Graham clearly embraced premillennialism. Christ's kingdom would arise from the ruins of earthly institutions, he proclaimed in *World Aflame* (1965): "Secular history . . . is doomed. . . . The whole world is hurtling toward a war greater than anything known before." Acknowledging his debt to Wilbur Smith, Graham speculated that the melting elements and "fervent heat" of 2 Peter referred to atomic fission, as God used nuclear means for earth's "purification."

In the early 1980s, however, social issues loomed larger in Graham's sermons. In Moscow in 1982, he called the nuclear arms race "a moral and spiritual issue that must concern us all" and offered a five-point disarmament program culminating in a ban on all nuclear, biochemical, and laser weapons. To evangelicals unsettled by this new activist emphasis, he described himself as a man "in process" still exploring "the deeper . . . implications of [his] faith." Graham's *Approaching Hoofbeats* (1983) offers a fascinating picture of this evolution, as it alternates between social meliorism and classic premillennial fatalism. The hoofbeats of the title were those of the four horses of the Apocalypse, conventionally taken to represent famine, pestilence, war, and death. Discussing each horse in the allegorical fashion favored by theological liberals, Graham addressed such issues as Third World poverty, public-health problems, and overpopulation; drought and famine; environmental hazards; and the arms race. Vividly evoking the horrors of modern war, he insisted that one cannot "sit silently by" in the face of the threat; the red horse symbolizing war "rides in warning to effect positive change." Jesus blessed the peacemakers, and Christians must work to slow the arms race and avoid nuclear holocaust. Graham even confessed that he should have done more over the years to promote peace and social justice.

Yet the classic premillennial outlook shaped *Approaching Hoofbeats* as well. History's final moments ("perhaps just ahead"), Graham wrote, will see "nuclear conflagrations, biological holocausts and chemical apocalypses rolling over the earth, bringing man to the edge of the precipice. History will 'bottom out' in the battle of Armageddon." Struggling to resolve the book's eschatological schizophrenia, he argued that while prophecy is sure, God may *delay* foreordained events in response to human effort. Therefore, we must never lapse into passivity in the face of such issues as the nuclear threat. Still, *whatever* we do, "ultimate peace" will come only when Christ reigns on earth.

In a nationally televised sermon in 1990, Graham, now in his early seventies, still vacillated between a premillennial orthodoxy and his newly awakened social conscience. Addressing the question "Are the Last Days Almost Here?" Graham insisted that they were: "We've become so technological and so wicked at the same time, that we have been on the verge of destroying our world. But . . . God is going to step in and not allow us to have an atomic war." How will God accomplish this purpose? He will "cleanse the earth by fire," just as he cleansed it by flood in Noah's day. The implication was not reassuring: Like the American troops who burned the Vietnam village in order to save it, God will destroy the earth to prevent wicked mankind from blowing it up. (Or, as one critic put it: "God so loved the world that he sent it World War III.")

At the same time, echoes of Graham's early-1980s' flirtation with social activism survived, at least vestigially, in this 1990 sermon. The arms race was "a spiritual and moral problem," he declared, and whatever humanity's ultimate destiny, Christians must speak out against it. The confusing message reflected the ambivalence of a man of conscience deeply rooted in one intellectual and theological tradition seeking to accommodate himself to another, very different one. Graham went perhaps as far as one could in adapting premillennialism to an ethic of social engagement with the nuclear threat and other issues of global import.

PROPHETIC BELIEF AND NUCLEAR POLICY

What influence, if any, did all these pronouncements by preachers and prophecy writers actually have on U.S. nuclear policy? The question is difficult, the evidence sketchy. Hal Lindsey insisted that the impact was direct and dramatic. He described earnest prophecy discussions with newspaper publishers, government officials, and military strategists. When he spoke at the American Air War College, "virtually the entire school turned out, including many officers accompanied by their wives." At the Pentagon, "hundreds . . . jamm[ed] the room" with more crowding outside. If we move beyond such self-serving anecdotal evidence, two lines of analysis suggest themselves: (1) the direct influence of premillennialist dogma on policymakers and (2) the more amorphous role of end-time belief in shaping public attitudes on issues of war and peace.

The direct influence of prophecy belief on nuclear decision-making surfaced as an issue in the 1980s, when the eschatological interests of several Reagan-administration officials became known. Secretary of Defense Caspar Weinberger, asked about the subject in 1982, replied: "I have read the Book of Revelation and yes, I believe the world is going to end—by an act of God, I hope—but every day I think that time is running out." Secretary of the Interior-designate James Watt, questioned at his confirmation hearing about preserving the environment for future generations, forthrightly replied: "I do not know how many future generations we can count on before the Lord returns." Reagan's surgeon general, C. Everett Koop, attended a 1971 prophecy conference in Jerusalem and reported on it for a leading premillennial journal.

The most sensational scenario, of course, was the election of a president who believed nuclear war inevitable and set out to help God bring it about. In *Kingdoms in Conflict* (1987), the former Nixon adviser turned born-again Christian Charles Colson offered a fictional account of just such a situation. Colson's "President Hopkins," an amalgam of Robertson and Falwell, spends his spare moments in the Oval Office reading Ezekiel and phoning premillennialist faculty members at "Mid-South Seminary." "I ran my campaign on the Bible, and I intend to run this nation on the Bible," he defiantly tells critics. Hopkins arranges the clandestine demolition of the Dome of the Rock, a Muslim sacred shrine on Jerusalem's Temple Mount, to make way for the prophesied rebuilding of the Jewish Temple, despite (or because of) his theological advisers' warnings that this will set the stage for Armageddon. As Colson's account ends, the Christian Broadcasting Network is playing "The Battle Hymn of the Republic," while the Dome of the Rock crumbles into ruin.

For a time in the 1980s, such a scenario seemed eerily plausible. Ronald Reagan's abiding interest in prophecy, dating from his youthful immersion in the theology of the Christian (Campbellite) Church, deepened in the 1960s and 1970s through contacts with Billy Graham, the Hollywood minister Donn Moomaw, the born-again entertainer Pat Boone, and other prophecy believers. "Apparently never in history," then-governor Reagan told *Christian Life* magazine in 1968, "have so many of the prophecies come true in such a relatively short time." *The Late Great Planet Earth* strengthened Reagan's beliefs, and at a 1971 political dinner in Sacramento shortly after a leftist coup in Libya (a nation mentioned in Ezekiel as one of Israel's invaders), he observed somberly: "That's a sign that the day of Armageddon isn't far off. . . . Everything is falling into place. It can't be long now. Ezekiel says that fire and brimstone will be rained upon the enemies of God's people. That must mean that they'll be destroyed by nuclear weapons."

During his White House years, while his wife, Nancy, communed with a San Francisco astrologer, Reagan's interests in prophecy continued. In 1983 he told a lobbyist for Israel: "You know, I turn back to your ancient prophets in the Old Testament and the signs foretelling Armageddon, and I find myself wondering if we're the generation that's going to see that come about. I don't know if you've noted any of those prophecies lately, but believe me, they certainly describe the times we're going through."

Asked about the subject by newsman Marvin Kalb in one of the 1984 presidential debates with Walter Mondale (as Nancy groaned "Oh, no" off camera), Reagan acknowledged a "philosophical" interest in Armageddon and noted that "a number of theologians" believed "the prophecies are coming together that portend that." But no one knew, he insisted (echoing Falwell and others), whether "Armageddon is 1000 years away or the day after tomorrow." In any event, Reagan concluded, he had "never seriously warned and said we must plan according to Armageddon." The issue faded in the late 1980s, as improved East-West relations eased fears of nuclear war. Reagan's successor, George Bush, while proclaiming himself a born-again Christian ("I'm a clear-cut affirmative to that"), did not, so far as one could tell, interest himself deeply in the arcana of Bible prophecy.

But for a time in the mid-1980s, the politics of prophecy elicited intense public discussion. The *New York Times* worried that "Armageddonist" advisers might subtly influence nuclear policy, and one hundred prominent religious leaders urged Reagan to disavow the dogma that nuclear holocaust is foreordained in the Bible. Such beliefs could lead to "historical fatalism," they cautioned, and prove self-fulfilling. People for the American Way, a liberal lobbying group, warned of the "disdain for peace" implicit in a belief in Armageddon. The columnist Hunter S. Thompson wrote in 1987, "The president is very keen on the Book of Revelation. I love it for the sharp and terrible power of the language, but [Reagan] really believes it." After quoting a particularly lurid passage from Revelation, Hunter went on: "A lot of acid freaks have been taken away in white jackets with extremely long sleeves for seeing things like that, but the visions normally don't last for more than 72 hours. Reagan, though, has believed in the coming of these hideous 'four beasts with six wings and full of eyes within' for something like 72 years."

Even some evangelicals expressed uneasiness about having a premillennialist in the Oval Office. An editor of *Sojourners,* the voice of a small but articulate band of evangelicals espousing the liberal-activist social agenda, warned of the politicization of prophecy: "The popular link between nuclear weapons and portions of apocalyptic scripture began as an innocent, if biblically shaky, attempt by simple people of faith to make some sense out of a new and horrifying evil. . . . But the linking of 'our' weapons and 'God's' plan became a part of presidential rhetoric, and frighteningly it has provided the one thing our military planners have always lacked—a religious justification for nuclear weapons."

On the other hand, evangelicals active in New Right politics denied that premillennial belief implied advocacy of nuclear war. Only a "small minority" of evangelicals, contended Harold Lindsell, a former editor of the evangelical journal *Christianity Today,* in 1984, opposed efforts to prevent nuclear holocaust as contrary to God's prophetic plan. Two of Falwell's associates, Ed Dobson and Ed Hindson, writing in the conservative journal *Policy Review* in 1986, insisted on God's sole responsibility for prophetic fulfillment. "A lot of talk about speeding up the apocalypse would be stopped," they complained, "if more people understood that prophecy cannot be altered." But despite such reassurances, nagging worries persisted that apocalyptic belief might inspire some future president or military leader to try, in Michael Barkun's fine phrase, "to make the inevitable, paradoxically, even more certain."

And how did nearly half a century's worth of books, articles, cassettes, films, and sermons (on national television and in local churches) that found nuclear war foreshadowed in prophecy shape the larger climate of public opinion within which politicians and policymakers operated? Few studies of nuclear attitudes include religious belief as a variable, but the limited data available do pinpoint prophetic belief as an important, and neglected, factor. In a 1984 Yankelovich poll, for example, 39 percent of the respondents said that biblical prophecies of earth's destruction by fire referred to nuclear war, with 25 percent convinced that God would spare them personally from the coming holocaust. Danny Collum, the *Sojourners* editor mentioned above, recalled the large urban Southern Baptist church he attended as a youth in the late 1960s and early 1970s as full of "lay, self-taught 'prophecy experts' who regularly turned Sunday School classes into seminars on the 'signs' of our apocalyptic nuclear times." The pastor of a Dallas-area Baptist church observed in 1989 that many of his parishioners professed little concern about the nuclear threat, either because they believed that God would never permit it, or that if it did come, it would be as "part of God's sovereign plan which cannot be altered."

Although Falwell's spokesmen Dobson and Hindson, writing in *Policy Review,* found no nuclear policy significance in premillennialism, the insistence of countless postwar prophecy writers on the futility of efforts to limit the arms race or to ease Cold War tensions had obvious policy implications. As Robert Glenn Gromacki declared flatly in *Are These the*

Last Days? (1970), disarmament "will never be achieved this side of the millennium." Charles R. Taylor in *The Destiny of America* (1972) found some antinuclear campaigners "very subversive" and under Communist influence. "Arms Control Agreements Always Fail," proclaimed Clifford Wilson and John Weldon in *1980s: Decade of Shock* (1978), as negotiations on the ill-fated SALT II treaty crept forward. In *The Late Great Planet Earth*, Lindsey warned that Antichrist would delude the world with promises of peace. The prophetic scriptures, he told *Eternity* magazine in 1977, underscored the need for "a strong [U.S.] military posture" and the readiness to use its military might.

With the politicization of Fundamentalism in the 1980s, such pronouncements increased. Through television and mass-market paperbacks, prophecy writers commented on nuclear policy issues from a conservative, promilitary perspective. Earlier writers had rejected official propaganda portraying the nation's growing nuclear arsenal as a guarantor of peace and had stressed that America would not escape the end-time holocaust. These themes did not wholly disappear in the 1980s, but many writers, increasingly mobilized into the ranks of the New Right, now treated God's prophetic plan and Reagan's military buildup as indistinguishable. Lindsey's 1981 best-seller, *The 1980s: Countdown to Armageddon*, was even more blatantly political than his earlier works. Rabidly nationalistic and virulently anti-Soviet (with charts showing the Russians' alleged nuclear superiority), *Countdown* insisted that the Bible "supports building a powerful military force," including more nuclear missiles, and urged readers to make themselves heard politically. A book more in tune with the beefed-up military spending and anti-Soviet rhetoric of the early Reagan presidency would be hard to imagine.

A strident chorus of 1980s writers—characterized by one critic as "the court prophets"—supported the weapons buildup and dismissed peace activism as at best "superficial window dressing" masking history's inexorable march to Armageddon. Falwell in 1983 lashed out at the nuclear-weapons freeze campaign movement as a "suicidal effort to force our country into . . . unilateral disarmament" and assure Communism's triumph. James Robison, the premillennialist television preacher who delivered an invocation at the 1984 Republican National Convention, proclaimed: "Any teaching of peace prior to [Christ's] return is heresy. . . . It's against the Word of God; it's Antichrist." In a 1985 novel about the end times, Antichrist wins a world following by espousing nuclear disarmament.

Even prophecy writer Harold Lindsell, the former editor of *Christianity Today,* while denying in his 1984 book that prophecy believers pined for nuclear war and further insisting that all "reasonable men, including Christians, should try to prevent any use of nuclear bombs . . . and wars of any kind," undercut this apparently forthright statement by insisting on the inevitability of end-time wars as "part of God's plan." Belying his conciliatory tone, Lindsell denounced peace activists for "helping the enemy," attacked the freeze campaign as KGB-inspired, implicitly endorsed Reagan's "Star Wars" proposal, and approvingly cited Edward Teller's debunking of the "myths" about the devastating effects of nuclear war.

Unquestionably this wave of blatantly political commentary on nuclear issues by prophecy popularizers helped shape the political culture, as millions of Americans absorbed supposedly Bible-based teachings proclaiming history's imminent and catastrophic end. As Robert Jewett of Garrett Theological Seminary observed in 1984, Reagan's musings on prophecy, like his reflections on other matters, were "uncannily close to the public pulse." Despite some interpreters' efforts to distinguish nuclear war from the end-time events foretold in Revelation, such subtleties escaped many believers, who, as the 1984 Yankelovich survey revealed, found "Armageddon" and "World War III" essentially indistinguishable. Many cultural observers outside the premillennial camp expressed fears that Armageddon theology would hasten the holocaust its proponents saw as preordained. As a British churchman put it, "One rather frightening by-product of this process of [prophetic] interpretation is that it is so easy to *create* the very situation which is being described, so that the interpretation . . . brings about its own fulfillment."

My own sense is that the connection between grassroots prophecy belief and nuclear-weapons policy, while real, was subterranean and indirect. Few post-1945 believers in prophecy consciously sought to bring on Armageddon as quickly as possible. Rather, convinced that the Bible foretells the end, and secure in the knowledge that believers will be spared, they tended toward passive acquiescence in the nuclear arms race and the Cold War. As Stephen O'Leary, a specialist in apocalyptic rhetoric at the University of Southern California, has argued, "The real issue is not . . . whether some born-again believer is going to get his hands on the button that could destroy all of us, but on the way this interpretation of end-time prophecy conditions all our expectations . . . , [making nuclear war seem] a perverse fulfillment of divine destiny." The assimilation of nuclear holocaust into the comfortably familiar premillennial scenario, agreed Eddie F. Carder, a young Southern Baptist minister critical of the prophetic views prevalent in his denomination, "encourage[s] social and political complacency." It "may lead to exciting preaching, attract a large following, and even pad the prophet's pocketbook," he concluded in 1989, but it "falls far short of responsible biblical interpretation."

One might argue that the prophecy popularizers, in compelling some readers who were not overtly political to confront the reality of nuclear war, unwittingly served the antinuclear cause. But this effect seems to have been at best minor and peripheral. Indeed, not only premillennialism's theology, but also its vocabulary, was more anesthetizing than energizing. In contrast to the rhetorical strategies of antinuclear activists, who translated the abstract calculus of nuclear war into gripping accounts of emotional trauma, radiation's medical effects, and the devastation a missile attack would bring to specific cities, the "nuclear war" of the prophecy writers had, with rare exceptions, little tangible reality or affective power. Although such writers spoke of billions killed, of cities obliterated, of oceans poisoned, of "a bloodbath of astounding proportions," their prose remained curiously inert. One reacts to it much as one responds to King Saul's smiting of the Amalekites recorded in 1 Samuel. Did the Amalekites bleed and moan? Did Amalekite children cry for their mothers?

The seventeenth-century biblical language retained by many prophecy writers—armies "perish"; God "slays" or "chastises" his enemies—further emasculated the prose. The distancing from reality built into the language of nuclear strategists, noted by Robert Jay Lifton and others, has its counterpart in the prophetic literature. The writers' theology may insist on the terrible literalness of these "inerrant" prophecies, but the rhetoric is mythic, a fairy tale domesticated through many tellings. The "billions of dead" are not flesh-and-blood human beings with families, hopes, and aspirations; they are eschatological zombies, signposts marking another stage in a sequence of familiar events.

Premillennialism's conceptual structure, as well as its rhetoric, encouraged skepticism toward efforts to reduce U.S.-Soviet nuclear competition. *Nations* are central to biblical prophecy. Of the Bible's more than 480 references to "nation" and "nations," some 70 occur in the books of Daniel, Ezekiel, and Revelation. During the Tribulation, Antichrist rules "all . . . nations." At Armageddon, where "the kings of the earth and of the whole world" gather, Jesus Christ returns "to smite the nations; and . . . rule them with a rod of iron." In the Millennium, Christ governs "all people, nations, and languages." In the prophecies, in short, *nations* remain intact to the end of history—and beyond.

Discussion of "the nations" pervaded the writings of John Darby, the nineteenth-century English evangelist and biblical scholar who formulated the scheme of prophetic interpretation embraced by many contemporary American prophecy believers. The fate of the nations also looms large in the work of the American Cyrus Scofield, who popularized Darby's scheme in his preaching and writings, including the popular *Scofield Reference Bible,* first published in 1909.

Post-1945 prophecy popularizers followed the nationalistic lead of Darby and Scofield. Doug Clark, in *Shockwaves of Armageddon,* citing such scriptures as Romans 13:1 ("the powers that be are ordained of God"), argued that nations—and the wars between them—are destined to survive to the end of history. And in the grammar of premillennialism, all forms of political organization beyond the national level are associated with Antichrist, and thus are deeply suspect. The evangelist Hilton Sutton drew laughter and applause in a 1988 appearance in Madison, Wisconsin, when he jeered at "the United Nothing in New York." Premillennial belief emphasizes the centrality of national power calculations in discussions of nuclear policy; encourages the view that nuclear-weapons competition among nations is a natural expression of the divine order of things; and deepens suspicions of any individual, organization, or movement seeking to address the issue from a supranational or global perspective.

How many U.S. premillennialists accepted the long series of governmental decisions that pushed the nuclear arms race to new levels of menace, in the belief that the entire process was inevitable? How many did *not* become involved in the late-1940s effort for international atomic-energy control, the test ban movement of the 1950s, or the nuclear-weapons freeze campaign of the early 1980s, in the conviction that such efforts were doomed to failure and even ran counter to God's plan for mankind? If national conflicts must go on to the end of time, and if nuclear cataclysm awaits us at the last turning of history's long path, then are not efforts to deviate from that course pointless and perhaps even impious? Believers' energies, the logic of premillennialism makes clear, are better spent in winning souls for Christ than in trying to shape world events.

Certainly it would be unwise to offer sweeping generalizations about all premillennialists, or to posit a simple cause-and-effect relationship between this belief system and an automatic acceptance of the inevitability of "wars and rumors of wars"—up to and including nuclear holocaust. Explaining premillennialism to *Policy Review* readers in 1986, Falwell's aides argued that only a "relatively small group" of "extreme fundamentalists" had "given up on the world" because of their eschatology and become "complacent about evils such as nuclear proliferation." How could Falwell support Reagan's Strategic Defense Initiative, they asked, if he thought no human effort could influence our nuclear fate? Yet the implications of premillennial doctrine, as well as the empirical evidence of public-opinion data and a mass of popular writing, suggests that the links between premillennialism and nuclear attitudes were stronger, and more unsettling, than these polemicists wished to concede.

Gordon Kaufman of Harvard Divinity School spoke to this issue in his 1982 presidential address to the American Academy of Religion. To find in prophecy the message that nuclear holocaust represents "the ultimate expression of God's sovereignty over history," he said, "is not only an ultimate evasion of our responsibility as human beings; it is demonically to invoke the divine will as a justification for that very evasion." To teach that nuclear cataclysm is inevitable (or, conversely, impossible because God would not permit it), he went on, means "cutting the nerve of human responsibility." In an age of a nuclear menace and of environmental hazards that almost defy comprehension, he concluded, "traditional images of divine providential care have become not only outmoded, they have become misleading and dangerous, and must be thoroughly reworked."

A similar perspective informed *Blessed Assurance,* A. G. Mojtabai's 1986 report on nuclear attitudes in Amarillo, home of the Pantex Corporation, a hydrogen-bomb assembly plant. Mojtabai quickly discovered that the worldview of Pantex workers and Amarillans generally was inseparable from their Fundamentalist religious beliefs—an interpenetration of the mundane and the sacred summed up in an Amarillo sign:

JESUS CHRIST IS KING OF KINGS
ALTERNATORS STARTED

Time and again in her interviews she found variations on a single core belief: God controls history; nuclear war, if it occurs, will not result from human action or inaction, but from God's prophetic plan. And, of course, whatever terrors lie ahead, believers will be spared. As one resident put it, "There's a possibility of nuclear war, but if it comes, it's because God allowed it. I believe as a Christian I'm ready to go home at any time—the world stinks." The Rev. Charles Jones, pastor of Amarillo's 2,600-member Second Baptist Church, echoed the point: "Some day we may blow ourselves up with all the bombs. . . . But I still believe God's going to be in control. . . . If He chooses to use nuclear war, then who am I to argue with that?" In complex and subtle ways, Mojtabai came to realize, premillennial doctrine enabled men and women abetting the nuclear arms race in the most direct way imaginable to distance themselves emotionally from the implications of their work. In this respect, Amarillo represented in microcosm vast stretches of the American religious and cultural landscape. As Mojtabai concluded: "The danger is not limited to possible actions by individuals in government or foreign policy positions, or working in nuclear weapons plants and launch sites, who might consider themselves instruments of Providence and decide to help the millennium along. It lurks everywhere, and deeply, in the habits of mind and heart of innumerable ordinary citizens who vote for those who help make policy."

Passivity, whatever its theological underpinnings, is also a political stance. Insofar as prophecy belief influenced citizens to avoid confronting nuclear issues in the Cold War era, it had direct political implications—implications that became explicit in the 1980s. "As the Fundamentalists moved into the partisan political arena," Danny Collum of *Sojourners* magazine noted in 1986, "they brought their theories about nuclear war and the endtime along with them"—theories that saw a certain inevitability to the military buildup and heightening of Cold War tension in the early Reagan era. In these years the premillennial eschatology that had saturated American religious culture for decades converged with a larger rightward thrust in the national political life in a synergistic process that, for a time at least, transformed the political landscape.

But has not Armageddon become passé? With the apparent end of the Cold War as the 1990s began, global nuclear conflict seemed a nightmare from which the world had blessedly awakened. Certainly the convulsive changes in the Soviet Union and Eastern Europe in these years had profound implications for prophecy belief. But given its durability and its exponents' resourcefulness in adapting their dramas to shifting events—not to mention the continued risk of nuclear confrontations, particularly in the volatile (and prophetically significant) Middle East—this theme seemed likely to continue to figure prominently among those invoked by prophecy writers in documenting humankind's bleak prospects. Like frugal homemakers, they had learned over the centuries to recycle their basic themes. The genre grows by accretion, rarely abandoning a theme, but simply adding new ones as world conditions change. Certainly a motif as powerful as the melting of the earth with fervent heat is unlikely to vanish entirely from the repertoire of prophetic themes. Should history take a more menacing turn (and who would confidently predict that it will not?), premillennialist images of a prophesied cataclysm will be available to make sense of events and offer reassurance to the redeemed, as men and women peer into the mists of an opaque and frightening future.

THE REAGAN ERA
The Freeze Campaign and After

At the time, the wave of nuclear fear that swept America in the early 1980s seemed far from unreasonable. The nuclear arms control process (never especially reassuring) had bogged down during the Carter years, and the Reagan White House showed no haste to resume them. Instead, a series of belligerent pronouncements emanated from Reagan and top administration officials, and Washington once again warned citizens to prepare for nuclear war by cooperating in an elaborate plan of "crisis relocation" from urban centers to small towns, to be implemented in times of international crisis.

In a now familiar pattern, this fear led to a surge of antinuclear activism. Beginning in wintry New England town meetings, the nuclear-weapons freeze campaign peaked in 1982–83. Once again,

nuclear themes and images pervaded the media and the culture, from poetry to pop music to television specials. By mid-decade, however, thanks in part to Reagan's "Strategic Defense Initiative" speech and in part to the general easing of Cold War tensions related to political changes in Russia, nuclear fear was in sharp decline.

As I noted earlier, these developments coincided with my own research on the atomic bomb's initial cultural impact and with the publication of *By the Bomb's Early Light*. I followed the nuclear-freeze campaign closely, participated in it, and commented on it. The brief entries in part 4 include reviews and journalistic pieces from this period that offer historical perspective on the freeze campaign, Reagan's "Star Wars" campaign, and the campus mood as activism faded.

10

THE BATTLE FOR PUBLIC OPINION IN THE 1940S AND THE 1980S

In a curious way, America's nuclear history in the early 1980s recapitulated early postwar patterns of opinion manipulation. While the Truman administration and the media had downplayed the bombs' deadly aftereffects, alarmed atomic scientists and their supporters had campaigned for the Acheson-Lilienthal international-control plan by portraying the horrors of atomic war in the most graphic terms conceivable.

In both cases, the manipulative techniques failed. Despite official censorship, the reality of radiation poisoning quickly became known. As for the fear campaign of the international-control activists, its principal effect, ironically, was probably to stimulate support for the Truman administration's frantic stockpiling of nuclear weapons in a desperate drive to "keep ahead of the Russians."

These parallels struck me as worth noting, and I did so in the two pieces reprinted below. The first, adapted from a brief review in the Fall 1985 issue of *Pacific Affairs,* compares Washington's efforts to manipulate public opinion in 1945 with similar deceptions by the Reagan administration.

The second, adapted from an article in the January 1986 *Bulletin of the Atomic Scientists,* recounts the ironic early history of activists' scare tactics as a way of critiquing the nuclear-freeze advocates who were terrifying audiences with blood-chilling images of global thermonuclear war. The immediate impetus for this essay was a talk given by the Australian pediatrician and nuclear-freeze activist Helen Caldicott to a large audience at the University of Wisconsin Medical School. Describing how she had cradled dying children in her arms, she mourned in advance the boys and girls who would die horribly in a nuclear war. Representing the nuclear arms race metaphorically as a deadly global epidemic, she showed slides of the inexorable spread of the "epidemic" that strongly suggested that the "patient" (humanity itself) had scant hope of survival. Though powerful, Caldicott's presentation left me skeptical, wondering about the utility of terror as a motivator for social action.

My ambivalent reaction to Caldicott's talk probably also reflected boyhood memories of lurid sermons on the torments of hell. These pious harangues had usually achieved their desired immediate result as tearful sinners rushed forward to seek salvation, but they had also left an aftertaste of cynicism and resentment. The manipulation of nuclear terror, I suspected, could prove similarly counterproductive.

A HISTORICAL VIEW OF OFFICIAL DECEPTION

From August 6, 1945, onward, the Truman administration sought to soothe the stomach-churning fear of the atomic future that the president's announcement had unleashed. In a calculated effort to shape the climate of public opinion, journalists close to the administration, like William L. Laurence of the *New York Times,* produced stories that dramatized the inspiring story of the Manhattan Project, pictured the shimmering peacetime promise of atomic energy, and portrayed the atomic bomb as the only alternative to a costly land invasion of Japan.

Washington also sought, with initial success, to control and sanitize the information that reached the American people about the effects of the bomb on the men, women, and children of Hiroshima and Nagasaki. This effort is illuminated by Wilfred Burchett's *Shadows of Hiroshima* (New York: Schocken Books, 1983), the final book of a prolific left-wing Australian journalist who died in 1983. Though heavily propagandistic in places, *Shadows of Hiroshima* has an important story to tell. Covering the Pacific war in 1945 for the London *Daily Express,* Burchett arrived in Tokyo shortly after the Japanese surrender and at once made his way to Hiroshima, which he reached on September 3, 1945. His arrival coincided with that of the first American reporters, a hand-picked group flown directly from Washington and carefully chaperoned by U.S. Occupation officials. Their leader was William L. Laurence, the Manhattan Project's official reporter—and unofficial public-relations mouthpiece.

In Hiroshima, Burchett observed the widespread incidence of radiation disease, though he did not know what it was. In a long dispatch published in the *Daily Express* on September 5, he described an "atomic plague" from which thousands of people uninjured in the blast itself were falling sick and dying. Returning to Tokyo on September 7, Burchett discovered that a news briefing had been called by Occupation officials to deny his story. When he reported his direct observations, the briefing officer told him: "I'm afraid you've fallen victim to Japanese propaganda." Whisked off to a hospital for "observation," he found on his release that his press credentials had been revoked and that his camera— containing a full roll of film from Hiroshima—and the original draft of his *Daily Express* story were missing. On September 12 and 13, under Laurence's prestigious byline, the *New York Times* carried two long stories reporting the official U.S. government position. The stories of radiation sickness coming out of Hiroshima and Nagasaki, Laurence insisted, were nothing but "Jap propaganda."

The early chapters of *Shadows of Hiroshima,* in which Burchett recounts these events of 1945, should be required reading for anyone seeking to understand the long history of deception and misinformation in Washington's treatment of the issues of radiation disease and radioactive fallout. The official effort to discredit Burchett's Hiroshima report in September 1945 in fact prefigured a pattern that would continue through the Bikini tests of 1946, the Eniwetok tests of 1954, a whole series of tests in the American Southwest, and decades of blandly optimistic civil-defense pronouncements ranging from Richard Gerstell's grotesquely upbeat *How to Survive an Atomic Bomb* of 1950 to the assurances of the Reagan-era Pentagon official T. K. Jones that, "with enough shovels we'll all make it" through a nuclear war.

A HISTORICAL VIEW OF SCARE TACTICS

To those conversant with the history of America's nuclear culture in the early postwar years, the role of fear in the contemporary antinuclear movement induces a strong sense of déjà vu. In fact, tactics very similar to those of Helen Caldicott and other present-day activists figured prominently in the strategy of their counterparts of forty years ago. These techniques gave rise to the same kinds of doubts and discussions about their efficacy four decades ago that we are witnessing again in the 1980s.

From the earliest moments of the atomic age, a spontaneous and well-justified surge of fear swept over the United States. The atomic scientists and other activists who rallied around the 1946 Acheson-Lilienthal plan for the international control of atomic energy quickly concluded that this gut reaction, rooted in the primal instinct of self-preservation, could be a potent instrument of political action. In 1946 and 1947, the politicization of terror became a major shaping force in American culture. In lectures, radio programs, and articles in such mass magazines as *Life* and *Collier's,* the American people were told of the horrors of atomic war in the most vivid imaginable terms.

"Mist of Death over New York," a 1947 *Reader's Digest* article, graphically portrayed an atomic explosion that spews poisonous radioactivity over New York City and its environs. "Within six weeks," noted the article, "389,101 New Yorkers were dead or missing," including looters shot by the National Guard, persons who drowned when they threw themselves into the river, and thousands crushed as they fled the city "in the worst panic known in all human history." In May 1947, seeking the assistance of J. Robert Oppenheimer on a similar article, a *Reader's Digest* editor wrote: "I think that we are both agreed that a sense of fear is probably necessary to break public apathy. I would therefore like to keep the Radioactive Warfare sequence as dramatic or sensational as I possibly can, to the utmost limit of underlying facts which are true or *which could be true.*"

As we have seen, another of these fear-inducing imaginings of atomic war, "The 36-Hour War," was published in *Life* in November 1945, illustrated with forbiddingly realistic drawings, including one of Manhattan Island as a rubble-strewn wasteland.

The public appeals of the organized scientists' movement initially rested almost wholly on fear. In any future international crisis, wrote W. A. Higinbotham of the Federation of American Scientists (FAS) in a 1946 *New York Times Magazine* article, "you will be haunted by the overpowering knowledge that if war is declared, you, your house, or your business may disappear in the next second." A January 1946 *Collier's* article by the chemist Harold C. Urey, a Nobel Prize winner from the University of Chicago, began candidly: "I write this to frighten you. I'm a frightened man, myself. All the scientists I know are frightened—frightened for their lives—and frightened for *your* life."

In this pre-television era many radio programs, often scripted with the cooperation of such activist groups as the FAS or the Atomic Scientists of Chicago (ASC), presented harrowing accounts of the aftermath of atomic war. One such program aired by a Chicago station early in 1946 described in vivid detail the effects of an atomic attack on Chicago and concluded: "No attempt at identification of bodies or burial ever took place. Chicago was simply closed, and the troops did not allow anyone to return."

This effort to intensify and prolong the spontaneous post-Hiroshima wave of atomic fear did not occur by chance. It arose from a deliberate calculation by advocates of the international control of atomic energy: From mass fear would spring a mass demand for the abolition of atomic weapons. As the Catholic journal *Commonweal* put it, "Fear may do what sheer morality could never do." If mankind survived, this editorial continued, "not conscience but the most basic of instincts will probably get the credit."

Acting on this belief, activists candidly discussed the practicalities of their fear campaign. As one Manhattan Project veteran commented in November 1945, only "the preaching of doom" could rally public opinion behind the outlawing of atomic weapons. The office manager for the Atomic Scientists of Chicago underscored this message in her correspondence with the ASC's public speakers. "Scare them a little, and incidentally give them some scientific background," she told one.

Although the atomic scientists consciously manipulated the public's fears, they—like the activists of the 1980s—did so from the highest motives. The frightening speeches, articles, and radio broadcasts invariably

ended with a call for support for what the activists saw as the sole alternative to ultimate human extinction—the international control of atomic
energy. Certain that the remedies they proposed offered the only hope,
these activists readily concluded that any measures necessary to rouse
public support for those remedies were justified.

Not everyone agreed that terrifying people was the best way to stir
them to action. The Danish physicist Niels Bohr criticized the fear campaign and urged a more upbeat emphasis on the potential of human
cooperation in the atomic age. The atomic prospect did indeed look
dark, observed the New York minister Harry Emerson Fosdick in a post-
Hiroshima radio sermon, "but no man or nation was ever yet frightened
into real brotherhood or peace."

Others warned that the ironic ultimate effect of the politically orchestrated campaign of fear might be deadened sensibility and apathy.
"The louder they shout to us, the more inaudible their voices become,"
observed the historian and cultural critic Lewis Mumford in 1946.

While the Atomic Energy Commission chairman David E. Lilienthal had tactical reasons to dwell on the upbeat side of the atomic prospect, he did offer a telling critique of the fearmongers. For two years,
Lilienthal observed in the summer of 1947, U.S. citizens had been "fed
a publicity diet of almost nothing else but horror stories." He went on
to caution: "Scaring the daylights out of everyone so no one can think,
inducing hysteria and unreasoning fear . . . is not going to get us any-
where. . . . Fear is an unreliable ally; it can never be depended upon to
produce good."

Such apprehensions were abundantly borne out. In January 1950, a
few months after the first Russian A-bomb test, President Truman gave
a green light to Edward Teller's hydrogen-bomb project, and the public overwhelmingly rallied behind that decision. As the terrible simplifi-
cations of Cold War thinking took hold, most Americans concluded
that safety lay in possessing more and bigger nuclear weapons than anyone else.

The rush to embrace the hydrogen bomb was closely linked to the
earlier fear campaign of the atomic scientists and the international-
control activists. Eugene Rabinowitch recognized this point in a bleak
editorial in the January 1951 *Bulletin of the Atomic Scientists*. From the

ominous perspective offered by the H-bomb project, "the clamor for the use of atomic weapons in Korea," and mounting evidence that a full-scale nuclear arms race was under way, Rabinowitch looked back on the scientists' movement and its important role in shaping public attitudes in the immediate postwar period. He concluded that the fear-based international-control campaign, in which he himself had figured prominently, had been worse than a failure: It had inadvertently encouraged the very reliance on atomic weapons the scientists had hoped to avoid. The scientists' insistence on the horrifying destructiveness of the atomic bomb had left the American people "half-educated." They had learned the lesson of the bomb's terrifying power but not the lesson that diplomacy and negotiations offered the best means of escaping the terror. The net effect was "despair and confusion." "While trying to frighten men into rationality," Rabinowitch concluded, "scientists have frightened many into abject fear or blind hatred."

As early as 1947, exhausted by their endless rounds of speaking and writing and demoralized by the failure of the international-control effort, many activist scientists began drifting away from political engagement. Although the scientists' movement's varied institutional expressions—the *Bulletin of the Atomic Scientists,* the FAS, and so forth—remained important, the movement's influence over public opinion and the media was largely gone by 1950.

This loss of influence had external causes, of course, including the policies pursued by the Soviet Union and the anti-Communist hysteria that engulfed the United States in the early Cold War years. But it was also linked to the scientists' somewhat naive political program and fear-based tactics. The collapse of the scientists' movement as a political force adds a dimension of irony to the skill and effectiveness with which, for a time, scientists had wielded their most potent and reliable instrument of persuasion: fear.

For years prior to 1945, fear had been a potent rhetorical theme in American political life. Franklin Roosevelt told Americans in 1933 that they had nothing to fear but fear itself, and in January 1941 he listed "freedom from fear" as one of the Four Freedoms for which America stood. Yet within a few years, a new and terrible fear of unfathomable magnitude had insinuated itself into American culture and consciousness. Activist scientists deliberately intensified this fear in pursuit of goals they wholeheartedly believed in. If only the reality of atomic destruction could be made vivid enough, they reasoned, surely America would rise up and demand that the nation's leaders act to eliminate the danger!

Many thousands of Americans responded in good faith to the scientists' challenge. They debated atomic issues, studied the Acheson-Lilienthal report, and wrote their congressmen and their newspaper editors. What was the result? Except for the Atomic Energy Act of 1946, which created the appearance of civilian control of atomic-energy matters on the domestic front, practically nothing. The international-control movement disintegrated, and the nuclear arms race began.

Looking back, it seems clear that scientists' reliance on rousing the public's fears of atomic war to an ever higher pitch, not the specific policies they advocated, comprises the major long-term significance of their movement. In one of the great ironies of the early atomic age, the spiraling arms race and the hysterical anti-Soviet mood of the early Cold War era—developments that most activist scientists bitterly deplored—were rooted in the very terror that they had themselves so assiduously cultivated.

The fear strategy of early postwar activists, despite its failure, set a precedent for all later antinuclear crusades. As a new generation of activists once again debated these troubling issues, one lesson of the 1945–50 experience seemed clear: Those who deliberately set out to exacerbate nuclear fear should be aware not only of the power but also of the volatility of the emotions they are arousing. Once fear is unleashed, the direction it will take is wholly unpredictable. Certainly the early activists learned—to their regret—that it is easier to terrify the public than it is to channel that terror into sustained, constructive political action.

▌▌

STAR WARS

The Cultural Implications of Reagan's Strategic Defense Initiative

On March 23, 1983, amid mounting public fears of nuclear war and a nuclear-freeze campaign that seemed to be gathering momentum, President Ronald Reagan offered a brilliantly crafted response. In a dramatic television address that caught even top Pentagon strategists off guard, Reagan unveiled his Strategic Defense Initiative (SDI), a multibillion-dollar military project to develop and deploy an impenetrable shield against nuclear missiles. Quickly dubbed "Star Wars" by the media and the public, Reagan's plan envisioned the use of incredibly complex computer technology to pinpoint incoming missiles, and futuristic laser weaponry to destroy them.

SDI eventually collapsed, or at least mutated into something considerably less grandiose, a victim of reduced Cold War tensions and of its own science-fiction aspects. For several years in the mid-1980s, however, it loomed large in public discourse—and in the military budget. As this fascinating episode unfolded, I was again struck (as I had been during the nuclear-freeze campaign) by parallels to earlier periods of America's nuclear history. In this essay, first published in the *Nation* magazine on January 10, 1987, I reflected on the cultural sources and ramifications of Star Wars, moving in a fairly freewheeling way from antebellum Transcendentalism to contemporary children's games.

SINCE PRESIDENT REAGAN'S memorable Star Wars address of March 1983, the technological feasibility of the Strategic Defense Initiative has been debated exhaustively. By contrast, its cultural and psychological implications have been largely ignored. This is particularly surprising because it is government-sponsored efforts to defend the civilian population against nuclear attack, rather than the buildup of offensive weapons, that have historically proved most unsettling to Americans and have left the deepest mark on our culture.

Ask any audience of Americans over thirty years of age about their nuclear memories, and what invariably come tumbling out—apart, perhaps, from the primal event, Hiroshima, and the frightening Cuban Missile Crisis—are recollections of civil defense: sirens, fallout shelters, CONELRAD radio alerts, crouching under schoolroom desks. These are the experiences evoked in the documentary film *Atomic Cafe* and in partially autobiographical novels like Tim O'Brien's *The Nuclear Age*. Now the government has embarked on the ultimate civil-defense project: Star Wars. The sky itself is to be converted into one vast schoolroom desk under which we will collectively huddle while Teacher hurls erasers at the marauding invaders.

What may be the cultural and psychological effects of this latest strategy? It is always risky to identify a single causal factor—even one as protean as SDI—in explaining or predicting cultural change. Nevertheless, a number of cultural developments may reasonably be anticipated if SDI research proceeds along its multibillion-dollar course and if some form of missile defense shield is eventually deployed. My speculation is somewhat disciplined by my research on the cultural impact of the atomic bomb in the first few years after World War II.

In the post-Hiroshima era, the atomic-bomb motif saturated American mass culture, from country music and cereal giveaways (Kix cereal's "Atomic 'Bomb' Ring" was especially popular) to jewelry design and skimpy bathing suits (the bikini). We may now expect all manner of SDI-derived images, concepts, and artifacts to show up in movies, television shows, and advertisements, and on the shelves of the neighborhood Toys "R" Us and Kmart.

One toy manufacturer has already introduced "Lazer Tag: The Game

That Moves with the Speed of Light." Along with alluring drawings of kids in Buck Rogers–style protective gear, the ads offer an enticing prospect: "Welcome to the age of Lazer Tag. Discover the exhilaration of one-on-one competition at the speed of light. Or a galactic free-for-all, where it's every man, woman and child for himself." A complete Lazer Tag set for two players, with all accessories, costs $316.

Such evidence can be accumulated with ease; the challenge is to assess its significance. The relationship between mass-culture ephemera and the shaping of popular attitudes toward public policy issues is highly complex. In the case of SDI, President Reagan's 1983 speech was preceded by a vogue for *Star Wars*–type video arcade games and, of course, by George Lucas's 1977 hit movie, *Star Wars,* which featured laser weapons and other futuristic forms of intergalactic ordnance. Many cultural observers have plausibly suggested that the video games and movies helped condition the public, especially the young, to imagine nuclear war as a high-tech game played on computers, with minimal human risk and involvement.

But the video games and the movies did not emerge from a void. Before the signing of the 1972 Anti-Ballistic Missile Treaty, there was extensive research on exotic antimissile technologies, and at least some of that research filtered into popular awareness. As early as 1962, General Curtis LeMay spoke publicly of "directed energy weapons" that would "strike with the speed of light" to destroy incoming missiles.

Rummaging even further back in our collective cultural memory, we find not only the Ur-hero Buck Rogers but the 1940 Warner Brothers' movie *Murder in the Air,* to which historian Stephen L. Vaughn has called our attention. This features a proto-SDI secret weapon called the Inertia Projector, whose mysterious rays can strike down incoming enemy aircraft from miles away. (*Murder in the Air,* by the way, starred a twenty-nine-year-old actor who had been signed by Warner Brothers a few years earlier—Ronald Reagan.)

Mass-culture fantasies and government weapons programs appear to be interwoven in complex ways. The fantasies lay the psychic groundwork for the weapons programs; the weapons programs in turn stimulate new fantasies. As SDI progresses, we should have ample opportunity to observe this phenomenon at work.

A striking feature of the post-1945 cultural climate has been the pervasive fear of nuclear attack. Before supersonic bombers, intercontinental ballistic missiles or missile-launching nuclear submarines, the characteristic nightmare was of nuclear blackmail: The components of an atomic bomb would be smuggled into the country, secretly assembled, and the product employed to force an American surrender. Give up, or say goodbye to New York! In a 1946 article, the physicist Edward Condon painted a terrifying picture of urban life in which every building, room, and filing cabinet potentially concealed an atomic bomb.

Within days of the president's March 1983 address, pundits and editorial writers were warning that SDI would still leave the nation vulnerable to other forms of nuclear attack, including the smuggled bombs that aroused such terrors in the late 1940s. In a country "protected" by SDI, nuclear fear would surely not diminish. It might even be more socially destructive, because the potential source of attack would now be so ubiquitous and innocuous—a fishing trawler, a diplomatic pouch, a shipping container of Stolichnaya vodka.

Under these circumstances a bunker mentality would probably develop rapidly, together with an accompanying obsession with secrecy and cultural conformity. In a remarkable 1947 essay on the social effects of the atomic bomb, Lewis Mumford imagined a society propelled by nuclear fear into a grim preoccupation with defense. In Mumford's scenario, the degraded, terrorized populace ekes out a miserable existence in a vast underground warren, dominated by an authoritarian government whose power rests on its control of the instruments of atomic war and by an elite of "scientists and technicians responsible for atomic production and anti-atomic defense."

The preoccupation with atomic secrecy that gripped the nation after Hiroshima would be more than matched by fears for the security of the exotic technologies being developed by SDI researchers. Already four million Americans hold security-rated jobs that are shielded from public scrutiny. The deployment of a Star Wars defensive network, with its vast infrastructure of supporting systems, would increase that number enormously.

SDI rests on a fundamentally nationalistic premise. In a world of nuclear menace and "evil empires," we must take our fate into our own hands. Its subtle and insidious subtext appeals to a dark and deeply rooted theme in U.S. culture, from the essays of Emerson to the mythology of the Old West. Self-reliance is best; draw the wagons into a tight circle. The upsurge of nationalism would be accompanied by an intensification of the myth of American innocence, one of the more tenacious themes in this country's cultural history. The conviction that our actions are by definition high-minded and pure crops up incessantly: in Andrew Jackson's sanctimonious justifications for removing Indians from Georgia in the 1830s; in the lofty rhetoric in which Woodrow Wilson enveloped his decision to enter the war in 1917 and his peacemaking efforts in 1919; and in President Truman's repeated postwar assurances that the United States viewed its atomic monopoly as a "sacred trust," never to be used for merely nationalistic ends.

Once Ronald Reagan shared his Star Wars dream with the world, both the Soviet Union and the system's domestic critics quickly pointed out that what appeared from the Oval Office as a benign defensive system could be viewed in a far more sinister light. In the Alice-in-Wonderland world of nuclear strategy, "defensive" systems turn into "offensive" ones with the slightest twist of the looking-glass. As former secretary of defense Robert McNamara notes in *Blundering into Disaster*, even a partial strategic defense system comports nicely with a first-strike strategy. Advocates of SDI respond to such criticism with self-righteous variations on the myth of national innocence. How could anyone suspect the virtuous United States of plotting anything so wicked and immoral? We are just not that kind of people.

Although the myth of national innocence is as strong as ever, public attitudes toward scientists and technicians remain profoundly ambivalent. These mixed feelings intensified with the explosion of the atomic bomb in August 1945. The same scientific discovery that had apparently brought an end to one terrible war simultaneously raised the specter of future wars of inconceivable destructiveness. An almost schizophrenic view of the scientist as public benefactor and as sinister impresario of death pervaded American culture.

In a time of highly visible, heavily publicized Star Wars research, this ambivalence would likely reach a new plane of intensity. On the one hand, the eager young Star Warriors pursuing their high-frontier experi-

ments at Lawrence Livermore National Laboratory and elsewhere will be
the Oppenheimers, Comptons, and Fermis of our age. The cultural prestige of science might be enormously enhanced, bringing further hefty
federal endowments for scientific research—at least for SDI. On the
other hand, that very process could also bring its antithesis—a powerful
reaction against science and its imperial pretensions—as the rest of us
increasingly realize our irrelevance in a world ruled by technology. As
Lord Zuckerman, former chief science adviser to the British government,
and others have pointed out, the split-second nature of SDI leaves no
alternative to total automation. Preprogrammed computers will command the entire apparatus; there will be no human intervention, no time
for human judgment.

Washington, of course, aided by the media, will do everything in
its power to allay these fears. In the late 1940s and early 1950s, as the
government stockpiled atomic bombs, developed advanced delivery systems, and organized research on the hydrogen bomb, a stream of euphoric propaganda poured forth from Washington, the radio networks,
and the popular press, portraying an exciting future of atomic transporta-
tion, cancer cures through nuclear medicine, atomic weather control,
and a brave new world of genetic manipulation. As we have seen, David
E. Lilienthal, the first chairman of the Atomic Energy Commission and
an enthusiastic cheerleader for the peaceful atom, made the circuit of
civic gatherings, religious conventions, and high school graduations, telling audiences to forget their atomic anxieties and focus instead on the
bright promise of atomic energy. That propaganda served an important
political function. It muted dissent and diverted public attention from
the buildup of atomic weapons.

We are witnessing the beginnings of a similar campaign today. As
SDI's critics challenge it on technological, strategic, and foreign-policy
grounds, proponents paint an increasingly rosy picture of the project's
beneficence for the civilian sector. Echoing Lilienthal's earlier pronouncements, Lieutenant General James Abrahamson, head of the Pentagon's SDI research project, vowed to "capitalize on the results of SDI
research and apply it across all facets of our economy and society." In
rhetoric eerily evocative of 1946, two leading Star Wars researchers at
Livermore have predicted that SDI laser technologies could also propel

giant solar reflectors into orbit to create a system of global meteorological control. They declared, "We can thereby demonstrate our racial competence for terraforming other planets for human use by first bringing our own one to its full potential."

The full, ripe flavor of this genre of SDI hype is well conveyed in "The Star Wars Spinoff," an article in the *New York Times Magazine* (August 24, 1986) by the science writer Malcolm W. Browne. In breathless prose, Browne offers a tantalizing sampler of the goodies that await us in the SDI cornucopia: Powerful new computer-modeling programs will enhance long-term weather forecasting and make possible detailed maps of the ocean floor; advances in computer pattern-recognition will at last enable us to develop robots to serve as "surrogate servants, laborers and bodyguards"; electron beams capable of penetrating human tissue at precise depths will be able to "hit a malignant tumor with pinpoint accuracy"; optic signaling and the substitution of such new synthetic crystals as gallium arsenide for the silicon chip will increase computer speed a thousandfold. To anyone who has pored over hundreds of late-1940s descriptions of the technological utopia to be expected from the invention of the atomic bomb, such rhetoric produces a profound sense of déjà vu—and a profound sense of depression.

The recently adopted Latin motto of the Army Strategic Defense Command is *Munimentum in Aethere Novis:* "Defense in Space." In a more innocent era, observers disturbed by the impact of technology found solace in the thought that whatever the machine's toll on earth, the starry skies above were immune to human folly. In his 1836 essay "Nature," Emerson offered the sky as a symbol of the possibilities of spiritual transcendence. In *Walden,* Thoreau describes how the clouds of steam from the intrusive Fitchburg railroad—his primary symbol of industrialization—escape to heaven while the noisy cars rumble on toward Boston.

This imaginative embrace of the heavens as a pristine alternative to the chaos of life on earth, long since undermined by the Wright brothers, has collapsed totally in the era of Star Wars. Space retains its symbolic power, but now as a vast stage set on which the deadly drama of Cold War military competition can be enacted on a literally cosmic scale.

12

ANOTHER CYCLE OF NUCLEAR ACTIVISM ENDS

Throughout America's nuclear history, as we have seen, cycles of heightened fear, activism, and cultural attention to the bomb gave way with surprising suddenness to intervals when the nuclear reality seemed to sink out of sight. Another such dramatic shift came in the later 1980s, as Soviet president Mikhail Gorbachev, who came to power in 1985, moved to liberalize Soviet politics and end the Cold War. The long-stalled arms-control process resumed, and by 1988, President Reagan was strolling in Red Square with the head of a state he had earlier denounced as an "evil empire."

Certainly, grave dangers remained. Thousands of nuclear missiles still existed; the prospect of nuclear exchanges in regional conflicts or nuclear blackmail by rogue states like Iraq or North Korea loomed on the horizon; and the world faced the massive challenge of dealing with tons of radioactive materials generated over a period of half a century—materials that would remain deadly for millennia. Nevertheless, the terrifying possibility of global thermonuclear war had clearly diminished radically, at least in the near term. The collective sigh of relief was almost audible.

Chapters 12 and 13, both written and first published in 1989, are products of this moment of transition. The brief book review that constitutes chapter 12, slightly modified from the version that appeared in the October 1989 *Bulletin of the Atomic Scientists,* comments on an upbeat and rather polemical study by a political scientist arguing that not only was the nuclear threat over, but that it had never been as serious as many had believed, and that the activists who had campaigned against it had been misled and deluded from the first.

I have included this review because the book in question captures the mood of relief—like a collective exhalation of breath after an extended period of tension—triggered by the mid-1980s improvement in U.S.-Soviet relations and the consequent decline of nuclear fear. It also serves as a useful reminder that successive antinuclear campaigns had not only won enthusiastic recruits, but had stirred skepticism and even hostility among those who considered challenges to the U.S. policy of deterrence through retaliatory readiness to be naive, if not profoundly threatening, to America's national-security interests.

SHOULD ANYONE still remain unaware of the precipitous decline of Cold War tensions since 1985 and the change in perceptions of the nuclear threat, a useful benchmark is John Mueller's *Retreat from Armageddon: The Obsolescence of Major War* (New York: Basic Books, 1989). Mueller's work, a freewheeling speculative essay embedded in a history of the Cold War, epitomizes the current U.S. mood of passivity, conservatism, and *glasnost*-induced optimism. The theme of the essay is easily stated: Just as the world outgrew slavery and dueling, so it is outgrowing war. In this model, World War II is an aberration brought on by one man, Adolph Hitler. In recent centuries, and especially since 1918, the West has been undergoing a profound ideological transformation in its view of war. No longer seen as romantic, manly, or purifying, war has come to be seen as "repulsive, immoral, and uncivilized." While noting that seventeen million people have died in war since 1945, Mueller, a University of Rochester political scientist, suggests that war will gradually fade from those regions where it vestigially survives, eventually to vanish entirely as a human social activity.

Regrettably, this appealing vision is based on selective and inadequately examined historical data. To blame World War II on one man, for example, is to neglect both the historical rootedness of Hitler's obsessions and the way the German masses rallied behind him. In general, Mueller emphasizes the power of ideology while paying little attention to economic interests and other material factors.

Humanity's shifting perception of war is a significant topic, but Mueller's treatment is disappointing. He considers only a few writers, none deeply, and almost wholly neglects the realms of fiction, music, the visual arts, and the mass media. At a time when intellectual historians are seeking to grasp more fully the relationship of ideas to their social milieus, and to understand more deeply the complex process of ideological transformation, *Retreat from Armageddon* seems facile. The changed view of war so central to Mueller's argument is only casually sketched, with somewhat random quotes that emerge from a social vacuum. The actual process of ideological change remains opaque. Similarly, the end of slavery, which Mueller stresses heavily for his analogy, is ascribed to inexplicable shifts in moral sensibility, while the rise of industrial capitalism, with its profound implications for the organization of labor, is largely ignored.

No utopianist, Mueller distinguishes his future scenario from the millennial vision of global cooperation and harmony. He foresees no changes in the present structure of nation-states, or in the struggles among them. Given this Hobbesian view, is it plausible that war, over the long haul, will lose its appeal as an option of last resort?

Mueller emphasizes rational decision-making, downplaying the way the line between "rational" and "irrational" can blur as leaders act under stressful, emotionally charged conditions. His rationalistic, schematic approach allows relatively little scope to unforeseen concatenations of events or to the infinite human capacity for novelty—a capacity with negative as well as positive implications. For all its speculative boldness, *Retreat from Armageddon* betrays a deficiency of historical imagination.

Despite its occasional caveats, this is in general a hopeful book. War is not endemic to the human condition; it is a learned social activity that can be unlearned. This perspective (so different from Reinhold Niebuhr's, for example) echoes in secular form the Victorian belief in inexorable progress through a divinely guided evolution, or the pre-1914 social gospel vision of the Kingdom of God pressing in on human history. Such an approach invites passivity on issues of war and peace.

Thanks to a sweeping change of consciousness, war is fading through a kind of historical inevitability, independent of further human effort, at least according to Mueller. As the more backward or more ideologically driven societies absorb the new consciousness from the West, war will be no more.

Like all such metahistorical theorizing, Mueller's conjectures are ultimately unprovable. As he himself cheerfully concedes, his book will be read in the future either as remarkably prescient, or as one more sorry example of wishful thinking about the human prospect.

But what of the other part of *Retreat from Armageddon*, its account of the Cold War? Here the work's historical thinness becomes particularly evident. In Mueller's drama, "international communism" dominates the stage. The role of the United States was entirely reactive, as it responded to the Communists' lingering ideological infatuation with war. The role of liberal capitalist ideology, or indeed of any ideology, in shaping U.S. policy is ignored. The Vietnam War is presented as a "sober and realistic" U.S. response to China's fomenting of wars of national liberation. Mueller argues that Washington's Vietnam policies were correct strategically (at least up to the collapse of Chinese influence in Indonesia), and flawed tactically only in underrating North Vietnam's will to resist. This version of recent history ignores a vast body of historical scholarship that over the past quarter century has offered a considerably more complex and nuanced understanding of the Cold War.

Mueller contends that nuclear weapons have played little role in postwar international relations. He presents President Truman's 1945 atomic-bomb decision as motivated solely by the desire to defeat Japan (again ignoring many studies suggesting a more complex interpretation); gives extended and uncritical attention to Alexander de Seversky's notorious 1946 argument that the atomic bomb's destructive power was much overrated; and downplays the significance of what he dismissively calls "the nuclear arms 'race.'" While treating rhetoric with great seriousness elsewhere in the book, he sees the history of nuclear threats and counterthreats during the worst of the Cold War as irrelevant "bluster," of no significance. Nuclear proliferation receives some attention, but it does not loom large in Mueller's optimistic scheme of things.

Since nuclear weapons are of little import, it follows that antinuclear activists must be deluded and misguided. Mueller pokes fun at the symbolic warning clock printed on the cover of each issue of the *Bulletin of the Atomic Scientists,* its hands positioned ominously at a few minutes before midnight. He dismisses the "antinuclear frenzy" of the early 1980s and flippantly caricatures the Catholic bishops' long and careful statement on nuclear war, *The Challenge of Peace* (1983), as "an airy pastoral letter declaring that it may be okay to threaten mass destruction but only if you didn't plan to do it."

Mueller's contempt for the antinuclear movement is understandable in view of his larger theories about the origins of the revulsion against war and his one-sided interpretation of the Cold War. Still, it is curious that he ascribes such importance to antiwar sentiment at one point in history and so little at another. Those who spoke out against conventional war early in the century were shaping a new human consciousness, but those who raised the alarm against nuclear war in recent years were irrelevant, misguided, and foolish. As Vice President George Bush said to his Democratic challenger, Michael Dukakis, in one of their televised debates during the 1988 presidential campaign, it must be wonderful to be so sure of oneself.

13

"You Must Keep Reminding Us"
Post–Cold War College Students Contemplate Nuclear Issues

As a visiting professor at Northwestern University in 1988–89, I taught an American Studies seminar entitled "Nuclear Weapons in American Culture" and with Carl Smith, director of the American Studies program, organized a conference on that subject. Coming at a moment when Cold War alarms and nuclear fears were rapidly diminishing, these experiences sharply reminded me how quickly the cultural barometer can change, and, more specifically, how rapidly nuclear awareness could fade, especially for the young. This essay, adapted from an article in the June 1989 *Bulletin of the Atomic Scientists,* reflects my experiences and impressions of that year. Rereading it in 1997, I am again struck by how much 1988–89 was a moment of transition—in the world situation, in domestic politics, and in the culture. While I and others of my generation vividly recalled the emotional intensity of the freeze campaign and continued to view the nuclear threat (however defined) as a matter of urgent and continuing concern, college students, already on the other side of an invisible fissure in the culture, were looking forward to the 1990s, a decade of different concerns and different issues, in which warnings of nuclear dangers would seem anachronistic and irrelevant. In some respects, this essay seems the most dated of any in the book. Yet it captures the moment of transition from one era to the next.

187

WHERE HAVE ALL the nuclear activists gone? The contrast between 1981–83 and 1988–89, in terms of nuclear awareness in the United States, could not be more striking. Then, massive Pentagon budget increases, "crisis relocation" plans, musings by a gung-ho secretary of state, Alexander Haig, about "nuclear warning shots," and belligerent presidential speeches lambasting the Soviet "evil empire" raised public attention to the nuclear threat to feverish levels. Nuclear-freeze activists rang doorbells, television programs like *The Day After* (1984) captured national attention, church groups issued manifestos and pronouncements, and thousands of protesters rallied in Central Park and across the country. *Time* featured a mushroom cloud on its cover for the first time in years. Since I was then working on a book on nuclear weapons in American thought and culture, invitations to speak or to participate in conferences and symposia on the subject poured in.

Six years later, public attention has faded. The restless media spotlight has moved on. The rallies and the referenda seem far in the past. Conferences and speaking invitations—somewhat to my relief—are less frequent. While a few books, films, and television productions conceived during the earlier period of nuclear awareness continue to appear, they seem misplaced in time, and stir little public response.

When public television announced a program in May 1988 in which a number of experts would discuss issues of nuclear strategy and nuclear disarmament, the *Los Angeles Times* television critic began his preview, "It sounds like an hour in PBS hell." When the strategists of Governor Michael Dukakis's presidential bid fought off efforts to add a no-first-use pledge to the 1988 Democratic platform (that is, a pledge that the United States would never again initiate use of nuclear weapons), and Dukakis refused to embrace the pledge himself, few protests were heard. W. Joseph Campbell of the *Hartford Courant* wrote in the summer of 1987: "The dramatic moments of the early 1980s, when arguments over freezing production and deployment of nuclear weapons could propel people into the streets by the thousands, nowadays are taunting memories. . . . Instead of gathering momentum . . . popular anti-nuclear activism has faltered, and the promise borne by the grassroots freeze movement has dissipated."

The reasons are not hard to find. Chief among them are President

Reagan's "Star Wars" proposal, with its technological quick-fix response to the nation's nuclear fears; the easing of U.S.-Soviet relations after Mikhail Gorbachev's rise to power in Moscow; and the 1989 INF Treaty, eliminating intermediate-range nuclear weapons from Europe. Amid all these developments, the nuclear-freeze movement in the United States went into hibernation, and an entire congeries of issues related to nuclear weaponry, nuclear power, and the nation's nuclear history seemed to vanish from the national consciousness.

This is strikingly reminiscent of the period after 1963, when a similar bout of nuclear amnesia gripped the American people following the signing of the test ban treaty. The columnist Stewart Alsop, describing the political climate in 1967—four years after the treaty—used phrases that seem strikingly apropos in 1989: "Writers rarely write about this subject anymore, and people hardly ever talk about it. In recent years there has been something like a conspiracy of silence about the threat of nuclear holocaust."

Despite jitters and protests over the prospect of "antimissile missiles" ringing America's cities that preceded the signing of the 1972 ABM (antiballistic missile) treaty, activists' energies did not fully revive until the late 1970s. During Jimmy Carter's presidency, a combination of events—including a campus-based campaign against nuclear power plants that culminated in 1979 with the Jane Fonda film *China Syndrome* and the near-disaster at Pennsylvania's Three Mile Island nuclear power plant—reawakened the public to the broader nuclear threat, leading to a wave of antinuclear protest in the early Reagan years.

The current decline in nuclear activism and cultural attention, and the parallels to earlier periods of apathy, have been sharply underscored for me while teaching at Northwestern University this year. My undergraduate students are bright, articulate, socially engaged, and concerned about public issues. They are a joy to teach. They are also very young. I am constantly made aware of the chasm that exists between us in terms of our nuclear memories and perspective. The college juniors of 1989 were most likely born in 1968 or 1969. Hiroshima, Bikini, civil defense, fallout shelters, the Cuban missile crisis, the test ban treaty, the ABM controversy—all this is ancient history to them, something known only secondhand. Even more recent events are part of the half-remembered world of childhood and adolescence. My students were about ten years old at the time of Three Mile Island, twelve when Ronald Reagan took office. Some remember seeing *The Day After* as teenagers. When I asked the undergraduates in my "Nuclear Weapons in American Culture" seminar about their earliest nuclear memory, a surprising number mentioned an episode on the early-1980s television series *Happy Days,* set in the 1950s, in which the central character (nicknamed "the Fonz") and his teenaged friends decide whether or not to build a family fallout shelter. (Producer Garry Marshall graciously supplied a video cassette of this episode, enabling the class to share a collective moment of nostalgia for its lost youth.)

My students' recollections of the freeze movement are hazy at best. One young woman remembers going to the 1982 antinuclear rally in Central Park with her mother. She recalls that the rally attracted "50,000 participants" (in fact, the total was over 500,000). My students' most vivid political memories are extremely recent: Reagan's Moscow trip, Soviet-American good fellowship, the INF Treaty, and the 1988 presidential campaign, in which nuclear issues barely surfaced.

With the activism of the early 1980s a thing of the past, today's college students typically encounter the nuclear reality in indirect ways, often through mass-culture channels. Rock lyrics occasionally have nuclear themes. Examples are "Guns in the Sky" (1987) an anti–Star Wars song by INXS; "Put Down That Weapon," by Midnight Oil; Sting's "Walking in Your Footsteps" (1983) and "Russians" (1984)—"How can I save my little boy, from Oppenheimer's deadly toy?"; and U2's "Seconds" (1981) and "Bullet the Blue Sky" (1987), in which droning guitars frighteningly simulate the sound of incoming missiles. One should note, however (as my students are quick to point out) that such songs represent only a tiny fraction of the total rock output. Their lyrics are often difficult to follow, and with rare exceptions they are not the most popular or frequently aired album tracks.

Movies like *Dr. Strangelove* keep nuclear memories alive, as do more recent films like *The Road Warriors* (1982), set in a brutal post–nuclear war future. Such role-playing games as *Gamma World* and *Twilight 2000* simply posit a world after nuclear war as a device for getting the action under way. As for coverage of the theme in lectures and textbooks, I suspect that the medium is the message: America's nuclear history tends to exist for most students at about the same affective level as Valley Forge, the Reconstruction era, Woodrow Wilson's Fourteen Points, and the New Deal.

As in the late 1970s, recent controversies about nuclear power plants—the battle over the Shoreham plant on Long Island, problems at the Department of Energy's Savannah River nuclear weapons plant in South Carolina, and the issue of nuclear waste disposal—seem more vivid in students' consciousness than the world's largely invisible nuclear-weapons arsenals, the seemingly remote and abstract threat of nuclear war, or the complex issue of nuclear proliferation among smaller nations.

For my students, the nuclear issue is subsumed into a larger set of environmental and ecological preoccupations. They are deeply and often passionately concerned about the fragile global habitat. Insofar as nuclear power or nuclear weapons contribute to this problem, they become the foci of attention. For example, in the current debate over the proposed nuclear waste dump site in Nevada (a state appropriately accustomed to high-stakes gambling), experts readily concede that the containment systems will probably not survive for more than a thousand years. From then on, our distant descendants will have to depend on the vagaries of a changing natural environment to protect them from the still lethal poisons we are burying today. This may speak to today's environmental consciousness more vividly than issues of missile deployment or details of arms-control proposals. As was true after 1963, most students readily confess that nuclear war per se does not loom large in their consciousness, and they express confidence that the easing of Cold War tensions has made a global nuclear conflict far less likely.

Ironically, the treatment of the nuclear issue by activists and the mass media in the early 1980s may be partially responsible for the decline of nuclear awareness in the current college generation. For understandable reasons, freeze activists and the media focused almost exclusively on the most terrifying of nuclear possibilities: global thermonuclear war and the related ecological horror of a worldwide "nuclear winter." Much less attention was devoted to the long-range and technically complex issue of radioactive waste disposal or to the possible use of nuclear weapons in regional conflicts. Amid widespread and legitimate terror over the prospect of worldwide nuclear holocaust, other lesser but still gravely important nuclear dangers tended to be left on the sidelines. As fears of a full-scale nuclear conflict between the United States and the Soviet Union faded, other urgent and menacing nuclear issues slipped down the memory hole as well.

Robert Jay Lifton recounts, in his 1982 book *Indefensible Weapons,* Michael Carey's mid-1970s interviews with some forty men and women who as schoolchildren had experienced the school drills and fallout-shelter controversies of the 1950s. Lifton comments on "the ubiquitous presence of the bomb" in the subjects' memories and consciousness. The same cannot, I think, be said of college students today. When my students recently read Tim O'Brien's novel *The Nuclear Age,* they found it largely unsatisfactory and expressed little but impatience for its nuclear war-obsessed hero. John Hersey's *Hiroshima* retains its power, but as an account of a remote, almost mythic event. Even such a major document as the 1983 pastoral letter of the American Catholic bishops, *The Challenge of Peace,* with its devastating ethical critique of the nuclear arms race and its profound skepticism about deterrence theory, stimulated little detailed discussion. It did, however, provoke considerable hostility for its theological framework—a framework hardly surprising considering the source.

In the spring of 1989, as part of the conference related to the seminar, Jonathan Schell visited the Northwestern campus. Schell's 1983 book *The Fate of the Earth* (which, like Hersey's *Hiroshima,* began as a *New Yorker* series) had become a best-seller for its reflections on the consequences of a global thermonuclear war that could not only extinguish all human life but even all memory that human beings had ever inhabited the planet. Schell received a respectful hearing from the large audience, but when he asked the students to articulate their own thoughts about such a prospect, he was greeted by a long and embarrassing silence. Nuclear war and its consequences, it seemed, simply did not figure very prominently, if at all, in their thoughts.

Since colleges and universities have historically functioned as seedbeds of political and social movements, my reading of the current campus mood not only suggests something about our situation at the moment, but also implies a discouraging prognosis for the renewal of antinuclear activism, at least in the short run. The collapse of the activist surge of the early 1980s reveals once again how susceptible the antinuclear movement is to shifts in the political winds, and how it collapses each time there is a small step toward ameliorating the threat.

Each generation must define its causes on the basis of its experience. On college and university campuses, where successive waves of students seem to come and go like fruit flies, a "generation" is not twenty or twenty-five years, but more like four. Just as the young scorn the styles, tastes, and slang not only of their parents but of their older siblings, as a way of asserting their own distinctive identity, they often cast a jaundiced eye on the issues deemed important by their elders. Even a cause as potent and seemingly timeless as preventing nuclear war, which loomed so large only yesterday, does not automatically speak with the same force to those who are products of a different cultural and political moment.

Today's students recognize *intellectually* how vulnerable we continue to be in the face of long-term nuclear menace, and how overwhelming is the work that remains if we are ever to be truly free of that menace. We need a comprehensive test ban, movement on the currently stalled negotiations for strategic arms reductions, progress on a wide range of confidence-building measures, and a serious global effort to grapple with the terrible risks inherent in nuclear proliferation. Students at the end of the 1980s understand all this in a cerebral way, but for most it is not emotionally vivid. As one woman student recently told me rather plaintively: "Those of you who lived through all those scary events have to keep reminding us that nuclear weapons really exist."

THE VIEW FROM THE NINETIES

ast-forward a full decade. By the mid-1990s, the Cold War was fading into memory, and the "nuclear threat" had mutated from its classic form—a nightmarish, world-destroying holocaust—into a series of still-menacing but less cosmic regional dangers and technical issues.

But these developments, welcome as they were, did not mean that the historical realities addressed in this book had suddenly vanished. For one thing, nuclear menace in forms both fanciful and serious remained very much alive in the mass culture, from popular fiction to movies, video games, and television programs. Further, Americans continued to wrestle with the meaning of the primal event that had started it all, the atomic destruction of two cities by the order of a U.S. president in August 1945. The fiftieth anniversary of the end of World War II, and of the nearly simultaneous Hiroshima and Nagasaki bombings, raised this still contentious issue in a particularly urgent form, inviting reflections on America's half-century effort to accommodate nuclear weapons into its strategic thinking, its ethics, and its culture.

14

NUCLEAR MENACE IN THE MASS CULTURE OF THE LATE COLD WAR ERA AND BEYOND

Paul Boyer and Eric Idsvoog

Despite the end of the Cold War, the waning of the nuclear arms race, and the disappearance of "global thermonuclear war" from pollsters' lists of Americans' greatest worries, U.S. mass culture of the late 1980s and the 1990s was saturated by nuclear themes. Images of nuclear menace continued to pervade the movies, video games, and mass-market fiction. This essay explores these continuities and reflects on what they tell us about American cultural anxieties as the nation moved into the uncharted terrain of the post–Cold War era.

This chapter is the product of a collaboration with Eric Idsvoog, an undergraduate at the University of Wisconsin-Madison who in the summer of 1996, funded by a professor/student research fellowship, investigated nuclear themes in the fiction and movies of the 1990s. This essay represents a shared process of research, discussion, analysis, and writing.

ON AUGUST 8, 1945, Anne O'Hare McCormick, writing in the *New York Times,* insisted that the atomic bomb had caused "an explosion in men's minds as shattering as the obliteration of Hiroshima." Whatever the appropriateness of McCormick's equation of mass death and mass psychology, an upsurge of "atomic" jokes, "atomic" drinks, and "atomic" sales, not to mention the many businesses that quickly incorporated the potent new word into their names, seemed to confirm her claim. From the beginning, advertisers, marketers, and mass-culture producers found the atomic bomb a potent and versatile image.

Within weeks of Hiroshima, movie marquees heralded *The House on 92nd Street,* a spy thriller hastily revised to incorporate in its plot "Process 97, the secret ingredient of the atomic bomb." By year's end, radio stations were airing the Slim Gaillard Quartet's "Atomic Cafe" and "When the Atomic Bomb Fell," a country song celebrating victory over the "cruel Jap."

The idea of nuclear weapons—and the terror they spawned—remained embedded in U.S. mass culture for the next forty years and beyond. This cultural output came in waves, however, paralleling cycles of activism and apathy. The fallout fears so pervasive from the mid-1950s to 1963, for example, produced a rich trove of cultural effluvia, including "mutant" movies featuring such radiation-spawned creatures as *The Beast from 2000 Fathoms* (1953), the giant ants of *Them!* (1954), *The Blob* (1958), and *The Incredible Shrinking Man* (1957). Nuclear anxiety often surfaced in the science-fiction television shows *The Outer Limits* and Rod Serling's *Twilight Zone,* and radioactive mishaps spawned a new generation of comic-book superheroes, including Spider-Man, the Fantastic Four, and the Incredible Hulk. As we have seen, this wave of atomic fear also gave rise to films adapted from nuclear-war novels, including *On the Beach* and *Dr. Strangelove.*

Similarly, the upsurge of nuclear fear and activism in the early Reagan years resonated in a variety of cultural forms, from poetry, novels, and science fiction to rock music, movies, and novels. The movies *War Games,* in which a high school hacker taps into the Pentagon's supercomputer and nearly triggers World War III, and *Testament,* which chronicles a California family's final days as radiation from a nuclear attack on San Francisco creeps northward, both debuted in 1983. In the 1983 made-for-TV movie *Special Bulletin,* terrorists threaten to destroy Charleston, South Carolina, with a nuclear weapon. The terrorist theme soon loomed large in post–Cold War mass culture.

The Day After (1984), a heavily publicized ABC-TV special, portrayed the effects of a Soviet nuclear attack on a Kansas town. With attention shifting from the nuclear-freeze campaign to President Reagan's Strategic Defense Initiative, *The Day After* missed the crest of the early-eighties' wave of nuclear fear and activism. Nevertheless, it unsettled many Americans—including children forbidden to watch it because of a parental-advisory message warning of its frightening content.

Nuclear jitters aided sales of at least three novels of the early 1980s: William Prochnau's *Trinity's Child* (1983), Frederick Forsyth's *Fourth Protocol* (1984), and Tom Clancy's best-selling *Hunt for Red October* (1984). In *Trinity's Child,* an unidentified nuclear missile explodes over a Russian city. The Soviets retaliate with a limited nuclear attack on the United States, forcing on American officials the agonizing choice of backing down or launching a full-scale nuclear counterattack that could jeopardize human survival.

In *The Fourth Protocol,* the British intelligence service narrowly forestalls a Soviet plot to detonate a nuclear device near a U.S. base in England and then pin the blame on the United States. The aim is to turn European public opinion against the United States, break up the NATO alliance, and open the way for a Soviet takeover of western Europe.

The Hunt for Red October, the first of Clancy's popular "Jack Ryan" novels of espionage, high-level intrigue, and military derring-do, told of a rogue Soviet submarine captain, Marko Ramius, who realizes that his sub has been selected to launch a nuclear first strike against the United States. As he desperately tries to defect to the West, the KGB falsely warns Washington that Ramius himself is the threat. As both Soviet and U.S. vessels close in, and as a nuclear showdown seems inevitable, only the CIA analyst Ryan grasps the truth, and by amazing heroics prevents World War III.

Even the novels and films in which nuclear themes seem incidental, or hover in the background, demonstrate the unease of these years. In Stephen King's 1979 thriller *The Dead Zone,* the clairvoyant protagonist attempts to assassinate the man he realizes will someday plunge the world into nuclear war. One of the many subplots of the 1983 James Bond film *Octopussy* involves a scheme by Kamal Khan (Louis Jourdain), a smuggler with ties to the Soviet Union, to plant a nuclear device on a U.S. Air Force base. In the 1985 movie *Back to the Future,* the eccentric scientist

Doc Brown, played by Christopher Lloyd, deploys a time-traveling vehicle powered by plutonium stolen from a nuclear-research facility by Libyan terrorists—another anticipation of a major post–Cold War nuclear theme. When the brain-eating zombies of *Return of the Living Dead* (1985) overrun a small town, the government fights back with (what else?) a nuclear bomb. In the potboiler movie *Weird Science* (1985), a nuclear missile disrupts a teenager's house party.

Some mass-culture output of the late 1970s and early 1980s interwove images of nuclear holocaust with fears of social breakdown and urban collapse. The anarchic society of the 1979 Australian film *Mad Max* and its sequels, *Mad Max 2* (1981; released in the United States in 1982 as *The Road Warriors*) and *Mad Max: Beyond Thunderdome* (1985), is presented as the aftermath of nuclear holocaust. As *The Road Warriors* opens, a scrolling text explains in mythic language how this debased, dog-eat-dog society came to be: "Two mighty tribes went to war, and touched off a blaze that engulfed them all." *Terminator* (1984) and *Terminator II: Judgment Day* (1991), both starring Arnold Schwarzenegger, offer nightmarish images of a post-holocaust Los Angeles of half-demolished buildings and wrecked playgrounds, where survivors desperately battle their own machines. Joining nuclear terror to fear of a computer-dominated world, the *Terminator* movies featured an omnipotent computer, Skynet, that has detonated all the world's nuclear weapons, destroying civilization. In *Terminator,* Schwarzenegger is a cyborg (the eponymous "Terminator") who arrives from the future, programmed to kill the person (still in utero) who is destined to lead a rebellion against Skynet. In *Terminator II,* Schwarzenegger has morphed into a robotic *defender* of the future rebel, now a young boy, against the powers that wish him dead.

William Gibson's 1984 science-fiction novel *Neuromancer* (which introduced the term "cyberspace") gives expression to a host of anxieties, including the existential terrors of a world dominated by powerful corporations possessing the technology to buy, sell, destroy, and even create human beings at will. The horror of nuclear weapons, while only one of Gibson's many themes, is powerfully invoked. One character, Peter Rivera, who can project his thoughts as holograms, generates this image of a city devastated by nuclear attack:

A dark wave of rubble rose against a colorless sky, beyond its crest the bleached, half-melted skeletons of city towers. The rubble wave was textured like a net, rusting steel rods twisted gracefully as fine string, vast slabs of concrete still clinging there. The foreground might once have been a city square; there was a sort of stump, something that suggested a fountain. At its base, the children and the soldier were frozen. . . . Children. Feral, in rags. Teeth glittering like knives. Sores on their contorted faces. The soldier on his back, mouth and throat open to the sky. They were feeding.

Even as these novels and films appeared, however, the Cold War and the nuclear arms race—realities woven tightly into the fabric of American life and culture—were ending. The sequence of now familiar events needs no elaboration: Mikhail Gorbachev's rise to power in 1985; his meetings with President Reagan; the fall of the Berlin Wall in 1989; Germany's reunification; the collapse of the Soviet Union itself in 1991.

Simultaneously, a series of nuclear-arms treaties, spawning a new set of acronyms—INF (1987), START I (1991), START II (1993)—reversed years of nuclear escalation. Negotiators also addressed complex issues related to dismantling nuclear weapons, the disposal of plutonium and other nuclear by-products, and the security of remaining missiles. President Bill Clinton, in his 1997 State of the Union address, called for renewed efforts toward nuclear disarmament and nonproliferation agreements. Clinton and Russian president Boris Yeltsin later that year agreed in principle on START III, aimed at cutting stockpiles to between 2,000 and 2,500 warheads by 2007.

THE MASS CULTURE RESPONDS

Given the historically cyclical pattern of Americans' cultural engagement with nuclear issues, which intensifies in times of heightened fear and activism and diminishes when fear and activism fade, one might have expected these events to have ushered in another cycle of cultural neglect. Don DeLillo's 1997 novel *Underworld,* exploring the cultural and psychological ramifications of America's half-century encounter with nuclear weapons, implicitly placed those ramifications in the past. The nuclear arms race and all its by-products had profoundly shaped, and warped, American life for decades after 1945, DeLillo suggested—but they were now history and could be grasped imaginatively and summed up novelistically.

In fact, however, the process of "cultural fallout" goes on—changed, certainly, but in some respects barely diminished. A decade after the Cold War's end, cultural concern with the nuclear menace was still pervasive. What the emotional and psychological effects of this outpouring of cultural material would be remained an interesting unanswered question.

Why this persistence? In contrast to the early 1950s, the federal government in the late 1980s and early 1990s did not downplay nuclear dangers with soothing propaganda about civil defense or the atom's peacetime uses. And in contrast to the post-1963 years, the late 1980s and 1990s did not see the emergence of such all-consuming issues as the Vietnam War, urban riots, or Watergate, which had earlier diverted attention from nuclear issues. On the contrary, the fiftieth anniversary of the atomic bombing of Japan and the controversy over the Smithsonian Institution's *Enola Gay* exhibit (see chapter 16) actually heightened nuclear awareness.

The language and imagery of the mass media and of everyday life in the later 1990s underscored the cultural persistence of the nuclear theme. We "nuke" foods in our microwaves. A PBS news commentator, speaking of a volatile political issue, says: "I don't want to get too close to this; it could be radioactive." A legislator criticizing a proposed bill observes on CNN: "It's like using a nuclear weapon to try to kill a fly." An antismoking activist admits in the *New York Times* that he "goes thermonuclear" when people ignore No Smoking signs. A Kentucky flood victim tells a reporter: "The only worse thing would be a nuclear disaster." Though the songs on the 1996 compact disk *Dr. Dre Presents . . . the Aftermath* did not deal with nuclear war, the cover featured a mushroom cloud, that generic, instantly recognizable symbol of menace. The third edition of the *American Heritage Dictionary* (1992) defined "apocalypse" as: "Great or total devastation: *the apocalypse of nuclear war*" (emphasis added). After half a century, in short, the language and the imagery of nuclear war so permeated U.S. culture that one hardly noticed them.

The mass media's imitative nature doubtless played a part as well. A theme that had inspired so many movies, novels, and television programs from the 1950s to the early 1980s clearly invited further exploitation, whatever the shifts in world realities. Just as Hollywood continued to churn out World War II movies long after the war was over, an occasional "nuclear" film or novel is hardly surprising.

Beyond all this, however, lay an additional and obvious causal factor: the persistence of nuclear hazards. The 1986 Chernobyl disaster revived fears of nuclear power. The cleanup of contaminated nuclear sites and the long-term storage of deadly radioactive waste (estimated by the Department of Energy to cost $230 billion or more for the United States alone) posed massive problems. By the mid-1990s, the United States possessed nearly one hundred tons of weapons-grade plutonium and almost one thousand tons of enriched uranium; Russia's stockpiles were even larger.

Further, despite significant moves toward nuclear disarmament, START II remained unratified by the Russian parliament, and Russian conservatives and military leaders ominously denounced Boris Yeltsin as a traitor for agreeing to START III in 1997. Even if fully implemented, these treaties would still leave Russia and the United States with several thousand nuclear warheads each—a stockpile that would have horrified the Americans of 1945, who had just seen what *two* atomic bombs, puny by 1990s standards, could accomplish.

Further, the continued presence of nuclear missiles, missile-grade materials, and atomic scientists in highly unstable regions of the former Soviet sphere (including Russia itself) spawned fears of nuclear blackmail or the clandestine transfer of nuclear materials or know-how to aspiring nuclear powers like North Korea, Iraq, or Libya—or even to small terrorist groups desperate to achieve their goals. In October 1997, a Russian nuclear scientist told a congressional committee that in the 1970s the Soviet KGB had had in its possession more than eighty suitcase-sized nuclear bombs; he added the alarming charge that this cache of microweapons had vanished in the breakdown of the chain of command after the Soviet Union's collapse. Commenting on this testimony, Senator Richard Lugar of Indiana warned of the danger of nuclear weapons falling into the wrong hands. (The FBI issued a statement denying that the eighty-four bombs were unaccounted for).

The uncertainties of the post–Cold War era, exacerbated by stories such as this, kept nuclear-related issues at the forefront of Americans' awareness and provided a rich lode of material for the mass culture of the late 1980s and 1990s. While nuclear fear may ultimately fade from American imagination and culture, it seems destined to have a very long half-life indeed.

THE LATE 1980s: YEARS OF TRANSITION

By a kind of cultural inertia, the nuclear preoccupations of the early 1980s persisted in U.S. mass culture as the decade wore on, despite the changing international climate, as projects already in the pipeline reached fruition. Tom Clancy, for example, followed *The Hunt for Red October* with *Red Storm Rising* (1986) and *The Cardinal of the Kremlin* (1988). In *The Cardinal of the Kremlin,* U.S. spies in the Kremlin seek information about Russia's missile-defense system. In *Red Storm Rising,* an interesting transitional novel, Clancy again takes the world to the brink of nuclear war, setting up a classic Cold War superpower confrontation while also introducing ambiguities and complexities that anticipated the post–Cold War era ahead. The action begins when Islamic fundamentalist terrorists destroy a major Soviet oil facility, crippling the nation's energy flow. Deciding on a desperate strategy, the KGB stages a coup and launches an invasion of western Europe as a prelude to seizing the oil-rich Persian Gulf.

The resulting war repeatedly threatens to go nuclear. When Moscow launches a surveillance satellite, U.S. authorities mistake it for an ICBM and nearly retaliate. As the Red Army faces defeat in conventional combat, pressures to play the nuclear card increase. In a showdown with the Soviet Defense Council, a Russian field commander, General Alekseyev, warns against this fateful step. Ridiculing the Defense Council chairman for urging the use of "tactical" nuclear weapons, Alekseyev fumes: "He's talking like one of those NATO idiots! There is no wall between a tactical and a strategic nuclear exchange, just a fuzzy line in the imagination of the amateurs and academics who advise their political leaders." Should the Defense Council proceed with its mad plan, he goes on, Russia's very survival "would be at the mercy of whichever NATO leader is the *least* stable." Seizing power, Alekseyev arranges a cease-fire with NATO and prevents nuclear war—by the narrowest of margins. In this scene, Clancy in fact powerfully critiqued NATO strategy, which included a nuclear first-use option if the Soviets invaded.

Cold War themes of nuclear menace pervade several movies of the late 1980s, in some cases reflecting the time lag in bringing novels to the screen. Frederick Forsyth's 1984 novel, *The Fourth Protocol,* for example, appeared as a movie (starring Michael Caine) in 1987. *The Hunt for Red October* reached movie screens in 1990, with Sean Connery and Alec Baldwin in the starring roles, although the international climate had changed radically since 1984. The made-for-TV movie *By Dawn's Early Light* (1990), the last of the "traditional" Cold War nuclear thrillers, was based on William Prochnau's novel *Trinity's Child,* published seven years earlier, when nuclear fear and activism had dominated U.S. life. In *Superman IV: The Quest for Peace* (1987), the Man of Steel belatedly emerges as a nuclear-freeze advocate, hurling the world's thermonuclear arsenals into the sun.

Other late-1980s novels and movies, however, moved beyond the familiar superpower showdown to explore more ambiguous post–Cold War forms of nuclear menace. In Stephen Hunter's 1989 novel, *Day before Midnight,* Russian commandos angered by Gorbachev's concessions seize a U.S. missile silo, intent on launching a nuclear war they can *win* through a decisive first strike. In the 1986 movie *The Manhattan Project,* a teenager eager to impress his girlfriend steals plutonium from a nuclear-weapons facility and constructs his own reactor.

In Roman Polanski's *Frantic* (1988), starring Harrison Ford, a young American couple, Richard and Sondra Walker, arrive in Paris to find that an airport mixup has left them with the wrong suitcase—one containing a nuclear triggering mechanism that a beautiful young French woman, Michelle, has smuggled into France for an Arab terrorist organization. Sondra is kidnapped, the detonator is nearly lost on a Paris rooftop, Richard is erotically attracted to Michelle, and many other plot twists ensue before the terrorists murder Michelle, the Walkers are reunited, and a disgusted Richard Walker throws the nuclear device into the Seine.

Mass-culture producers continued to exploit the nuclear theme as the 1990s dawned. But as the full implications of the Soviet collapse became apparent, this protean theme assumed a variety of forms fascinating and revealing in their diversity.

COLD WAR NOSTALGIA

For Americans accustomed to "the Soviet threat" and the icy reassurance of a superpower balance of terror, the abrupt transformation of world realities proved disorienting. As Harry Angstrom complains in John Updike's 1990 novel, *Rabbit at Rest:* "It's like nobody's in charge of the other side any more. I miss it, the cold war. It gave you a reason to get up in the morning." In the same vein, a character in the 1995 movie *Crimson Tide* pines for "the good ol' days of the Cold War, [when] the Russians could . . . be depended upon to do what was in their own best interest."

Reflecting this almost nostalgic mood, some mass-culture products emulated the Tom Clancy novels of the later 1980s in continuing to portray Russia as America's adversary, and global holocaust as imminent, even as the Cold War and the nuclear arms race wound down. Reluctant to abandon such a rich theme, the mass-culture producers only slowly acknowledged that a new order had dawned. Whatever the evidence to the contrary, the Cold War and its stark polarities—Washington vs. Moscow; NATO vs. Warsaw Pact; good vs. evil—together with the nuclear confrontation that was its by-product, would surely survive! In *Star Trek: First Contact* (1996), a U.S. nuclear missile left over from World War III is discovered in the distant future. Cold Wars may come and go, but in the mythic realm of *Star Trek,* global nuclear holocaust still awaits.

The burgeoning world of teenage video games, played in arcades and on home consoles, offered another arena of Cold War nostalgia in late-1990s mass culture. A game called *Soviet Strike* remained popular. *Silent Steel* featured a nuclear-armed submarine. "They said the cold war was over," snarled the promotional copy; "—it ain't." An ad for *Tunnel B1* warned darkly: "Welcome to your tomb. The light at the end of the tunnel is a heat-seeking thermonuclear missile."

Like the *Mad Max* movies, several futuristic urban-combat video games ascribed the devastation and anarchy of their virtual cities to nuclear attack. Ads for *Fallout* promised a "Postnuclear Adventure." Mushroom clouds proliferated, as did such terms as "overkill," "ground zero," "meltdown," and "radioactive fog." One company promoted a game called *Scorched Planet*. Ads for another new game of the later 1990s, *MDK,* featured images of blasted cities and proclaimed: "On a good day, only 1.5 billion people will die."

But while the video game industry continued to exploit Cold War hostilities and nuclear showdowns, it also responded to changing realities. In Nintendo's *Dixie Kong's Double Trouble,* the villains were thinly disguised as "Kremlings." In *Soviet Strike,* the covert operations squad posted in eastern Europe to "make sure the cold war stays in the fridge" deploys such conventional weaponry as Apache helicopters, and snowplows to bulldoze Warsaw Pact encampments, but *not* nuclear weapons.

In a variation on a long-term trend in the game world, many 1990s video games preserved the Cold War's absolutist moral framework while shifting the confrontation to some faraway time. *King's Field II* was set in King Alfred's England; *Blood Omen: Legacy of Kain* unfolded in a vaguely medieval age, where the forces of righteousness struggle against usurpers bent on imposing a reign of terror. In *Realms of the Haunting,* "the Battleground between Ultimate Good and Evil" is set in an apocalyptic future age.

The video games *Red Alert* and *P.T.O. II* (Pacific Theater of Operations) were particularly ingenious in avoiding scenarios of nuclear holocaust while preserving the Cold War's black-and-white moral polarities. *Red Alert* melded World War II and the Cold War. The action unfolds in the pre-nuclear 1940s, but the enemy is the Soviet Union, not Nazi Germany. (A time traveler kills Adolph Hitler, preventing the rise of Nazism, but also enabling the Soviet Union to invade Europe.) The player at last gets to engage in full-scale war with Russia—but with 1940s weaponry, not including a nuclear option.

Players of *P.T.O. II* refought World War II in the Pacific "from Pearl Harbor to unconditional surrender," as the ads proclaimed. But the game rewrites history in one crucial respect: The options do *not* include the atomic bomb. The player must devise strategies for defeating Japan *without* the "winning weapon" that scientists presented to Truman in July 1945.

SOURCES OF NUCLEAR MENACE

Chaos in the Former Soviet Sphere

"Go to one of the old Soviet republics," says a character in the 1996 movie *Broken Arrow*, "—they'll fix you up with a couple [of nuclear weapons] for the price of a BMW." While the Cold War and threats of global nuclear holocaust lived on in some novels, movies, and video games of the late 1980s and the 1990s, the more typical strategy was to adapt to the changed realities and offer more plausible scenarios of nuclear menace. Once the Soviet Union's collapse deprived Americans of a single, well-defined enemy, the mass culture introduced a multiplicity of threats, less terrifying than the ultimate nightmare of world cataclysm, but in some ways more troubling just because of their amorphous, hydra-headed nature.

Upheaval in eastern Europe, turmoil in the former Soviet republics (some of which housed nuclear-weapons facilities), and disorder verging on anarchy in Russia itself offered ample raw material for mass-culture narratives of nuclear danger arising within the former Soviet sphere. Like Stephen Hunter's *Day before Midnight*, several novels and movies of the 1990s featured dissident groups or criminal elements in the domain once ruled by Moscow that seize nuclear weapons or engage in nuclear black-mail. In the action movie *Jackie Chan's First Strike* (1997), Chan pursues Russian mobsters who have stolen a nuclear warhead. Stephen Coonts's novel *The Red Horseman* (1993) involves corrupt Soviet military leaders who orchestrate a Chernobyl-like disaster to cover their theft of war-heads from a base near the crippled reactor. In Tom Clancy's well-named 1991 novel, *The Sum of All Fears*, a complex tale with many interwoven plotlines, one leader of the terrorist group that plots a nuclear detona-tion in the United States is Günther Bock, an East German Communist. Dismayed by capitalist America's triumph and by Moscow's betrayal of Marxism, and embittered by his wife's suicide in a West German prison, Bock seeks his apocalyptic revenge. In *Sword of Orion,* Robin White's 1993 novel of nuclear menace, the Russian Pavel Markelov, a disgruntled intelligence agent left jobless by the Soviet Union's collapse, plays a key role.

The 1995 Hollywood thriller *Crimson Tide* similarly viewed political turmoil in Russia as the spawning ground of nuclear holocaust. The plot, drawn from current headlines, featured an ultra-nationalist demagogue, Vladimir Radchenko, who exploits the international protests against Russia's brutal crushing of the breakaway province of Chechnya. Rallying dissident military officers against the Russian president, Radchenko gains control of much of eastern Russia, including Vladivostok, a nuclear missile base and home port to a fleet of nuclear-armed submarines. As the situation deteriorates and a nuclear attack on America appears imminent, the Pentagon orders the commander of the nuclear sub *Alabama,* Captain Ramsey (Gene Hackman), to launch ten nuclear missiles on Vladivostok. A second command follows, but technical difficulties prevent its delivery. Ramsey's subordinate, Executive Officer Hunter (Denzel Washington), urges that the launch be delayed until the second command can be read, but Ramsey insists on proceeding. After a tense period of verbal sparring, physical conflict, and a near-fatal attack by a Russian submarine, the second message finally arrives: Radchenko has surrendered, the attack order is canceled, and global holocaust is averted—for the moment.

Rogue States, Terrorist Groups

A closely related plotline in many novels and movies of the 1990s dealing with nuclear menace involved the acquisition of warheads or fissionable materials from the former Soviet Union by hostile states or terrorists from various trouble spots, often assisted by greedy middlemen. Sometimes, the terrorists are generic, with no specific identification. In the 1992 movie *Under Siege,* armed men seize a decommissioned U.S. battleship transporting nuclear missiles, with the intent of selling them to vaguely described foreign "investors."

Most often, however, reflecting another major preoccupation of the 1990s, the terrorists were explicitly identified as Muslim. Even in *Under*

Siege, the ultimate recipients of the stolen missiles are at one point generically referred to as "François and Muhammed." The enemy in Arnold Schwarzenegger's 1994 action comedy *True Lies* is the "Crimson Jihad," a band of Islamic fundamentalists led by the fanatic Aziz (played by Art Malik, a British-reared Pakistani who earlier starred in *A Passage to India* and the PBS special *A Jewel in the Crown*). Schwarzenegger plays Harry Tasker, a computer salesman who leads a double life as a member of the Omega Sector, a secret antiterrorist unit. Tasker and his Omega Sector associates battle Aziz and the Crimson Jihad, who have acquired a nuclear warhead from a former Soviet republic and threaten to destroy the Florida Keys unless their demands are met.

In Robin White's *Sword of Orion,* the disgruntled Russian intelligence agent Markelov helps Hezb Islami, a Muslim faction in Afghanistan, hijack a Russian army unit transporting a hydrogen bomb for dismantling. Hezb Islami then resorts to nuclear blackmail to force the cancellation of Afghan elections from which they have been excluded. After many plot twists, Russian and U.S. security forces find the bomb and disarm it.

The anti-Islamic strain in this material illustrates the skill of mass-culture producers at combining multiple sources of anxiety. Linking nuclear uneasiness with the much-publicized menace of "Islamic terrorism" (reenforced by such acts as the 1988 downing of Pan Am 103 over Scotland and the 1993 World Trade Center bombing), the mass-culture industry both reflected and aggravated these anxieties. Reacting to the stereotyping, Muslims picketed *True Lies* and otherwise protested movies and fiction that portrayed members of their faith in negative terms.

In a variation on this theme, the source of menace was a hostile state intent on acquiring stolen nuclear components or co-opting renegade scientists. As early as 1976, in an episode entitled "The Plutonium Connection," the PBS science program *Nova* had documented how readily nuclear-weapons materials and know-how could be obtained. In the same vein, a 1989 television movie, *The Terror Trade: Buying the Bomb,* documented the nuclear black market. It is no surprise, then, to find this theme in popular fiction and films of the edgy post–Cold War era.

Several novels in this vein gained force by drawing on actual situations and familiar events. In Clancy's *Sum of All Fears,* the East German

Communist Günther Bock joins forces with Palestinian extremists funded by Iran and led by the fanatic Ismael Qati. When Jack Ryan (now deputy director of the CIA) proposes a Mideast peace plan that involves Palestinian acceptance of Israel's existence and shared rule in Jerusalem, Qati's followers grow desperate. Their opportunity comes when a farmer discovers an atomic bomb in the wreckage of an Israeli plane that crashed in Syria in the 1973 Yom Kippur War. Ibrahim Ghosn, a Palestinian bomb expert working for Qati, and Manfred Fromm, an East German nuclear engineer, upgrade the aging fission bomb to a thermonuclear weapon of devastating power. The terrorists conceal this superbomb outside Denver's Skydome and detonate it during the Super Bowl (a nice touch), while Fromm and Bock simultaneously instigate a confrontation between U.S. and Soviet troops in Berlin. The aim is to revive the Cold War, which the Palestinians hope to turn to their advantage.

The plot nearly succeeds. Owing to last-minute glitches the bomb proves less devastating than expected, but the American president, Robert Fowler, rashly blames fanatical elements in a disintegrating Soviet Union, and prepares a massive nuclear retaliation. He is egged on in this misguided course by his hysterical national security adviser, who is also his mistress. (Clancy's novels are nothing if not imaginative.) But Jack Ryan, convinced that the bombing is the work of terrorists, not a Soviet plot, commandeers the White House hotline, negotiates a stand-down with the Russian leader, and captures Qati and his co-conspirators. Once again, global cataclysm is averted by the narrowest of margins.

Frederick Forsyth's more realistic *Fist of God* (1994), unfolds during the Persian Gulf War and, according to the blurb, tells "the utterly convincing story of what may actually have happened behind the headlines." Using the names of actual persons, among them U.S. secretary of state James Baker and Iraqi foreign minister Tariq Aziz, Forsyth offers a fictionalized account of the efforts of an international team of specialists to find and destroy Iraq's nuclear bomb.

Like countless nuclear disarmament activists of the past, these authors evoked the horrors of nuclear war as a means of heightening the drama of their story. Of the bomb-hunting team in *The Fist of God*, Forsyth writes: "They did not need to be scientists to know that the first explosion would kill more than a hundred thousand young soldiers.

Within hours, the radiation cloud, sucking up billions of tons of active sand from the desert, would begin to drift, covering everything in its path with death."

Many authors took pains to link their fictions to real-world conditions. In an afterword to *The Fist of God,* Forsyth warned of unstable or dictatorial regimes' ready access to nuclear technology, and accurately summarized how Iraqi strongman Saddam Hussein (in the novel) made the country a nuclear power: "For a decade the regime of the Republic of Iraq was allowed to arm itself to a frightening level by a combination of political foolishness, bureaucratic blindness, and corporate greed." Tom Clancy, in an afterword to *The Sum of All Fears,* made a similar point: any "sufficiently wealthy individual could, over a period of from five to ten years, produce a multi-stage thermonuclear device." And delivery of such a doomsday weapon, he added, "is child's play."

As Forsyth's novel suggests, the mass-culture industry of the 1990s found in Saddam Hussein an all-purpose villain. As the ads for the video game *Back to Baghdad* proclaim: "Time to Finish the Job . . . Time to Go Back to Baghdad." This is, indeed, what happens in R. J. Pinero's *Ultimatum* (1994), the story of a second Gulf War (led by President Clinton) against a nuclear-armed Saddam. Charlie Sheen's 1991 comedy *Hot Shots!,* a parodic vision of the same theme, involves a mission to destroy Saddam's nuclear-weapons facility. In the cathartic and (for Americans) deeply satisfying climax of Coonts's *Red Horseman,* after Saddam has acquired the stolen warheads, they are recovered, Saddam and the renegade Russians are captured, and Saddam is shot through the heart by one of his Russian partners in crime.

Saddam Hussein's Iraq in the 1990s replaced the Soviet Union as the paradigmatic nuclear threat. Demonized by the media (often with good reason), Iraq and its supreme ruler were seen as unambiguously evil and menacing. Having long associated nuclear danger with a single, clearly defined enemy, Americans for a time elevated Saddam (sometimes in tandem with North Korea's Kim Il Sung) to that role.

While "Islamic terrorists" were the preferred villains in these dramas of nuclear menace, other candidates surfaced as well. Tom Clancy's *Debt of Honor* (1994) linked lingering nuclear fears with worries about America's trade imbalance with Japan. When a horrible accident involving defective gas tanks on imported Japanese cars leads Congress to slam the door on Japanese imports, the corporate leaders who (in Clancy's world) control Japan retaliate with a combination of economic and military measures. Their campaign includes undermining the U.S. economy, gaining access to oil resources, and recovering the Mariana Islands, lost in World War II.

To the shock of U.S. officials, Japan's military offensive includes a nuclear threat. Having acquired deactivated SS19 missiles from Russia, supposedly for peaceful purposes, the Japanese have secretly built a small but deadly arsenal of twenty MIRV missiles, each with seven separately targeted warheads, giving Japan the capacity "to cut the heart out of 140 American cities."

Once again, indomitable Jack Ryan (now national security adviser) rises to the challenge, utilizing a combination of diplomacy, military measures, and parachute commando drops in Japan. The nuclear threat is forestalled, and an embargo threat forces Japan's surrender. (Advised by Ryan, the president rejects the Truman option of 1945 and magnanimously rules out an atomic attack on Japan.) Ryan becomes vice president at the end of *Debt of Honor,* preparing the way for Clancy's next novel, *Executive Orders* (1996), in which he achieves the position for which he is obviously destined: president of the United States.

A disgruntled Bosnian Serb, resentful of America's intervention in the Balkans conflict, is the villain of the 1997 nuclear-menace film *The Peacemaker.* Working with unscrupulous Russian middlemen, he hijacks a trainload of nuclear weapons scheduled for demolition, smuggles one into New York City, and prepares to detonate it. (This plotline revived a fifty-year-old scenario of atomic horror on America's shores that first surfaced in the immediate post-Hiroshima period, before the era of ICBMs.) Only Nicole Kidman, playing the acting head of the "White House Nuclear Smuggling Group," aided by sidekick George Clooney, fresh from his starring role in the hit television series *E.R.,* foil the plot and save Manhattan. "The Cold War Is Back, Nuclear Bombs and All," the *New York Times* captioned its review of *The Peacemaker.*

Nuclear Technology Run Amok

The hazards of nuclear technology past and present deepened America's realization that the Cold War's end did not erase nuclear danger from the world. Even if all the missiles were deactivated, the legacy of decades of nuclear testing would remain, along with the problem of disposing of tons of radioactive waste that would remain deadly for thousands of years, and the threat of more nuclear power plant malfunctions like those at Three Mile Island in 1979 and Chernobyl in 1986. These issues, too, figured largely in the representations of nuclear danger in post–Cold War mass culture.

Harking back to the 1950s, several movies probed the nuclear-weapons tests and the medical experiments with radioactive substances conducted in those years. *Nightbreaker* (1989), starring Martin Sheen and Emilio Estevez, explored the U.S. government's secret radiation testing of civilians in the 1950s. In *Desert Bloom* (1986), set in the Nevada of the 1950s, John Voight plays Jack Chismore, a gas-station operator obsessed with the comings and goings of military brass involved in the top-secret atomic tests at a nearby site. A coming-of-age story, *Desert Bloom* alternates the tensions in Chismore's family with his rising anxiety about the government's mysterious activities.

A series of documentaries heightened public awareness of the dangers of nuclear technology. *Building Bombs* (1994), an Academy Award nominee, dealt with mismanagement at the Savannah River nuclear-weapons facility in South Carolina. *Plutonium Circus* (1995) focused on the Pantex hydrogen-bomb assembly plant in Amarillo, a subject A. G. Mojtabai had earlier explored in *Blessed Assurance: Living with the Bomb in Amarillo.*

Technological failure as a source of nuclear menace also propels several Hollywood movies of the 1990s. In *The Cape* (1996), a nuclear-powered Russian spy satellite malfunctions and threatens to crash to earth, spewing deadly radioactivity. An emergency NASA shuttle mission—including a Russian cosmonaut, in the spirit of post–Cold War amity—averts the catastrophe by the usual hair's-breadth margin.

Fear of nuclear technology assumed many guises in 1990s mass culture. The video game *Blast Corps* involved transporting decommissioned nuclear warheads through populated areas where one mistake means catastrophe. In the movie *Naked Gun 2½: The Smell of Fear* (1991), a parody of the techno-menace theme, the bumbling antihero Frank Drebin (Leslie Nielsen) battles the nuclear power industry (as well as the oil, gas, and coal industries), which will do anything to thwart a new national policy favoring safer, less exploitative energy sources. In a 1991 episode of the animated television comedy *The Simpsons,* dim-witted Homer Simpson, a nuclear power plant worker, manages by sheer dumb luck to prevent a meltdown. (He plays "eenie-meenie-miney-moe" to decide which button to push.) Hailed as a hero, he lectures at other plants on crisis management. In the 1986 movie *Class of Nuke 'Em High* and its 1991 and 1994 sequels, all of which update many 1950s potboilers, mutants from a nearby nuclear waste spill invade a suburban New Jersey high school.

Terrorists, Loners, Madmen

At the dawn of the atomic age, long before hydrogen bombs, ICBMs, nuclear submarines, and SAC armadas, the media seethed with anxious speculation about foreign agents who could smuggle in the components of an atomic bomb, secretly assemble it, and bring America to its knees. Half a century later, after decades when nuclear fears had focused on the Soviet superpower and on sophisticated doomsday technologies, the media turned again to the smaller-scale worries that had first surfaced in 1945 and 1946. Marching through 1990s novels and movies of nuclear menace is a parade of bomb-brandishing terrorists, crazed madmen, grudge-bearing loners, or normally rational individuals driven over the edge by the stress of doomsday decision-making.

A striking motif of these nuclear narratives is the villains' irrationality. However menacing the nuclear prospect during the Cold War, people at least had the reassurance—or the comforting illusion—that the arms race was being managed from the top by responsible leaders of reason and restraint. As this assurance faded in the 1990s, the mass media reflected the resulting apprehensions. Nearly every work cited in this essay involves a highly unstable character. Ismael Qati, the mastermind in Clancy's *Sum of All Fears,* to cite but one example, is not only a religious fanatic; he is also dying, with nothing to lose. The villain of *The Peacemaker,* a cultivated, mild-mannered Sarajevo piano teacher, initially gives no hint of his double life as a nuclear terrorist plotting the destruction of New York City.

The madmen are sometimes heads of state, or are at least near centers of power. Forsyth's *Fist of God* portrays Saddam Hussein as an erratic, sadistic leader willing to use any means, including nuclear devastation, to achieve his evil goals. The rantings of Vladimir Radchenko, the ultra-nationalist Russian who threatens nuclear devastation in *Crimson Tide,* echo the scary sound bites of the actual Russian neofascist Vladimir Zhirinovsky.

Sometimes, as we have seen, the individuals who precipitate the crisis are motivated not by religious zeal or political ideology, but simply by resentment or personal grievance. Günther Bock in *The Sum of All Fears* is a disgruntled loner with a bone to pick against those who have done him wrong.

Nor are these menacing loners always foreigners. In an America rattled by domestic terrorism, homegrown mad bombers, and antigovernment militias, such anxieties readily found their way into the novels and movies of nuclear menace. While Captain Ramsey in *Crimson Tide* is not insane, his rigidly authoritarian personality borders on the irrational. In one scene, his contorted face dramatically illuminated by a demonic glow, he threatens to kill one of his own crew in his desperate eagerness to launch his missiles. *The Sum of All Fears* contains a similar scene, in which President Fowler, emotionally unhinged by the nuclear blast at the Super Bowl, frantically prepares to retaliate against Russia.

In the 1996 film *Broken Arrow,* John Travolta plays Major Deakins, a Utah-based Stealth bomber pilot embittered by his low status, paltry pay, and lack of promotion. Slipping over the edge of sanity, he takes off with two live nuclear warheads and threatens to obliterate Denver unless his blackmail demands are met. Fortunately for Denver, Deakins's friend and copilot Captain Hale (Christian Slater), with an assist from a resourceful park ranger, foils the plot and saves the city.

In *Under Siege,* the crisis is initiated by a former CIA operative, William Strannix (Tommy Lee Jones), seeking revenge on the agency for having ordered him killed during an abortive earlier operation. Strannix's insanity manifests itself as an obsession with the "Looney Tunes" cartoon series. (Perhaps he saw the Tom and Jerry episode "'Tomic Energy.") Assembling a ragtag band of terrorists, and aided by the corrupt and greedy Commander Krill, skipper of the USS *Missouri,* Strannix organizes the raid to steal the nuclear missiles aboard the decommissioned battleship on its final voyage.

The "alienated loner" formula is repeated in *Under Siege 2: Dark Territory* (1995). In this sequel, a computer genius gone bad (Eric Bogosian) develops a CD-ROM that enables him to control a super-sophisticated experimental U.S. spy satellite that is also capable of raining nuclear devastation upon the earth. Bogosian, who designed the satellite in the first place, has now reprogrammed it to obliterate Washington, D.C., unless the federal government pays him one billion dollars. (How he plans to spend the ransom money remains unexplained.) Again the embittered lone madman, who had once contributed his technical genius to the government's purposes, turns on that same government as the enemy.

The angry-loner-as-nuclear-menace theme was parodied in "Sideshow Bob's Last Gleaming," a 1995 *Simpsons* episode in which an embittered ex-TV clown discovers a discarded ten-megaton missile in a trash barrel at an air force base. Resorting to nuclear blackmail, Sideshow Bob threatens to detonate the bomb unless all television is eliminated. When Lisa Simpson pleads, "Don't do it—that would be taking the easy way out," he replies, "I quite agree," and detonates the bomb. But it is a dud; Bob has missed the consumer advisory pasted on the missile: "Best before 1959." This episode exploits the familiar ephemera of America's nuclear history. As Sideshow Bob prepares to detonate the bomb, he whistles "We'll Meet Again," which Kubrick had used in *Dr. Strangelove,* while Maggie Simpson plucks petals from a daisy, evoking the anti-Goldwater television commercial from the 1964 presidential campaign. In a world without television, one character mutters grimly, "the survivors will envy the dead."

The madman scenario presumed that the nuclear option was never a rational alternative. This presumption (which also underlies the black humor of *Dr. Strangelove*) appears in President Truman's 1953 State of the Union address, quoted earlier: "The war of the future would be one in which man could extinguish millions of lives at one blow. . . . Such a war is not possible for rational man. We know this, but we dare not assume that others would not yield to the temptation science is now placing in their hands."

Truman's faith in "rational man," and his certainty that "we" would never use the bomb, ring hollow, coming only eight years after Hiroshima. The ironies become explicit in *Crimson Tide* when a crewman aboard the USS *Alabama,* in a moment of self-consciousness rare in this cultural material, insists that the Russian nationalist Radchenko must be a "dangerous lunatic" for threatening nuclear war to achieve his goals. Another crewman retorts: "What's that make us, since we're the only one who's ever dropped a nuclear bomb on anyone?" A heated discussion of the Hiroshima decision ensues, as the nuclear past and possible nuclear future intertwine.

Stephen Hunter's *Day before Midnight* offers another twist on the madman motif. Arkady Pashin, mastermind of the Russian commandos who seize a U.S. missile silo, is repeatedly dismissed as "crazy" or "nuts." Yet his plan possesses a certain rationality. His first strike will not only assure victory for the Soviet Union, but also cripple the U.S. nuclear arsenal. Rather than await an eventual world-destroying nuclear Armageddon, he will start a war that will leave only *half* the world in ruins. As he explains, "The fact is, I'll kill only a few hundred million. I'll *save* billions. I'm the man who saved the world." Pashin is mad, yet his first-strike strategy is the brainchild of "Peter Thiokol," a famous U.S. strategic theorist. "Thiokol's" logic, in turn, echoes arguments seriously put forward by actual American military figures early in the Cold War (see chapter 4).

Paralleling the "alienated loner" theme, in many post–Cold War cultural productions *one's own government* is the enemy. In a 1994 opinion poll, only about 20 percent of Americans (down from about 80 percent in 1964) expressed confidence that the government "always or almost always does the right thing," and the mass culture mirrored this skepticism. In *The Hunt for Red October* and *Red Storm Rising,* lower-level military figures frantically seek to thwart their own government's insane plans for a nuclear first strike. In *Under Siege,* the CIA has ordered the death of one of its own. In the horror movie *Return of the Living Dead,* because secret government experiments have produced the zombies that terrorize the city, the government must and does destroy the city with a nuclear bomb to prevent the zombies from spreading.

The premise of Kevin J. Anderson's *Ground Zero* (1995), based on the Fox network's popular *X-Files* series of the 1990s, is that despite the Cold War's end, government nuclear-weapons research continues. In a scene reminiscent of the "peaceful atom" propaganda of earlier days, visitors to the "Teller Nuclear Research Facility" view an upbeat video that glorifies the vast promise of atomic research, offers soothing reassurances about the facility's safety, and pooh-poohs the alleged dangers of radiation. In these stories, as in the *X-Files* series as a whole, official candor is an illusion; those in power invariably conceal the truth.

Even when not overtly sinister and deceptive, the governments in these novels and movies are impersonal, unthinking, inhumane bureaucracies. As an East German official says of NATO's nuclear-war strategizing in *Red Storm Rising,* "Their government reports are written by computers to be read by calculators. Just like ours. Just like ours."

The post–Cold War mass culture visions of nuclear menace portray a world not of government versus government, but of individuals maneuvering in an anarchic, film noir–like environment. Loners like Deakins in *Broken Arrow,* Strannix in *Under Siege,* or Bock in *The Sum of All Fears* take desperate measures against the irrational, dangerous, or unfair actions of their superiors. But the nuclear catastrophes threatened by such alienated individuals are typically averted by *other* loners who must act in the face of the inept stupidity of *their* superiors. Tom Clancy's Jack Ryan and General Alekseyev are only two of many such intelligent loners thwarted by bumbling, wrongheaded higher-ups. In *Under Siege,* a low-ranking cook, Casey Ryback (Steven Seagal), emerges as the hero, foiling the embittered Strannix. Seagal reprises his Casey Ryback role in *Under Siege 2: Dark Territory,* saving Washington, D.C., from destruction at the hands of a mad computer genius.

In the movie *Bloodfist IV: Ground Zero* (1994), an obscure military courier battles the terrorists who overrun a U.S. Air Force base to commandeer its nuclear weapons. The hero of Hunter's *Day before Midnight* is a semiliterate Vietnam War veteran released from military prison to help repel the missile-silo invaders. At the end, an army general soberly reflects that it wasn't the "professionals" who prevented catastrophe, but "the regular people, the Rest of Us."

Amoral Scientists

Brilliant but amoral scientists and technocrats often appear nearly as pathological as the nuclear madmen in these novels and films. Drawing on a very old "mad scientist" motif in Western culture, the representation of science and scientists in this material is usually of the Dr. Frankenstein variety. A central theme of America's nuclear discourse from 1945 on— atomic energy as the ultimate example of scientific discovery out- stripping ethics—took on fresh life as the moral certitudes of the Cold War era faded. Without a clear enemy, the ethical rationalizations for nuclear scientists and technologists seemed more ambiguous than ever.

In Clancy's *Sum of All Fears,* the nuclear engineer Manfred Fromm epitomizes the unscrupulous genius motivated solely by a project's tech- nical challenges. Employed to repair and upgrade the aging fission bomb acquired by the Palestinians, Fromm displays no interest in how the weapon will be used. In Forsyth's *Fist of God,* the giant cannon that is to launch Iraq's sole nuclear weapon is the brainchild of Gerry Bull, a politi- cally naive weapons designer embittered because his ideas have been re- peatedly rejected by his superiors.

Terminator II adds a feminist twist to the amoral scientist theme. A brilliant nuclear scientist realizes too late that his technical discoveries have horrendous implications. In a self-justificatory mood he asks rhe- torically, "How were we supposed to know?" At this, the mother of the boy who is destined to lead the anti-Skynet rebellion explodes: "Right. How were you supposed to know. . . . Men like you built the hydrogen bomb. Men like you thought it up. You think you're so creative. You don't know what it's like to really create something, to create a life, to feel it growing inside you. All you know how to create is death and destruction."

This mordant view of science pervades Kevin J. Anderson's *Ground Zero.* In the opening chapter, a mysterious burst of radiation kills Dr. Emil Gregory, the nuclear-weapons designer in charge of Project Bright Anvil, which is supposed to develop a radiation-free nuclear bomb. Re- flecting on the problematic nature of such research in the post–Cold War era, an FBI agent investigating Gregory's death muses: "Here we are, still building bombs to fight against the bad guys—yet we're not at all certain who the bad guys are anymore."

But Gregory's successor as head of Bright Anvil defends the project in classic technocratic language: "Is a gun manufacturer responsible for the people killed in convenience-store robberies? My team has created a *tool* for our government to use, a *resource* for our foreign policy experts. . . . I have no more business dictating this country's foreign policy than . . . a politician has coming into my laboratory and telling me how to run my experiments." Warming to his subject, however, the scientist quickly abandons his apolitical, technocratic pose: "Bright Anvil is *fallout free,* man! . . . It removes the big political stigma of using a nuclear weapon. Bright Anvil finally makes nuclear weapons *usable,* not just bluff cards. . . . If some nutcase like Saddam Hussein or Moammar Khadaffi [of Libya] wants to lob their own homemade uranium bomb at New Jersey, I want to make sure that our country has the means either to defend itself or strike back."

As a foil to this morally obtuse breed of scientist, the novel introduces Miriel Bremen, a former Bright Anvil scientist who, after a visit to Hiroshima and Nagasaki, has founded the protest group Stop Nuclear Madness! Shortly before a planned test of Bright Anvil on a Pacific atoll, Bremen arrives with Ryan Kamida, the sole survivor of a group of Pacific Islanders displaced by a U.S. nuclear test in the 1950s. Kamida brings with him a barrel of dark powder—the ashes of his people and the mysterious focal point of their collective spiritual energy. In the novel's climactic scene—a classic *X-Files* denouement—the atoll, along with the Bright Anvil scientists and their weapon, vanish in a mysterious burst of radioactive energy such as had earlier vaporized Dr. Gregory. History has come full circle. The human spirit has triumphed over amoral science.

Although themes of nuclear menace clearly pervaded post–Cold War mass culture, documenting nuclear-related material and cataloging its themes and motifs tell us little about its meaning and influence. The nuclear strand in a complex plot may, in fact, be relatively unimportant, hardly noticed consciously by readers, moviegoers, or video game players.

The H-bombs, ICBMs, and nuclear devices that litter these mass-culture products are often little more than gimmicks. In many of the post–Cold War films— *Under Siege, Broken Arrow, Jackie Chan's First Strike,* and others—the nuclear bombs or missiles appear quite unthreatening: We see the weapons, but not the destruction. In *Jackie Chan's First Strike,* the characters toss around a "uranium core" concealed in an ordinary oxygen tank. ("Talk about good clean fun," observed the *New York*

Times reviewer, "here it is.") While these films exploit the hard-wired cultural awareness that nuclear weapons are scary and dangerous things, they rarely bother to dramatize their actual effects. In the 1996 block-buster *Independence Day,* a futile attempt to use nuclear warheads to de-stroy the alien spaceship threatening Washington is little more than a minor diversion amid the spectacular special effects.

Despite these caveats, however, the pervasiveness of this theme in post–Cold War mass culture demands that anyone interested in the con-tinuing effects of the nuclear reality in contemporary America sit up and take notice. So, too, do the ways in which the danger was presented. Representations of nuclear menace in the 1990s differed radically from those of the 1950s or even the early 1980s. No longer involving two superpowers posturing across an Iron Curtain, the menace now unfolded in a destabilized, decentered world where deadly hazards arise in unex-pected places and assume many guises. The emblematic slogan of this new genre of nuclear horror might be the incantatory phrase used on *The X-Files:* "Trust no one." The prospect of a future in which nuclear weapons and nuclear know-how form a constant of the human condition is hardly reassuring.

Equally sobering is the fact that so many of these plots deal (admit-tedly in fanciful ways) with actual post–Cold War nuclear realities: the hazards of nuclear-waste disposal, the dangers of nuclear weapons and nuclear materials in highly unstable if not anarchic settings, the risk that dictatorial regimes or terrorist groups could acquire doomsday weapons. To be sure, the nightmarish prospect of global annihilation envisioned by Cold War movies, novels, and nonfiction writers like Robert Jay Lif-ton and Jonathan Schell had clearly faded by the end of the 1990s. But in place of one big menace, the latest wave of nuclear novels, movies, video games, and science fiction stories featured a mass of complex and shadowy dangers hardly less unsettling in their cumulative effect.

The opportunistic way these themes are often treated, noted above, is itself noteworthy. Many earlier works in this genre had been marked by profound moral seriousness. Science-fiction stories like Walter Miller Jr.'s *A Canticle for Leibowitz* (1959); the songs of Tom Lehrer; and movies like *On the Beach, Dr. Strangelove, China Syndrome,* or even *The Day the Earth Stood Still* (1951), with its message of global cooperation or global annihilation, were deeply engaged with the issues they addressed in a fictionalized or satirical way. With some exceptions, post–Cold War novelists, moviemakers, and video game designers exploited nuclear danger mainly for its capacity to stir fear and build tension. Seriousness of purpose beyond the desire to elicit a passing frisson of fear was rarely evident. As Dean Devlin, cowriter and producer of *Independence Day*, conceded: "Our movie is pretty obvious. The closest we get to a social statement is to play upon the idea that as we approach the millennium, and we're no longer worried about a nuclear threat, the question is, Will there be an apocalypse, and if so, how will it come?" *Time* magazine's comment on *Independence Day* suggests the impact of this "social statement": "You leave saying 'Wow!' instead of a speculative 'Hmmm.'" (Interestingly, the one filmmaker who continued in the 1990s to bring moral seriousness to the nuclear theme was the octogenarian Japanese director Akira Kurosawa. His *Rhapsody in August* of 1991, for example, evokes an aging Japanese woman's memories of the bombing of Nagasaki.)

Whatever the level of trivialization, one thing was clear as the twentieth century ended. Neither the reality of nuclear danger nor the continued presence of nuclear fear in American mass culture had disappeared with the end of the Cold War. Like the radiation-affected creatures in the science-fiction stories and movies of the 1950s, the cultural expression of that fear had simply mutated into sometimes bizarre new forms.

15

HIROSHIMA IN AMERICAN MEMORY

The year 1995—the fiftieth anniversary of both the end of World War II and the beginning of the atomic age—had powerful emotional overtones for America. When Michael J. Hogan, editor of the journal *Diplomatic History,* invited me to contribute to a special commemorative issue on the Hiroshima and Nagasaki bombings, I readily accepted. The invitation not only provided an opportunity for me to revisit my own memories of August 1945 and of a 1958 visit to Hiroshima but also to explore further the continuing role of Hiroshima in America's cultural and political discourse. Ten years earlier, in 1985, I had written an essay for the *New Republic* on Americans' immediate reaction to President Truman's atomic-bomb announcement (see chapter 2). In the 1995 essay below, I broadened the focus to reflect on the continued polemical and metaphorical resonance of Hiroshima in U.S. life from 1945 to the present. Drawing on my earlier work as well as on considerable fresh research, I once again rethought America's effort to come to terms with these protean events that refused to recede quietly into history, instead remaining vividly alive in the nation's collective memory.

The essay from which chapter 15 is adapted appeared in the Spring 1995 issue of *Diplomatic History.* This special issue, also including essays by Barton J. Bernstein, Herbert P. Bix, John W. Dower, Michael J. Hogan, Seitsu Tachibana, and J. Samuel Walker, was subsequently reprinted in Michael J. Hogan, ed., *Hiroshima in History and Memory* (New York: Cambridge University Press, 1996). Both versions included full scholarly citations, omitted here.

THE FIFTIETH ANNIVERSARY of the atomic bombing of Hiroshima invites reflection on the role of this event in American memory. For half a century now, the word "Hiroshima" has resonated in U.S. culture and public discourse, as its meaning has been debated, contested, and exploited. For me, a 1958 visit to that city drove home the ambiguous quality of the memory. As my train entered the station, several Japanese passengers around me, smiling and apparently full of civic pride, repeated "Hiroshima: atomic bomb. Hiroshima: atomic bomb" for the benefit of the visiting American. How to respond? I felt acute embarrassment, yet my seatmates seemed clearly pleased to remind me of the event that had made their city famous. This memory now mingles with earlier recollections of my first confused encounter with Hiroshima, in a newspaper on August 6, 1945, four days after my tenth birthday. With the Hiroshima-Nagasaki bombings now half a century in the past, perhaps the moment is opportune to explore our long effort to come to terms with Hiroshima—the city, the event, and the symbol.

At least since the Romans leveled Carthage in 146 B.C., thereby imposing the first "Carthaginian peace," the names of certain sites have taken on powerful symbolic meaning. "Waterloo" evokes irrevocable defeat; "Gettysburg," the Civil War's turning point. "Verdun" has become shorthand for the futility of trench warfare, while "Guernica" and "Dresden" stir thoughts of the slaughter of civilians from the air. Allusions to "Pearl Harbor" rallied Americans during World War II, while the chambers of commerce of Buchenwald and Dachau face an uphill task in extricating their towns from associations that are only too familiar—and gruesome. In more recent times, "Dien Bien Phu" and "Bay of Pigs" took on their own symbolic resonances.

Clearly certain place names serve as a shorthand in cultural discourse, based on a shared understanding of their symbolic meaning. When the event alluded to is sufficiently remote, the name is drained of emotion and serves a purely rhetorical function. We speak of a "Carthaginian peace" or say that someone "met his Waterloo" with little conscious awareness of the specific events or the specific towns in North Africa or Belgium that gave rise to these expressions. Hiroshima is another place name set apart by history, but unlike Carthage or Waterloo, its symbolic meaning continues to evoke passionate emotional responses.

For many Americans, that meaning is clear and unambiguous. Since 1945, Hiroshima, sometimes paired with Nagasaki, has been shorthand for the destructive capability of nuclear weapons. In medieval cartography, Jerusalem was the navel of the world. In nuclear geography, it is Hiroshima. In *We Can Do It!* (1985), a "Kids' Peace Book" with definitions for each letter of the alphabet, the entry for "H" reads:

> **H is for Hiroshima.** *Hiroshima* is a city in Japan, where an atomic bomb was dropped many years ago in 1945. Thousands of people lost their lives and the city was destroyed. That's why we say "NO MORE HIROSHIMAS!" H is also for *hope, happiness,* and *harmony.* That's what the world needs instead. Another H is for *hug.*

The page is illustrated with a drawing of a boy hugging his grandmother as she writes a protest letter, while grandpa sits nearby knitting a scarf with the slogan: "No more Hiroshimas!" In this rhetorical usage, to which we shall return, Hiroshima was removed from history and treated as a semimythic symbol of atomic menace. In the passive voice of the above passage, for example, the bomb *was dropped,* a city *was destroyed,* with no hint of *who* dropped the bomb or destroyed the city, or why. Such dehistoricizing characterizes not just juvenile peace literature but much of the rhetorical invocation of "Hiroshima" by antinuclear activists over the years.

But the peace activists' use of "Hiroshima" is only part of a multivocal discourse. At the other end of the spectrum, millions of Americans have over the years shared the view enunciated by President Harry S. Truman when he announced that a new weapon had destroyed the "military base" of Hiroshima: that the atomic bomb was a wholly justified means of defeating a treacherous foe. In Truman's geographic calculus, "Hiroshima" avenged "Pearl Harbor." More important, the argument runs, the bomb saved thousands of American lives that would have been lost in an invasion of Japan. In the immediate postwar period, most Americans embraced this view. As Eugene Rabinowitch, editor of the *Bulletin of the Atomic Scientists,* recalled in 1956: "With few exceptions, public opinion rejoiced over Hiroshima and Nagasaki as demonstrations of American technical ingenuity and military ascendency."

The lack of detailed visual evidence of the bomb's effects reinforced this initial positive response. Occupation authorities censored reports from the city and suppressed the more horrifying films and photographs of corpses and maimed survivors. Americans initially saw only images of the awesome mushroom cloud, which, as historian James Farrell has observed, presented the bomb as "a new but natural event, free of human agency." Indeed, Farrell notes, both elements of the quickly adopted compound term "mushroom cloud" suggested an unmediated natural phenomenon.

As we saw in chapter 3, Henry Stimson's 1947 *Harper's Magazine* article "The Decision to Use the Atomic Bomb" was part of a high-level effort to justify the use of the bomb and to define the meaning of Hiroshima and Nagasaki for Americans. The president of Harvard, James Conant, a key figure in nuclear policymaking, both prodded Stimson, the former secretary of war, to publish his apologia, and edited the first draft (ghostwritten by McGeorge Bundy, the son of Stimson's wartime aide Harvey Bundy) to make sure it struck the appropriate justificatory note. Despite much revisionist scholarship on Truman's decision, the mantra "the atomic bomb prevented an invasion and saved American lives" is still repeated, particularly by veterans convinced that it saved *their* lives.

This argument, more often expressed orally than in print, found its boldest—not to say its most reckless—articulation in Paul Fussell's 1981 *New Republic* essay "Hiroshima: A Soldier's View," later revised and published in Fussell's *Thank God for the Atomic Bomb* (1988). Having spent the spring and summer of 1945 as an infantryman in France expecting imminent reassignment to the Pacific, Fussell implied that only persons in his precarious situation had the moral authority to evaluate the A-bomb decision. He pointed out that one critic of that decision, political scientist Michael Walzer, was only ten years old in 1945. Revisionist historian Michael Sherry, he jeered, "was eight months old, in danger only of falling out of his pram." "The farther from the scene of horror," he said, "the easier the talk." "The invasion was definitely on," Fussell asserted, "as I know because I was to be in it." With equal assurance he dismissed the claim that postwar power calculations influenced Truman's decision: "Of course no one was focusing on anything as portentous as that, which reflects a historian's tidy hindsight. The U.S. government was engaged not in that sort of momentous thing but in ending the war conclusively, as well as irrationally Remembering Pearl Harbor with a vengeance."

Certainly the testimony of historical actors is useful, but Fussell moved beyond merely presenting combat soldiers' perspective to an anti-intellectualism that ignored a large body of scholarship directly relevant to his topic. Fussell notwithstanding, most historians now view Japan as teetering on the brink of collapse by early August 1945 and agree that postwar considerations did indeed influence Truman's decision. By ignoring or ridiculing the relevant scholarship, Fussell vastly oversimplifies highly complex issues. Nevertheless, his outburst merits notice as an articulation of a widely held and culturally influential view of the bomb decision—and of the meaning of Hiroshima.

But the more familiar cultural role of the word "Hiroshima" has been as a symbol of what must never happen again. It is the definitive object lesson of nuclear horror. If the bomb's full meaning in terms of human suffering did not at first grip the American consciousness, the fact of the destruction of a *city* certainly did. In this sense, Conant's view of the salutary effects of actually dropping the bomb on a crowded metropolis proved prescient. While the obliteration of two cities did not lead to international control, as Conant had hoped it would, it did help to inspire successive antinuclear campaigns. The cautionary theme emerged quickly. Within hours of Truman's announcement, radio commentators and editorial writers somberly noted that the fate of Hiroshima could await any American city. For many atomic scientists, euphoria over the Alamogordo test and the Hiroshima blast quickly changed to dismay as the human toll became apparent in classified reports. Many Manhattan Project veterans plunged into the campaign for international control with speeches and articles in which future Hiroshimas figured as the fearful alternative to the Acheson-Lilienthal plan. The image of Hiroshima as a preview of the atomic future gripped the American consciousness in August 1945, not to be dislodged thereafter.

John Hersey's *Hiroshima* (1946) deepened popular perceptions of the word's meaning: not just the destruction of "a city," but the death and suffering of scores of thousands of individual men, women, and children, each with his or her own story. A skilled journalist, Hersey translated the mind-numbing statistics into a gripping interwoven narrative of six individuals. Of the first 339 readers to write Hersey, 301 offered glowing praise. Such articles were essential, observed one, "to counteract the 4th of July attitude most people hold in regards to the atom bomb." Another described "a fitful, dream-laden night" after finishing the article. The San Francisco poet William Dickey later recalled his initial encounter with Hersey's work:

> I sat in the car one summer
> during lunch breaks at the frozen food plant, reading
> *Hiroshima*
> when it first came out. The picture that is in my mind
> is of people, vaporized by an unexpected sun
> and only their shadows left burned into the wall behind them.
> In their eyes it was shock of noon forever.

While Hersey's work deepened emotional sensibilities, it had a broader cultural impact as well. As William F. Buckley Jr. later observed, its appearance in a leading periodical "was both a spiritual acknowledgment of the transcendent magnitude of the event, and an invitation to analytical meditation on its implications." With his cool, understated prose, Hersey helped position Hiroshima at the core of the debate over nuclear weapons—past, present, and future. In successive campaigns against the nuclear arms race, "Hiroshima" offered a stark, one-word encapsulation of the alternative. In the lexicon of symbolic geography, it was often linked to Alamogordo and Bikini as representations of the three faces of atomic danger: modern science, the bomb itself, and more terrible instruments of thermonuclear destruction around the corner.

But the politico-cultural role of Hiroshima memories, brought to a keen edge by John Hersey in 1946, fluctuated over the years with the cycles of activism and quiescence in America's long encounter with the nuclear threat. As Michael Mandelbaum observed in 1984, "Americans have normally ignored the nuclear peril. Each episode of public anxiety about the bomb has given way to longer periods in which nuclear weapons issues were the preoccupation of the nuclear specialists alone." With the onset of the Cold War, the Soviet A-bomb test in 1949, and Truman's green light to the hydrogen-bomb project, Hiroshima and Nagasaki, like nuclear awareness in general, faded from public consciousness. Takashi Nagai's *We of Nagasaki* (1951) offered gripping testimony similar to that of Hersey's *Hiroshima,* but in an altered cultural and political climate, the work attracted much less attention.

As activism revived in the mid-1950s, now aimed at halting nuclear testing and its deadly by-product of radioactive fallout, campaigners again invoked "Hiroshima," this time as an example of the lethal effects of radiation and as a benchmark to demonstrate the escalating nuclear threat. The H-bomb, they repeatedly emphasized, was "a thousand times more powerful" than the Hiroshima bomb.

The resurgence of Hiroshima memories that accompanied the test ban campaign had many sources. Michihiko Hachiya's classic *Hiroshima Diary* (1955), published on the tenth anniversary of the bombing, brought the event sharply back into focus. So, too, did the "Hiroshima Maidens," twenty-five disfigured survivors of the blast who in 1955 arrived in the United States for reconstructive surgery. The project had originated with Kiyoshi Tanimoto, a Methodist minister featured in Hersey's *Hiroshima.* Promoted by the antinuclear activist Norman Cousins, editor of the *Saturday Review,* the project gained national attention on May 11, 1955, when Ralph Edwards's popular television show, *This Is Your Life,* showcased Tanimoto. The program evoked the terror of the bombing and featured a handshake between Tanimoto and Captain Robert Lewis, copilot of the *Enola Gay,* who gave the minister a check for the Hiroshima Maidens. Edwards invited viewers to contribute, and twenty thousand letters poured in. The 138 operations performed on the young women had mixed results, and the death of one from cardiac arrest under anesthesia clouded the project. But despite criticism in Japan about the "publicity stunt" and the U.S. State Department's reservations, the project helped restore Hiroshima to the forefront of memory while furthering the test ban cause.

As the test ban campaign intensified, so, too, did the cultural resonance of Hiroshima. "Nuclear War in St. Louis" (1959), the documentary-style narrative written by St. Louis antinuclear activists and published in the *Saturday Review,* was based on data from Hiroshima and

Nagasaki. Edita Morris's novel *Flowers of Hiroshima* (1959), an exploration of the bomb's physical and psychological effects, was the work of an antinuclear activist who with her husband operated a center in Hiroshima for atomic-bomb survivors. Betty Jean Lifton's documentary film *A Thousand Cranes,* on child victims of the bomb, appeared in 1962.

In a different medium, Alain Resnais's 1959 film *Hiroshima Mon Amour,* widely shown in the United States, portrayed a brief affair between a Hiroshima architect (played by Eiji Okada) and a French actress (Emmanuelle Riva) who has come to the city to make an antiwar film. With a screenplay by Marguerite Duras, *Hiroshima Mon Amour* juxtaposed grainy images of the devastated city of 1945 with the actress's recollections of a doomed wartime romance with a German soldier. As the images of destruction give way to scenes of bustling postwar Hiroshima, so the actress's wartime memories fade. But though the theme is one of forgetfulness, the atomic-bomb scenes early in the movie conveyed their own message to audiences of 1959.

In 1962, as the test ban campaign crested, Robert Jay Lifton, an associate professor of psychiatry at Yale, completing a year of research on Japanese youth, turned to a different project. Traveling to Hiroshima, Lifton interviewed some seventy *hibakusha* ("explosion-affected persons"). Reporting his findings and speculations in a 1964 article in *Psychiatry,* then more fully in *Death in Life: Survivors of Hiroshima* (1967) and subsequent writings, Lifton advanced the concept of "psychic numbing" to explain how survivors dealt with their bomb memories and their guilt over escaping death when so many had not. Broadening his focus, Lifton speculated that psychic numbing could also illuminate patterns of nuclear denial in entire societies that faced not the reality but the *possibility* of nuclear annihilation. "The encounter of people in Hiroshima with the atomic bomb has specific bearing upon all nuclear age existence," he wrote; "a better understanding of what lies behind this word, this name of a city, might enable us to take a small step forward in coming to terms with that existence."

Cultural historians tended to be critical of Lifton's bolder hypotheses for their lack of historical specificity. Lifton's model, they suggested, did not explain the alternating cycles of engagement, apparent apathy, and renewed engagement that characterized Americans' response to the bomb. It tended to reduce the complex texture of actual lived experience to a single procrustean psychological formula.

Nevertheless, Lifton's explanatory framework, and perhaps even more his clear moral engagement with nuclear issues, proved highly influential, as evidenced by the fact that *Death in Life* won the prestigious National Book Award for 1967. And in using Hiroshima as the template for the phenomenon of "psychic numbing," he kept the city in the forefront of awareness.

British science writer Jacob Bronowski, reviewing *Death in Life* in the June 1968 *Scientific American,* made the point explicitly. The psychic numbing exhibited by the *hibakusha* of Hiroshima, he suggested, could help explain the decline of nuclear awareness in the later 1960s:

> Twenty years is too long for sorrow, which time does not so much heal as blunt. . . . In that ebb tide of conscience . . . the moral impulse of 1945 has been eroded. We might have supposed that the sense of guilt had been washed away without a trace, had not Professor Lifton discovered it still haunting (of all people) the survivors of Hiroshima. The discovery gives his quiet and penetrating book a kind of cosmic irony that, more than any burst of righteousness, ought to shake us all out of our somnambulism.

Lifton and Bronowski thus contributed to what by 1967 had become a well-established practice of using Hiroshima heuristically. The fate of this city and its inhabitants in 1945, they suggested, could illuminate the larger psychic dynamics of the nuclear age.

The next surge of U.S. nuclear activism, arising in the late 1970s and cresting in the nuclear-freeze campaign of the early 1980s, once more brought Hiroshima to the cultural forefront. As in the late 1950s and early 1960s, activists again contrasted the puny Hiroshima bomb with modern nuclear firepower. The poet Sharon Doubiago, for example, noting that the missiles carried by one Trident submarine packed the explosive might of 2,040 Hiroshima-sized bombs, wrote in 1982:

> *Say the word Hiroshima*
> *Reflect on its meaning for one second*

Say and understand Hiroshima again.
Say and understand Hiroshima two thousand and forty times.

Testament, a 1983 television movie set in a northern California town as radiation from an attack on San Francisco creeps nearer, included an impaired Japanese-American boy called Hiroshi—a common Japanese name, but one obviously chosen for its historical resonance. The courses on nuclear war introduced on many college and university campuses in the early 1980s typically began with Hiroshima and assigned John Hersey's now classic work. For several years, Wisconsin antinuclear activists launched paper lanterns on the Mississippi River on August 6, emulating an annual commemorative ceremony held in Hiroshima on that date. Robert Penn Warren's 1983 poem "New Dawn" imagined the moment just after the Hiroshima blast, as the *Enola Gay* streaks away:

> Now, far behind, from the center of
> The immense, purple-streaked, dark mushroom that,
>   there, towers
> To obscure whatever lies below,
> A plume, positive but delicate as a dream,
> Of pure whiteness, unmoved by breath
>   of any wind,
> Mounts
>
> Above the dark mushroom,
> It grows high—high, higher—
> In its own triumphant beauty

Hiroshima also provided freeze advocates with a wealth of medical evidence. In 1947 the National Academy of Sciences, with funding from the Atomic Energy Commission, had launched a research project in Hiroshima on the bomb's radiological effects. By the 1980s, links had emerged between A-bomb exposure and heightened incidence of cataracts, leukemia, multiple myeloma, and other cancers. Persons exposed in utero or in infancy exhibited abnormally high rates of small head and body size and mental retardation. Such antinuclear organizations as Physicians for Social Responsibility (PSR) used this evidence to build opposition to nuclear weapons. References to Hiroshima dotted *The*

Final Epidemic, a 1981 collection of essays by scientists and physicians on the effects of nuclear war. At a 1982 Washington conference of educators concerned with the nuclear threat, Dr. Stuart Finch of Rutgers Medical School presented medical data from Hiroshima and expressed the hope that it would help deter "any future use of nuclear energy as an instrument of war."

Meanwhile, Robert Jay Lifton continued to explore the larger applicability of the Hiroshima experience. At the 1982 conference mentioned above, Lifton returned to his now familiar theme: "Hiroshima is important to us, it is a text for us, and we must embrace it and learn from it." He also stressed, however, that Hiroshima could be a misleading text. Just as the "small" 1945 bomb served to dramatize the vastly larger destructive power of the H-bomb, so Lifton contrasted the *hibakusha* experience with the incomparably greater psychological impact of global thermonuclear war. At Hiroshima, outsiders had quickly arrived to aid the survivors; in a full-scale thermonuclear war, little outside aid would be available—the whole world would become "Hiroshima." Beyond the statistics of death, destruction, and long-term medical consequences, Lifton contended, Hiroshima had introduced a new image into human self-awareness: a "radical sense of futurelessness" that undercut people's hopes of living on through their work or their offspring. After August 1945, such forms of symbolic immortality could no longer be presumed. All this, he suggested, lay embedded in the historical meaning of Hiroshima and set it forever apart from other cities that had become symbols of war's horror.

A variety of literary works helped reawaken Hiroshima memories in the late 1970s and early 1980s. Eleanor Coerr's children's book *Sadako and the Thousand Paper Cranes* (1979) told of a young bomb survivor, dying of leukemia, who tried to fold a thousand paper cranes, believing this would cure her. She died short of her goal, but her classmates completed the project. In 1982 Harper's issued a paperback edition of *Children of Hiroshima,* a long out-of-print collection of writings by youthful survivors. *Atomic Aftermath,* an anthology of short stories about Hiroshima by Japanese authors, published in Japan in 1983, appeared in U.S. bookstores in an English edition the following year. In Kim Stanley Robinson's 1984 science-fiction story, "The Lucky Strike," the *Enola Gay* crashes en route to Hiroshima, killing all aboard. The bombardier of the backup crew has qualms of conscience and releases the bomb far outside the city, with few casualties. This "demonstration shot" ends the war, but the bombardier is executed for disobeying orders. The activist climate of the early 1980s also assured a larger audience for Nasuji Ibuse's brilliant *Black Rain,* a novel exploring the long-term effects of the Hiroshima bombing on a young woman and her relatives. Originally serialized in a Japanese magazine, Ibuse's work appeared in English in 1967–68 in the small-circulation *Japan Quarterly,* but a 1985 Bantam paperback edition introduced it to a wider public.

PSR lecturers, instructors in college nuclear-age history courses, and organizers of nuclear-freeze rallies made effective use of films of Hiroshima's devastation and photographs of survivors, including the horrifying (and once suppressed) documentary film *Hiroshima-Nagasaki 1945.* But the visual evocations of Hiroshima came in many forms. The artist Robert Morris's ambitious 1981 installation "Journado del Muerto," a highly theatrical and politically engaged work exhibited by Washington's Hirshhorn Museum in 1981–82, included large photographs of Hiroshima in ruins and close-ups of burn victims, together with replicas of missiles and photographs of Manhattan Project scientists. *Unforgettable Fire* (1977), originally shown on Japanese television, offered gripping watercolors by Hiroshima survivors. In the preface, Japanese television executive Soji Matsumoto stressed its contemporary relevance: "Thirty years have passed since the A-bomb was dropped. The memory of how things were in Hiroshima at that time is being forgotten. It is therefore necessary to appeal to the people of Japan and of the world that there be 'No More Hiroshimas.' . . . To publish a collection of these pictures as a book is very significant, since we are living in a world in which the diffusion of nuclear weapons is threatening the existence of all humanity."

In 1982, a San Francisco publisher issued "I Saw It," cartoonist Keiji Nakazawa's comic book–format account of the bombing, which he had lived through as a boy. In 1985 came a U.S. edition of the powerful *Hiroshima Murals* by the Japanese artists Iri and Toshi Maruki. A 1986 documentary film about the Marukis and their work, by historian John Dower and filmmaker John Junkerman, received an Academy Award nomination. Toshi Maruki also wrote and illustrated *Hiroshima no Pika*

(1982), a children's book about a Hiroshima family caught in the bombing. Like Hersey's *Hiroshima,* these fresh visual images—from naive watercolors, comic books, and children's stories to works by well-known artists—restored human and historical immediacy to an image constantly at risk of being dulled by familiarity or drained of specificity by repeated use for symbolic or rhetorical purposes.

Aging Hiroshima survivors added emotional intensity to the nuclear-freeze campaign. Several *hibakusha* spoke at the June 1982 Central Park rally and participated in a television special on PBS. At a Washington forum arranged by Senate sponsors of the freeze resolution, four survivors recounted their memories. One, Dr. Mitsuo Tomosawa, fifteen years old in 1945, recalled lying awake all night on August 6 listening to the moans from a nearby hospital.

The attention generated in August 1985 by the fortieth anniversary of the atomic bombings of Japan also served to focus renewed attention on Hiroshima. *Time,* in the issue that featured a cover photograph of the mushroom cloud over Hiroshima, published a special section, "The Atomic Age," that included a lengthy essay about Yoshitaka Kawamoto, director of Hiroshima's Peace Memorial Museum and himself a bomb survivor. The Yale sociologist Kai Erikson, in a fortieth-anniversary essay in the *Nation,* reflected on Hiroshima's significance for the present: "We need to attend to such histories as this . . . because they provide the clearest illustrations we have of what human beings can do . . . when they find themselves in moments of crisis and literally have more destructive power at their disposal than they know what to do with. That is as good an argument for disarming as any that can be imagined."

Hiroshima memories were often explicitly used by freeze activists to awaken people to the nuclear danger. As the editor of *Atomic Aftermath* put it: "The short stories included herein are not merely literary expressions, composed by looking back at the past. . . . They are also highly significant vehicles for thinking about the contemporary world over which hangs the awesome threat of vastly expanded nuclear arsenals." More luridly, Peter Wyden's 1984 popular history *Day One: Before Hiroshima and After* contained a stark prefatory legend: "One millisecond after you read this, you and one billion other people could begin to perish."

From fall 1945 through the 1980s, in short, the role of Hiroshima in American memory was linked to the shifting rhythms of confrontation with the threat of nuclear war and with campaigns to reduce that threat. In an official environment marked by concealment and evasion, Hiroshima remained jaggedly real. The missiles were out of sight, underground or underwater, their horror only potential, but what happened at Hiroshima (and Nagasaki) could be instantly grasped and invoked: the print of a woman's blouse fabric burned into her skin, a battered pocket watch forever frozen at 8:15 A.M., shadowy images of human beings vaporized by the blast. Such evidence offered a permanent reminder that the nuclear threat was not simply potential or theoretical. An actual city had been destroyed, actual human beings had died. As Robert Lifton wrote in 1980, "We require Hiroshima and its images to give substance to our own terrors, however inadequately that city represents what would happen now if thermonuclear weapons were dropped on a human population. As much as we must decry the atomic bombings of Hiroshima and Nagasaki, it is possible that these cities already have contributed significantly to our tenuous hold on the imagery of extinction. They have kept alive our imagination of holocaust and, perhaps, helped to keep us alive as well."

Hiroshima memories subversively undercut the techno-rational vocabulary of the nuclear theorists. Artifacts from the shattered city, whether survivors' narratives, photographs or watercolors, or the prose of a Hersey or an Ibuse, cut through the strategists' bloodless prose. As Jean Bethke Elshtain has observed, "Human beings think most often in images; a terrible or delightful picture comes into our minds and then we seek to find words to express it, to capture it, to make it somehow manageable. Thus it is with the possibility of nuclear war. Our images are fixed. The scenes of utter destruction at Hiroshima and Nagasaki; two cities laid waste; people disappeared, remaining as shadows on cement or persisting in a terrible and painful twilight zone of lingering death from radiation."

But precisely how, if at all, did Hiroshima memories actually affect nuclear policy? Evidence of *direct* influence on policymakers is scant. When I asked former secretary of defense Robert McNamara in 1985 if he could recall any film, novel, painting, or other imaginative work that had shaped his view of nuclear war, he candidly replied: "No, I don't think so. . . . I was so associated with the Defense Department and writings related to the Defense Department that were . . . scientific, or technical, or political in character that I think it was those rather than artistic expression that influenced my thinking."

But the effect of Hiroshima images on grassroots opinion, and thus in defining the parameters within which policymakers operate, while difficult to quantify, has surely been important. From 1945 through the 1980s, antinuclear activists used films, photographs, paintings, journalistic accounts, firsthand testimony, fiction, and poetry based on the Hiroshima and Nagasaki bombings to convey the human meaning of nuclear attack, rouse awareness of the continuing threat, and build support for disarmament.

A few scholars, usually antinuclear activists themselves, have attempted to measure this effect. In the late 1960s, disturbed by widespread apathy about the nuclear threat, the sociologists Donald Granberg and Norman Faye showed the harrowing documentary film *Hiroshima-Nagasaki 1945* to students at the University of Missouri and then measured the results by questionnaire. After several screenings they reported: "It was our impression that the film was doing what we wanted: making concrete something that is ordinarily seen as an abstraction, and sensitizing people to the victims and potential victims of nuclear war." The questionnaires confirmed this impression: The film increased most students' "anxiety regarding nuclear war, decrease[d] the desire to survive a nuclear war, raise[d] the sufficient provocation threshold, and lower[ed] the maximum tolerable casualty threshold."

A decade later, a doctoral student in history at Illinois State University devised a teaching unit on Hiroshima and then tested its results on undergraduates at Illinois State and on students in an Indiana high school. The unit included films documenting the devastation and suffering caused by the Hiroshima bombing, as well as material on Truman's atomic-bomb decision. Results were mixed. For example, the high school students who completed the study unit showed greater agreement with the statement "War is not a satisfactory way to settle disputes" and heightened awareness of the "danger of nuclear extinction," but they also showed greater agreement with the statements "The dropping of the atomic bomb was a moral act" and "The bomb was used to save lives and shorten the war." Apparently the visual material from Hiroshima heightened apprehensions about a future nuclear war, while the print material convinced some students that Truman's 1945 decision was justifiable and wise.

Other research suggested that many factors shaped attitudes toward nuclear-related issues, and thus toward the meaning of Hiroshima. In an attitudinal study of 477 Californians conducted in 1969–70, for example, the sociologist Vincent Jeffries found the greatest readiness to accept nuclear war in defense of "our national interests" among the generation born before 1927, and the least readiness among those born between 1943 and 1949. In other words, Americans who had learned of Hiroshima as adults, and who had lived with the knowledge the longest, showed a higher tolerance for nuclear war than did those with no direct memories of the event. Such evidence casts doubt on the assumption, often implicit in the antinuclear camp, that the sharper the Hiroshima memories, the greater the aversion to nuclear war. For the older age group, news of the atomic bomb had come in a specific historical context: at the close of a popular war against a hated enemy. The younger and more vehemently antinuclear group in Jeffries's study, by contrast, knew Hiroshima and Nagasaki in a more culturally mediated, less historically rooted framework.

Political ideology as well as age affected how one read the Hiroshima story. For example, from the 1950s through the 1980s, antinuclear activists cited medical data from Hiroshima to show the long-term radiological hazards of nuclear war. But others used the same evidence for different purposes. In 1955, just as the "Hiroshima Maidens" arrived, the conservative *U.S. News & World Report* published an upbeat interview with Dr. Robert H. Holmes, director of the Hiroshima research project. The boldface summaries accompanying the interview conveyed the magazine's rose-tinted slant on the story: "In 190,000 survivors: 100 cases of leukemia, some mild eye cataracts, the next generation is normal . . . No genetic changes thus far in the first generation . . . Many within 2,000 meters did not show radiation effects . . . Only 15 percent of deaths due solely to radiation . . . Children of survivors appear happy, well adjusted . . . Usually fertility returns with general health . . . The Atomic Age is here, let's not be afraid of it."

Three photographs illustrated the story: a devastated Hiroshima in 1945; a healthy-looking young survivor being measured by a kindly researcher; and three generations of a Hiroshima family, including a boy born before August 1945, one in utero when the bomb fell, and one born after the bombing, all apparently in the bloom of health. At the time this cheerful feature appeared, *U.S. News* was faithfully echoing the government's theme that through civil defense, atomic war would not be so bad. The message was clear: Hiroshima had been destroyed, but recovery had been quick, and all was now well.

Religious beliefs influenced perceptions of Hiroshima's meaning as well. For some biblical literalists (see chapter 9), the annihilation of two cities and the prospect of a vastly more destructive nuclear war represented essential steps in a foreordained sequence of end-time events. In this providential narrative, Hiroshima functioned not as a cautionary example but as a sign pointing to a glorious future as God's divine plan unfolded.

Not only was the meaning of "Hiroshima" contested, but the repeated use of this image by activists always carried the risk of exploiting the actual event and of subordinating it to one's own agenda. Paul Goodman addressed this risk in a sardonic and doubtlessly unfair comment on *Death in Life:* "The survivors of Hiroshima, Dr. Lifton has shown us, are certainly fucked up, but they are not so fucked up as Dr. Lifton. After all, it is rather much to drop an atom bomb on people and then to come ask them how they feel about it." Hiroyuki Agawa made a similar point in his 1957 novel *Devil's Heritage,* which bitterly attacked the U.S. medical research project in Hiroshima for treating the *hibakusha* like guinea pigs. As Hiroshima memories were transmuted into literature and visual images, and as cautionary lessons were drawn from the ordeal of the city and its inhabitants, the reality of what actually happened on August 6, 1945—and why—sometimes seemed to blur. As the Japanese architect repeatedly tells the French actress in *Hiroshima Mon Amour,* when she describes the photographs and artifacts displayed in the city's atomic-bomb museum, "You have seen nothing."

The issues involved in manipulating and imaginatively reworking historical events can become exceedingly complex. In *Death in Life*, Lifton reflected perceptively on the symbolic status of Hiroshima, distinguishing it from other cities devastated by war: "When we hear reports about the Hiroshima bomb, our emotions are not exactly the same as when confronted with equivalent evidence of bomb destruction in London, Amsterdam, Hamburg, Dresden, or Tokyo. These cities, to be sure, convey their own messages of man's capacity and inclination to assault himself. But with Hiroshima (and her neglected historical sister, Nagasaki) something more is involved: a dimension of totality, a sense of ultimate annihilation—of cities, nations, the world."

Yet this unique emotional power rested in part on extracting "Hiroshima" from history and elevating it to the realm of metaphor. Lifton himself, with admirable motives, contributed to this process, as he made the psychically numbed *hibakusha* symbols of a numbed world. But he was hardly alone. Many who spoke out against nuclear war over the decades used memories of Hiroshima in this instrumental and potentially exploitative fashion. For some activists, invoking "Hiroshima" became a way to avoid hard thinking, an emotional button that could always be pressed, a high-voltage jolt to any discourse.

But the effect of this jolt could not always be anticipated. For some, it simply roused terror. The Australian pediatrician and antinuclear activist Helen Caldicott (see chapter 10) faced criticism in the early 1980s for what some saw as her irresponsible manipulation of fearful images. For others, repeated exposure to the "Hiroshima" image seems to have produced the very numbing that Lifton deplored. Symbols—even the most potent ones—decay over time. As Andy Warhol once observed: "When you see a gruesome picture over and over again, it doesn't really have any effect." Hiroshima was not immune to this process. As early as 1981 a journalist wrote: "Hiroshima has become one more historical cliché, like Lexington or the Battle of New Orleans." Contributing to this deadening process was the ubiquitous practice of using Hiroshima as a convenient date marker in book titles, as in *The American Past: A History of the United States from Concord to Hiroshima; Cold War America: From Hiroshima to Watergate;* or *From Harding to Hiroshima: An Anecdotal History of the United States from 1923 to 1945*. New imaginative works in different genres helped revive the image, but as 1945 receded further into the past, the loss of immediacy and resonance that eventually envelops even the most horrendous or momentous historical events inevitably took its toll.

Hiroshima, then, has clearly played a crucial and a complex role in post-war American thought and culture. The slowly dimming memory of August 6, 1945, has functioned as a palimpsest on which many different fears, expectations, and political agendas have been imprinted. In the realm of cultural imagery, "Hiroshima" has functioned as a kind of empty vessel, replicating the literal void created in August 1945. As one survivor described his experience immediately after the bombing: "I climbed Hijiyama hill and looked down. I saw that Hiroshima had disappeared. . . . Hiroshima just didn't exist." As the actual city was rebuilt and became the bustling metropolis of today, the "Hiroshima" of the imagination floated free, playing its ambiguous role in the first half century of our encounter with nuclear weapons.

And what of the future? Will Hiroshima gradually fade from our cultural and political discourse? The Cold War is over, and while nuclear menaces remain, the threats of the superpower nuclear arms race and of global thermonuclear holocaust have clearly ebbed. Under these circumstances, cultural attention to Hiroshima—always closely linked to broader cycles of nuclear awareness and activism—has diminished sharply. "For most people," the historian Richard Minear observed in 1993, "Hiroshima has become a non-issue."

Such judgments, of course, are relative. Hiroshima is obviously in no danger of vanishing entirely from the arena of either scholarly or cultural discourse. *Atomic Ghost,* a 1995 anthology of nuclear-age poetry contains several poems about the city and its fate. Evidence for its continued power to stir the imagination is provided, too, by a recent three-act play about Hiroshima by Walter A. Davis, a professor of English at Ohio State University. The drama begins realistically, in 1989 at an Ohio shopping mall, with a book-signing by Paul Tibbets, the *Enola Gay* pilot (an actual event in which Davis participated as a protester bearing a sign proclaiming: "Mourn: Hiroshima Was Mass Murder"). But it soon takes a surreal and expressionistic turn. Tibbets, kidnapped by a historian, recalls his career, and Truman, Stimson, Oppenheimer, and a group of *hibakusha* make appearances. In a hallucinatory final scene suggesting the enduring vitality of the Hiroshima memory, the historian shoots Tibbets, but the former pilot "rises from the dead and reclaims his spot and begins again to sign copies of his book for the queue in a never-ending process."

Meanwhile, however, the ranks of those who actually remember the events of fifty years ago grow thinner. In another twenty-five years, when "Hiroshima" is nearly as remote as "Verdun" is today, what will be its symbolic status? If the danger of nuclear war continues to lessen, it will probably join Carthage and Waterloo in the graveyard of dead symbols, drained of urgency, a shorthand convenience for textbook writers.

But given the human capacity for mischief and the nuclear knowledge that is now an ineradicable part of our mental storehouse, the chances seem at least even for Hiroshima to play its symbolic role again, as the world confronts the nuclear threat in some new form. In Helen Caldicott's epidemiological language, the virus has entered a latent phase, but it survives. We still live with the new reality encoded in that innocuous-looking metal sphere as it lazily drifted six miles down from the *Enola Gay* to a point 570 meters above the Aioi Bridge: epicenter of the nuclear age.

16

THE *ENOLA GAY* CONTROVERSY AND THE PERILS OF "HISTORICAL REVISIONISM"

As the fiftieth anniversary of the Hiroshima and Nagasaki bombings neared, a long-planned exhibit at the Smithsonian Institution's National Air and Space Museum (NASM) became the focus of a bitter dispute. As early as 1989, NASM officials had decided to mount a major exhibit on the atomic bombing of Japan, using as a centerpiece the *Enola Gay*, the plane that dropped the Hiroshima bomb. Developed by the museum curators in consultation with historians and other scholars, the planned exhibit included, along with the technical and military aspects of the story, exhibits conveying the bombs' immediate effects; the role of the atomic bomb in the early Cold War; and a spectrum of opinion about the decision to drop the bomb, pro and con. The critical voices included not only "revisionist" historians, but also respected figures of 1945—including political and military leaders—who at one time sharply questioned Truman's decision.

As word of the exhibit spread, vocal protest erupted from veterans' organizations and Washington politicians, who insisted that the exhibit be patriotic and celebratory. Reacting to the pressure, the Smithsonian scuttled its original plans, radically scaled back the exhibit, and eliminated all textual and visual material that could conceivably rouse controversy.

This heavily publicized dispute—one of several involving government-funded exhibits around the same time—attracted much attention among historians. When my friends

246

Edward Linenthal of the University of Wisconsin–Oshkosh and Tom Engelhardt of Henry Holt (in an earlier incarnation the editor at Pantheon with whom I had worked on *By the Bomb's Early Light*), asked me to contribute to a collection of essays on the controversy, I agreed.

This concluding chapter is adapted from the essay I wrote for that book, *History Wars: The* Enola Gay *and Other Battles for the American Past* (New York: Metropolitan Books, Henry Holt, 1996). Seeking to place the 1995 controversy in the larger context of America's nuclear history, it sums up my fifteen-year scholarly engagement with the bomb—and an episodic personal involvement that covers nearly my entire life.

———————

"AS SOON AS you bring historians in, you run into problems. You get distortions." This comment might well have been made by one of the Washington politicians or veterans' organizations that in 1994 attacked the Smithsonian Institution's plans for an exhibit observing the fiftieth anniversary of the atomic bombings of Hiroshima and Nagasaki. In fact, a Shinto priest at Japan's Yasukuni shrine to the nation's war dead made it while criticizing proposals to add an educational component to the shrine's commemorative functions. The priest's comment reminds us of the universality of the suspicions and hostility that historians can arouse when they become involved in matters about which great numbers of citizens feel passionate emotion.

With the fiftieth anniversary of the Second World War's final events behind us, we can perhaps begin to gain some perspective on the remarkable rancor the commemorative effort unleashed. The storm center of the controversy was, of course, the proposed *Enola Gay* exhibit at the Smithsonian's Air and Space Museum, which was to feature extensive treatment of the current state of historical scholarship on the decision to drop the atomic bomb and the ending of the war, as well as the bombs' immediate effects on the people of Hiroshima and Nagasaki and the long-term implications of the development and use of nuclear weapons. As early drafts of the exhibit text became known, the 180,000-

member Air Force Association, the 3-million-member American Legion, a small group calling itself the Committee for the Restoration and Proud Display of the *Enola Gay*, and conservative members of Congress, some genuinely offended, some sensing the issue's demagogic potential, denounced the exhibit as "anti-American," insensitive to veterans, and overly sympathetic to the bomb victims.

Enola Gay pilot Paul Tibbets blasted the planned exhibit as "a package of insults." President Bill Clinton, attuned as always to the ever-shifting currents of public opinion, aligned himself with the veterans' organizations and unqualifiedly endorsed the actions of his predecessor in the White House half a century before. Editorial opinion overwhelmingly lined up against the Smithsonian. The right-wing politician Pat Buchanan detected a sinister conspiracy in the whole affair: "In all this, friends, there is something less benign than the timidity of academics desperate to be seen as politically correct. What is under way is a sleepless campaign to inculcate in American youth a revulsion toward America's past."

Numerous meetings and extensive modifications in the exhibit text did no good. When the smoke cleared, the exhibit had been scrapped; the museum director had been forced out; and Republicans in Congress (joined by a few Democrats) were gearing up for hearings that for a time threatened to turn into a McCarthyite witch-hunt for the sinister and disloyal persons responsible for the shameful exhibit. When the Senate hearings began in May 1995, Chairman Ted Stevens (R.-Alaska) asked ominously: "What went wrong with [the Smithsonian's] management practices, and what steps have been taken to correct the revisionist and 'politically correct' bias that was contained in the original script?" (Though marked by senatorial rancor and ill-temper, the hearings actually proved fairly tepid and inconclusive.)

Reeling and shell-shocked, the Smithsonian mounted a cautious, scaled-back exhibit that simply portrayed the fuselage of the *Enola Gay* and videos of the crew, with minimal historical context on President Truman's decision, the bomb's human toll, or the long-term consequences of its use. The air force historian Richard P. Hallion dismissed the new exhibit as "a beer can with a label." Another historian, Kai Bird, modifying the chilling term "ethnic cleansing" coined by the genocidal Bosnian Serbs, spoke of a "historical cleansing" of the museum. A cartoon in the *Boston Globe* pictured a totally empty museum with an official announcing: "We're returning to our original mission as the air and space museum." An ironic outcome of the episode, as we shall see, was that far more Americans undoubtedly became aware of the scholarly debate over the atomic-bomb decision than would otherwise have been the case.

While the Smithsonian flap attracted the most public attention, the fiftieth-anniversary cultural struggle over the meaning of Hiroshima and Nagasaki erupted on other fronts as well, even in the arcane realm of postage-stamp design. Because of their ubiquity, lowly postage stamps represent a significant visual means by which a nation's historical perception can be shaped; hence the controversy over a proposed stamp commemorating the atomic bomb. The original U.S. Postal Service plan was to issue an "atomic bomb" stamp as part of an ongoing series recalling the major landmarks of World War II. Those planned for 1995 release would have noted the principal events of 1945, including the atomic bombings—certainly the most notable war events of that year apart from the actual capitulation of Germany and Japan.

Planning went forward in the recesses of the postal bureaucracy. At one point I received a telephone call from a historian friend who had been asked to evaluate an early draft of the proposed stamp. (I had not realized until then how carefully the planned textual and visual content of stamps is reviewed and evaluated. The Citizens Stamp Advisory Committee oversees the process, consulting specialists in various fields.) In this version, the mushroom cloud appeared to float in space, with no hint that a city lay below; the historical tag line read (as I recall) "Atomic Bombs Level Hiroshima and Nagasaki." I immediately agreed with my friend that some geographic features should be included to link the bomb to its target, and that the word "Level"—with its bland and even positive connotations (as in, "This is absolutely on the level")—be replaced by a more accurate phrase, perhaps "Atomic Bombs *Destroy* Hiroshima and Nagasaki." In fact, the message was softened, rather than made more precise, eventually evolving into: "Atomic Bombs Hasten War's End."

But the entire issue soon became moot. In December 1994, under protest from the Japanese government, with whom his administration was already embroiled in trade conflicts, President Bill Clinton canceled the much-revised stamp entirely, relegating it to the limbo reserved for postage stamps that never actually reach the nation's post offices.

In one way or another, across America, journalists, pundits, and ordinary citizens found themselves unexpectedly wrestling with the historical meaning of Hiroshima and Nagasaki in the angry months leading up to the fiftieth anniversary of the bombings. In a Gallup poll jointly commissioned by *USA Today* and the Cable News Network, 59 percent of Americans expressed approval of Truman's decision, with 35 percent disapproving. Fifty years after the event, Americans remained uncertain and deeply divided about its meaning.

THE BOMB AND THE "GOOD WAR"

Why do Hiroshima and Nagasaki stir so restlessly in our national psyche after the passage of half a century? Why do we have such trouble not only reaching consensus about how we should view these events, but even discussing them calmly and rationally? The fiftieth anniversaries of Pearl Harbor, D Day, Germany's surrender, and other landmarks of World War II were observed by public ceremonies and general agreement about their significance, but Hiroshima and Nagasaki generated only recrimination and angry debate.

One reason Americans have had so much trouble coming to terms with Hiroshima and Nagasaki lies in the fact that what our atomic bombs did to those cities did not lend itself to the prevailing public view of World War II as the "Good War"—a noble struggle against forces that threatened not only Western values but the survival of civilization itself. Particularly in the aftermath of the bitterly divisive Vietnam conflict, Americans looked back nostalgically to the 1941–45 period as a time when the nation's aims were unambiguously clear and just, a time when nearly all citizens had rallied behind the government. This show of unanimity was sharply at variance with the turmoil of the 1960s. No campus protesters in 1944 had accused Franklin Roosevelt of being a baby killer; no one had dubbed the conflict "Stimson's War." On the contrary, World War II symbolized a moment of shared national purpose and unity in a righteous cause. Studs Terkel's decision to call his 1984 oral history of

World War II *The "Good War"* helped fix this image in the public mind (though his quotation marks suggest certain reservations about the appropriateness of the popular label).

Of course, even without the atomic bomb, this version of the war elided some awkward realities. The Roosevelt administration's grudging response to the plight of European Jewry, the arrest and internment of Japanese-American citizens, black-market chiselers and wartime profiteers, the persistence of racism in the military and on the home front, the incineration of Dresden and other German cities, and the firebombing of Tokyo on the night of March 10–11, 1945 (in which more people may have died than initially perished at Hiroshima), all complicate the Norman Rockwell image of the war. Historians have explored these darker facets of the conflict, and some history textbooks deal with them, but they have not cast much of a shadow in either the public memory or the media's treatment of the war.

Although the popular image of the "Good War" involved selective memory and the downplaying of certain awkward facts, it also contained much truth. By and large—and certainly in contrast to the Vietnam era—1941–45 *did* mark a time of national unity and moral clarity. The bombings of Hiroshima and Nagasaki have long complicated this picture of a crusade pursued by a unified nation employing wholly justifiable means. They are the misshapen pieces that prevent us from completing the puzzle in an entirely satisfactory fashion. While some of the awkward realities noted above were partially redressed as the years passed—survivors of internment camps were belatedly compensated; a Holocaust memorial arose in Washington; the civil-rights movement erased some more blatant forms of racial segregation—the issues posed by the atomic annihilation of two cities remained contested terrain. As the semicentennial approached in 1995, the subject seemed further from closure than ever. Once the anniversary passed, the controversy no longer dominated the front pages, but the wounds and animosities remained.

The inability to fit the destruction of Hiroshima and Nagasaki comfortably into the "Good War" paradigm did not prevent those events from figuring prominently in the politics and culture of the Cold War years. As we saw in chapter 15, the very uncertainty that surrounded the meaning of those acts made them available for a variety of polemical uses.

President Truman initially presented the Manhattan Project as an awe-inspiring scientific achievement and defended his decision to drop the bomb as a fully justifiable action that had ended the war, saved untold thousands of American lives, and repaid Japan for Pearl Harbor, the Bataan Death March, and other atrocities. As the wartime enemy became the postwar ally, the argument that the bomb "saved American lives" was sometimes expanded to encompass the contention that it had also assured the survival of thousands of *Japanese* who would otherwise have been killed in the invasion that supposedly would have become inevitable had the bombs not been dropped. On the evidence of public opinion polls, a huge majority of Americans initially accepted this justification for the atomic destruction of Hiroshima and Nagasaki, and a majority—though a steadily dwindling one—has continued to do so ever since.

This popular endorsement of the government's rationale for the dropping of two atomic bombs in 1945 may in part reflect the public's insulation from the human consequences of that action. From the first, Washington officialdom, often with the support of the media, offered for public consumption a selective, sanitized version of these events. In Japan, as Wilfred Burchett's memoir *Shadows of Hiroshima* describes, U.S. Occupation authorities strictly censored photographs and films showing bomb victims. Medical data on both the short-term blast-and-fire effects and the long-term consequences of radiation exposure (not only at Hiroshima and Nagasaki but also at later nuclear test sites in the Marshall Islands and the American Southwest) were kept from the public or discussed in bland and general terms.

Preceding the publication of Henry Stimson's highly influential—and artfully misleading—1947 essay on the atomic-bomb decision, Stimson and his collaborators made their purpose crystal clear in letters discussing the article: to influence the larger public by reaching teachers and other opinion molders. In James Conant's words, the aim was to combat the "sentimentalism" that, if not resisted, could "have a great deal of influence on the next generation." Conant continued in a September 1946 letter to Harvey Bundy, "A small minority, if it represents the type of person who is both sentimental and verbally minded and in contact with youth, may result in a distortion of history." From such concerns the Stimson essay took shape, and in the years that followed, it played a significant role in sustaining the official version of events and warding off the inroads of "sentimentality" that Conant so feared.

Hollywood films like *The Beginning or the End* (1947), a ludicrously fictionalized version of the Manhattan Project and the decision to drop the bomb, and *Above and Beyond* (1953), a formulaic tale of marital discord and reconciliation supposedly based on the life of Paul W. Tibbets Jr., the pilot for the Hiroshima mission, further shored up the official government version. Since most Americans very much wanted to believe the fundamental message of all this propaganda—that dropping the bomb was essential, wholly justified, and fully in keeping with the nation's high war aims—the opinion-molding effort proved highly effective. The subtle process of creating a dominant hegemonic discourse (to use Gramscian analytic terms) unfolded in almost textbook fashion in the shaping of postwar American attitudes about the atomic bombing of Japan.

The campaign to forestall criticism of Truman's decision was part of a larger government and media effort throughout the early postwar period to soothe atomic fears and play down the true effects of nuclear weapons. In its August 11, 1951, issue, to cite only one of hundreds of examples, *Collier's* magazine published "Patty, the Atomic Pig." The article was based on an actual incident in which a piglet that was part of the "Noah's Ark" of goats, pigs, rats, and other experimental animals assembled for the July 1946 Operation Crossroads nuclear test at Bikini atoll was later found swimming in the radioactive waters of Bikini lagoon. The *Collier's* story, presented as a whimsical fairy tale, began: "Once upon a time, there was a great group of generals, admirals, scientists, newsmen and curious people who wanted to know more about atomic explosions." Illustrated with cute drawings, the story imagined Patty's thoughts before the blast ("'My, oh, my,' thought the little piglet, 'What will become of us all?'") and her adventures afterwards ("Patricia swam as fast as she could thrash her little legs, holding her nose high out of the water"). Patty not only survives (no scary radiation-exposure hazards here!) but grows to be a six-hundred-pound porker under the benevolent care of kindly scientists at the Naval Medical Research Institute at Bethesda, Maryland, and ends her days as a coddled exhibit in a zoo. Sugar-coated propaganda like this, part of a mountain of material in the

media that reinforced the government's version both of the 1945 bombings and of Washington's subsequent nuclear program, served to deflect
and neutralize serious scrutiny of the meaning and the implications of
atomic weaponry, past, present, or future.

For all its power and pervasiveness, however, the official justification
for the atomic bombing of Hiroshima and Nagasaki never achieved absolute dominance; a "counterhegemonic discourse" was present from the
beginning. The Hiroshima announcement immediately seized the attention of theologians, ethicists, pacifists, religious leaders, and other Americans concerned about the moral implications of war. Many pointed to
the instantaneous annihilation of that city, and then of Nagasaki, as the
logical (and chilling) culmination of a long twentieth-century process by
which the rhetoric of "total war" radically undermined the centuries-old
"just war" doctrine (most fully articulated by Roman Catholic theologians) that sought to shield civilian populations from the worst horrors
of wartime.

The distinction between civilians and combatants had broken down
badly in the course of World War II. The leaders of all the belligerent nations, including President Roosevelt, spoke the language of "total war,"
insisting that every citizen, not just the military forces, share in the
struggle. Wartime vegetable plots became "victory gardens"; the sale of
government bonds became "victory drives." Even children were milita-
rized. I vividly recall the pressures in my third- and fourth-grade classes
at Fairview Elementary School in Dayton, Ohio, to buy war stamps, col-
lect scrap metal, and turn in pencil stubs for the graphite they contained.
(Worried about what my pacifist parents might think of these efforts, I
once asked my teacher to return a pencil stub I had contributed, leading
her to ridicule me before the class as an "Indian giver.") If an entire society is mobilized for war, the argument goes, the entire society also becomes a legitimate target of war. President Truman, justifying the atomic
bombing of Hiroshima and Nagasaki, accurately pointed out that they
were centers of military production—just as were Seattle, Los Angeles,
and countless other U.S. cities.

The atomic bombing was only the culminating act in the breaking
down of a never wholly inviolable ethical barrier—already breached in
World War I by Germany's U-boat attacks on passenger ships, at Guer-

nica and Nanking in the 1930s, in the Nazi V-2 raids on London, Antwerp, and other Allied cities, and in the Allied firebombings of Hamburg, Dresden, Tokyo, and other teeming urban centers. But the Manhattan Project's technological gift to President Truman rendered the mass extermination of civilians vastly more efficient, radically raising the stakes of the larger postwar debate over the viability of the just-war doctrine and the ethical implications of the total-war language so enthusiastically embraced by wartime leaders.

Hiroshima and Nagasaki also naturally pervaded the discourse of antinuclear campaigners. As the Cold War deepened, and waves of nuclear fear periodically swept the nation, activists regularly invoked the two cities' names as reminders of what must never happen again. As we have seen, in each period of heightened nuclear fear and activism from 1945 onward, Hiroshima and Nagasaki did polemical duty as emblems of a global fate to be avoided at all costs.

HISTORIANS CONFRONT THE BOMB

Despite the use of "Hiroshima" and "Nagasaki" as shorthand points of reference in various public discourses, the origins and consequences of the actual atomic bombings of August 6 and 9, 1945, already obscured by official censorship and deception, grew steadily dimmer in public memory with the passing years. In the early 1960s, however, historians and other scholars turned a fresh eye on those events, and especially on President Truman's decision to authorize the military use of the awesome new superweapon at a moment when Japan's warmaking capability was near collapse. Their cumulative findings made it increasingly hard for informed observers to view this decision from the simplistic and uncritical perspective of 1945.

Even from the earliest moments of the atomic age, some had challenged the official rationale for dropping the bomb. In a radio broadcast on April 26, 1946, the liberal news commentator Raymond Gram Swing said: "I have heard it argued that the bomb dropped on Hiroshima was in effect dropped on the Russians, since it was not needed to bring the Japanese war to a close, but to establish and demonstrate a vast margin of power superiority over the Soviet Union." The British scientist P. M. S.

Blackett, a political radical, developed the same argument in a 1948 work, *Fear, War, and the Bomb.*

Not all the criticism came from the left. General Dwight D. Eisenhower and other military figures expressed reservations about Truman's resort to the atomic bomb, as did such Republican stalwarts as Herbert Hoover and John Foster Dulles. Indeed, in the 1950s it was often right-wing publications, such as William F. Buckley's *National Review,* that voiced retroactive skepticism about this momentous decision taken by a Democratic president.

But not until the 1960s did this dissident viewpoint gain a significant scholarly hearing. In *Japan Subdued: The Atomic Bomb and the End of World War II* (1961), Herbert Feis, while generally supportive of Truman's action, became the first major American historian to suggest that the calculations underlying it might have been more complex than official dogma conceded.

Only in 1965, though, with the publication of Gar Alperovitz's *Atomic Diplomacy,* did an American academic radically challenge the received interpretation. Why the rush to deploy the new weapon when some top leaders of Tokyo's wartime government were urgently signaling a desire to end the fighting, asked Alperovitz? Why did Washington so vehemently insist on "unconditional surrender" prior to August 6, only to do an abrupt about-face and accept a whopping condition—Emperor Hirohito could remain on his throne—as soon as the bombs were dropped?

Any meaningful response to these questions, Alperovitz concluded, required attention to broader strategic and economic considerations. A dramatic demonstration of the atomic bomb's destructive power, he suggested, promised to introduce a potent new factor in U.S. dealings with the Soviet Union, a wartime ally already shaping up as a postwar adversary. Doubtless the passions of war, the impulse to avenge Pearl Harbor, Japanese atrocities, and the appeal of ending the war with a fantastic display of American firepower rather than by painstaking negotiations (which would later have to be explained to a restive public) all played their role—especially after the desperate and bloody Okinawa campaign of March–June 1945. But other considerations entered the picture as well, considerations that scholars began to probe with increasing insistence.

Despite Truman's later claims, suggested Alperovitz (and soon other scholars as well), the grim prospect of a land invasion of the Japanese main islands, tentatively scheduled to begin November 1, was not necessarily paramount in the president's mind in late July and early August 1945. He was in fact, they argued, more concerned with how, precisely, the war might be ended in the coming few weeks or even days. If a spectacular American blow demonstrating an awesome new secret weapon, not Russia's imminent declaration of war (pledged by Stalin at Yalta and again at Potsdam), were seen as having forced Japan's capitulation, America's role in postwar Japan and in Asia, as well as Washington's bargaining posture vis-à-vis the Soviet Union in shaping the politics and the economy of postwar Europe, might be vastly enhanced.

Combing the primary sources, Alperovitz—and an impressive group of historians that eventually included Martin Sherwin of Tufts University; Barton Bernstein of Stanford University; Robert Messer of the University of Illinois–Chicago; Michael Sherry of Northwestern University; J. Samuel Walker, historian of the U.S. Nuclear Regulatory Commission; James S. Hershberg, director of the Cold War History Project at the Woodrow Wilson International Center; such independent scholars as Stanley Goldberg and Kai Bird; and a number of others—documented a variety of considerations that clearly seemed relevant to a full understanding of Truman's decision. Stanley Goldberg, for example, emphasized that Truman and his inner circle of atomic advisers, including General Leslie R. Groves, majordomo of the Manhattan Project, feared an angry public and congressional reaction if they failed to use a new weapon that they had secretly spent billions to develop. Hershberg, in a massively researched biography of James Conant, a member of the Interim Committee that advised Truman on atomic matters, revealed that the high-minded university president favored demonstrating the bomb's power in the most awesome possible way—by destroying a city—as the best hope of rallying world support for postwar international control of atomic energy.

Meanwhile, John Dower's *War without Mercy: Race and Power in the*

Pacific War (1986) documented the racism that pervaded America's anti-Japanese wartime propaganda (as well as Japan's anti-American wartime propaganda). *Eagle against the Sun: The American War with Japan* (1985) by the historian Ronald Spector (a Vietnam veteran and member of the U.S. Marine Corps Reserves) similarly emphasized the centrality of racism on both sides. This, too, it seemed, must be factored into the equation when evaluating Truman's readiness to drop two atomic bombs on a defeated Asian nation.

Washington's original justification for the A-bomb decision arose in the specific context of the immediate postwar period, when wartime passions still ran high, and the Cold War and the nuclear arms race were just taking shape. The post-1965 wave of critical scholarship about the bomb was shaped by a very different historical moment. Alperovitz, born in 1936, represented a younger generation of historians who came of age politically in Cold War America, when the bomb (now called a "thermonuclear weapon") evoked not so much the memory of victory over Japan as thoughts of nuclear tests, radioactive fallout, a grim struggle with the Soviet Union, and the threat of a world-destroying thermonuclear holocaust. As an undergraduate at the University of Wisconsin, Alperovitz encountered the historian William Appleman Williams, who was radically revising diplomatic history by insisting on the primacy of economic factors—especially the influence of corporate capitalism—in shaping U.S. foreign policy.

After earning an M.A. in economics at Berkeley and a stint as legislative assistant to Robert Kastenmeier, a Wisconsin congressman known for his antimilitarist views, Alperovitz entered a doctoral program in political economy at Cambridge University, where he read with economist Joan Robinson, who, like Williams, stressed the interplay of politics, economics, and diplomacy. Alperovitz's 1963 dissertation (published two years later by Simon and Schuster) was a product of all these experiences. Reflecting Joan Robinson's influence, his initial thesis topic had not been the atomic-bomb decision but wartime Washington's economic and political planning for postwar eastern Europe. This led him first to the larger topic of how Washington policymakers viewed the Soviet Union, and then to how these postwar calculations influenced the Truman administration's strategy for ending the Pacific war. The specific issue of the atomic bomb was originally quite peripheral to his research focus.

When *Atomic Diplomacy* appeared in 1965 (timed by the publisher to coincide with the twentieth anniversary of the Hiroshima and Nagasaki bombings), reviewers and scholars at once recognized it as a thoroughgoing challenge to a version of the atomic-bomb story that for two decades had enjoyed broad public assent and minimal critical scrutiny. The book and the times were made for each other. Early in 1965, President Lyndon Johnson massively escalated the Vietnam War—and he did so with a decision to launch an intensive bombing campaign against North Vietnam (after running as a peace candidate against Barry Goldwater a few months earlier). That year saw the first major stirrings of an antiwar movement that soon came to question the official version of the war and the bombing campaign against the North Vietnamese. It was a propitious moment, indeed, to probe the motives that might have led an earlier American president to call tremendous destructive power down on an Asian people.

Not surprisingly, the critical reassessment of the A-bomb decision launched by Alperovitz steadily gained ground after 1965 within academia, especially among younger scholars, as a succession of events eroded the credibility of public officials and their pronouncements: the optimistic bulletins that flowed from Vietnam as the body bags and the shocking television images multiplied; the New Left's ideological assault on "the Establishment"; Henry Kissinger's secret bombing of Cambodia and wiretapping of his own staff; and, of course, the tangle of official crimes collectively known as Watergate, which ended with a discredited Richard Nixon driven from office.

The timing of Martin Sherwin's *A World Destroyed: The Atomic Bomb and the Grand Alliance* (1975), another major contribution to the scholarly critique of the atomic-bomb decision, further illustrates the link between the reassessment of Truman's action and the broader political climate. Like *Atomic Diplomacy,* Sherwin's book was based on his Ph.D. thesis, completed at UCLA in 1971 as the controversy over the Vietnam War raged, and revised for publication as newspaper headlines screamed of secret Cambodia bombings, the explosive Pentagon Papers, the

Watergate hearings, and a president's forced resignation. These were not times that fostered the uncritical acceptance of official versions of public events! Indeed, the political-cultural climate of 1965–75 almost demanded the skeptical reassessment of accepted historical interpretations and even of the fundamental assumption—a legacy of World War II, really—that the government's version of the truth was ipso facto trustworthy, disinterested, and reliable.

All this unfolded just as new methodological approaches and new areas of research were transforming the history profession. The rethinking of the Hiroshima-Nagasaki bombings was, in fact, only part of a much broader process whereby an older historiography that had focused mainly on elites—political, military, social, intellectual, or cultural—gave way to a "new social history" more attuned to the experiences of ordinary people, particularly the underclass, and more critical of the actions of policymakers, statesmen, corporate leaders, generals, and others who wield power. In the phrase of the day, the new social historians, some using computer-based quantitative techniques, proposed to study history "from the bottom up." In diplomatic history, the focus shifted from treaties and conferences to the larger economic, cultural, and ideological framework within which foreign-policy processes unfold.

These new historiographical emphases, coupled with the broader political and cultural currents that flowed across America in the wake of Vietnam and Watergate, encouraged a skeptical reassessment of the received wisdom on many topics. Inevitably this reassessment included attention to the events of August 6 and 9, 1945, that had taken the lives of well over one hundred thousand human beings (including long-term deaths related to radiation exposure) and laid the groundwork for an ever more dangerous nuclear arms race between the United States and the Soviet Union.

ATOMIC BOMB SCHOLARSHIP IN THE ARENA OF PUBLIC OPINION

By around 1980, the reassessment of the A-bomb decision launched by Alperovitz and others had been generally welcomed as stimulating and provocative. Within the guild, it was widely viewed as another manifestation of the familiar process by which historians continually reassess the past and question received interpretations. Debated at scholarly conferences and dissected in journal articles, the new analytic hypotheses were beginning to make their appearance in college textbooks and in classroom lectures.

For most Americans, however, historians' debates on this topic remained arcane and remote, a matter of no concern. While the work of Alperovitz, Sherwin, and others certainly had some broader impact through the major newspapers, intellectual reviews, and journals of opinion, the received wisdom about the justice of the atomic-bomb decision generally retained its sway in grassroots America. For those who had embraced the "Good War" paradigm, any questioning of Truman's oft-repeated justification of his action challenged an image of World War II that had become a cornerstone of national self-identity. If the motives for dropping the atomic bomb could be probed and problematized by historians, what part of the American past was safe from skeptical critical scrutiny? As historian Michael Kammen wrote in the aftermath of the Smithsonian debacle and other cultural battles involving conflicting interpretations of the American past, "Historians become notably controversial when they do not perpetuate myths, when they do not transmit the received and conventional wisdom, when they challenge the comforting presence of a stabilized past"—and, it may be added, when news of what they are up to finally gets out. Perhaps no issue of the postwar era confirmed this generalization more dramatically than the angry struggle over who would finally determine the meaning of Hiroshima and Nagasaki: historians or "the people."

Exacerbating the populist (or pseudopopulist) reaction against the scholarship of the atomic-bomb historians was the widespread practice (adopted by many historians as well as by nonhistorians) of attaching to such scholarship the label "revisionist." Historians *were* engaged in a process of revision, of course, but when the term was applied exclusively to this one group, it suggested that they were deviants who had departed from accepted norms of professional practice. In fact, these scholars were revisionists only in the sense that all good scholars are revisionists, continually questioning and revising standard interpretations on the basis of new evidence, deeper analysis, or the fresh perspectives offered by the passage of time.

Allusions to "*the* revisionist school" of atomic-bomb historians also conveyed a certain conspiratorial implication, as though these scholars had colluded, presumably with sinister or subversive motives, to concoct and foist on an unsuspecting public a single, agreed-upon new version of history. In fact (as anyone familiar with American intellectual life would assume), the "revisionists" were a diverse and contentious crew, representing a wide range of often conflicting viewpoints that were based on different research findings and different weighings of the facts. Barton Bernstein, for example, criticized Gar Alperovitz for talking of Truman's "decision" to drop the bomb when in fact, in Bernstein's view, Truman inherited from the Roosevelt administration both the assumption that the bomb would be used and a tolerance for destroying entire cities. As a new president in office for only a few months, Bernstein argued, Truman had simply fallen back on inherited assumptions and practices when confronted with the successful Alamogordo test. Bernstein also took both Alperovitz and Sherwin to task for treating as a virtual certainty the possibility that the war could have been ended well before the planned invasion date of November 1, 1945, without the atomic bomb. While agreeing that other alternatives were available and should have been tried, he remained skeptical about whether or not they would have succeeded in forcing Tokyo's surrender. Other historians criticized Alperovitz, Sherwin, and others who were assessing the A-bomb decision for concentrating too much on U.S. sources and paying insufficient attention to the Japanese archives.

Certainly, most historians who addressed the question agreed that the factors shaping Truman's actions in the war's climactic days were too complex to be summed up in a single, easily recited formula ("It saved American lives, ended the war, and repaid Japan for Pearl Harbor")—a formula that, if not demonstrably false, was demonstrably inadequate. But beyond this, one would be hard put, despite accusations to the contrary, to identify a monolithic "revisionist" position. The process of historical reassessment on this subject is continually evolving, as it is on every topic of sufficient complexity to attract historians' interest, with a variety of arguments and hypotheses in play at any given moment.

That the fury over historians' treatment of the Hiroshima-Nagasaki bombings exploded so spectacularly in 1994–95 was linked, I think, not only to the fiftieth-anniversary observances, but also to the fact that U.S. society was racked by new kinds of cultural conflict and political turmoil in the 1990s. Conditioned by four decades of black-and-white Cold War thinking, many Americans in the aftermath of the Soviet Union's collapse seemed to transfer the same outlook to the domestic sphere. From this perspective, the angry denunciations of the "revisionists" as unpatriotic and contemptible, and the refusal to grant their findings any shred of legitimacy, became simply another manifestation of a political climate marked by inflammatory, polarizing rhetoric.

In this climate, the low-level irritation felt by many ordinary citizens, especially older Americans and World War II veterans, at historians who questioned an article of national faith was exacerbated and amplified by a vocal army of jingoistic politicians, editorial writers, and radio talk-show hosts who saw this as another emotion-laden wedge issue—like attacking the National Endowment for the Arts for promoting obscenity; or advocating Constitutional amendments permitting school prayer, requiring a balanced budget, and banning flag desecration. By such issues the New Right defined itself, rallied the faithful, and demonized its enemies.

Conservative presidential aspirants made sure the issue would remain divisive and inflammatory. Senator Bob Dole, in a red-meat speech to the American Legion in September 1995, denounced the Smithsonian's original *Enola Gay* exhibit as another example of the insidious work of "intellectual elites" and other "arbiters of political correctness" who were contemptuous of patriotism, scornful of veterans and their sacrifices, and intent on waging "war on traditional American values."

But even in this volatile climate, popular attitudes toward the atomic-bomb decision continued to resist easy generalization. Over the years, different groups had diverged markedly in their judgments about Truman's action. So, too, in the 1990s. The aggregate results of a 1995 Gallup poll concealed important variations in opinion on the basis of gender, race, and age. The rate of approval of Truman's action, for instance, was notably higher for men than for women. (A similar gender gap emerges in almost every poll dealing with military issues, including defense spending, the use of force to achieve U.S. aims, armed interventions like the Persian Gulf War, and so forth.) As to race and ethnicity—

no surprise here—a significantly higher percentage of whites approved the atomic-bomb decision than did African Americans, Hispanics, or Asian Americans. From the first, nonwhite groups had raised the issue of racism in the A-bomb context and posed awkward questions about whether President Truman would have dropped the atomic bomb on Germans if the European war had continued into the summer of 1945. (Given the firebombing attacks that turned German cities into crematoriums, it is by no means clear that Truman would have refrained from using the bomb on white Europeans—but the nagging What if? can never be answered with certainty.)

Another key division that shows up in public-opinion data as early as the 1960s, and again quite sharply in the 1995 poll, is a generational one. Broadly speaking, as we have seen, the older generation that remembered World War II and that initially associated the atomic bomb with Japan's surrender and frenzied V-J Day celebrations tended to be strongest in the conviction that dropping the bomb was justified. Succeeding generations, having very different associations with nuclear weapons and no direct memories of the war, tended to be more critical of Truman's action.

Of course, none of these correlations of gender, race, or age is absolute. Other factors, including religious beliefs, political views, and variations in individual temperament, enter in as well. Any generalization about how "the American people" have viewed these issues remains open to qualification and skeptical challenge.

It would be misleading to frame the *Enola Gay* controversy as a simple conflict between historians (or academics) on the one hand and the general public on the other. Some historians continued to accept the Truman administration's justification for dropping the bomb as sufficient; a few attacked the "revisionists" as scornfully as any conservative politician or outraged veteran. Academia is no tranquil domain cut off from the passions and ideological disputes that agitate the larger society.

Nevertheless, broadly speaking, the controversy of 1994–95 did expose a considerable chasm between the methodology of historians and the way many Americans think about the past, especially that portion of it falling within their own experiences and memories. Historians con stantly challenge the received wisdom and established interpretations of events. This is what we do. Usually this process unfolds in scholarly journals or at professional gatherings out of the public eye. As new interpretations filter into textbooks and classrooms, they may eventually modify the general public's historical understanding, but the shift is typically gradual and almost imperceptible.

Occasionally, however, the disjuncture between the scholarly approach to history and the public's highly personal, even semimythic view of the past is exposed with stark clarity, usually when the ongoing process of historical revision and reassessment focuses on an issue about which many citizens feel passionately, or that has great patriotic resonance. Such a moment occurred in 1913, for example, when Charles A. Beard argued in his *Economic Interpretation of the Constitution of the United States* that the Founding Fathers had in fact pursued public policies that served their pecuniary interests. Beard was roundly vilified. He had questioned the motives of patriots revered by every schoolchild! This controversy over an issue of historical interpretation unfolded at a moment of highly charged ideological conflict, as conservatives and reformers battled over the government's role in regulating capitalism.

A similar phenomenon, I suspect, underlay the reaction, ranging from annoyance to rage, roused by the historical profession's ongoing examination of the atomic-bomb decision—a long-term scholarly project that the *Enola Gay* controversy suddenly thrust into public view. As the Air Force Association demanded in one of many press releases aimed at discrediting the Smithsonian exhibit, "All revisionist speculation should be eliminated." The Shinto priest at Japan's Yasukuni war shrine could not have put it better.

This reaction was undoubtedly intensified by the fact that August 1945 remained a part of older Americans' living memory. As Edward T. Linenthal pointed out in a perceptive essay in the February 10, 1995, *Chronicle of Higher Education,* the fiftieth anniversaries of great public events, the "last hurrah" for most survivors, tend to bring out in a particularly volatile way the continuing tension between the commemorative impulse and critical historical scholarship.

This particular fiftieth anniversary cast in bold relief a gap that had been developing for years between the American historical profession and a significant portion of the American people. I myself had become acutely aware of this discontinuity in the early 1980s when, as the nuclear-freeze campaign unfolded and I pursued my research on the atomic bomb's cultural fallout, I often lectured to community groups. When asked about Truman's A-bomb decision (as I almost invariably was), I would discuss the work of Alperovitz, Sherwin, and others as interpretive approaches that merited consideration. But often the questioner would have none of it, especially if he (usually it was a male) remembered World War II, and most especially if he was a veteran convinced—beyond all argument—that the atomic bomb had saved his life.

In August 1995, when I published an essay in the *Chronicle of Higher Education* reviewing the controversy over the A-bomb decision and (as I thought) offering a fairly balanced, uncontroversial assessment of the cultural issues and faultlines it had exposed, the response was revealing. While fellow historians and other scholars reacted positively, the scattered responses from outside academia proved uniformly hostile. One early-morning telephone call, for example, came from a North Carolinian who, though born after the war, was the son of a veteran who had fought in the Pacific. My caller therefore insisted that he also owed *his* life to the atomic bomb, since if his future father had died in an invasion of Japan, he, the son, would never have been conceived. To him, any questioning of the assumption that the atomic bomb "saved American lives" represented a kind of existential challenge.

Shortly after this call, a Louisiana investment counselor wrote a sarcasm-filled letter that attacked me as a typical "off-the-wall," anti-American academic eager to besmirch the United States while glossing over all of Japan's misdeeds. He concluded with this thrust: "I await your political comments on the justification of the war between Athens and Sparta. I am sure that you have an opinion on this and I welcome your comments."

Those who articulate such responses are not interested in debate. For them, unquestioning support for Truman's atomic-bomb decision becomes a test of patriotism. In fact, they reject the legitimacy of the historical enterprise. What right have you, a mere academic, such critics are really asking, to publish dissenting views on matters about which true patriots cannot possibly hold differing opinions? As my Louisiana correspondent put it: "*No one can doubt* that this horrible weapon saved American lives" (emphasis added). That precisely this assertion is, in fact, a matter of considerable doubt, and certainly open to historical inquiry and discussion, was a position whose legitimacy he simply could not acknowledge. He was left, therefore, with no alternative but to impugn the character and the integrity of those who do hold it. The confrontation between popular memory and patriotic affirmation, on the one hand, and the norms of historical research and argument on the other, could hardly be more starkly revealed.

When even columnists (and World War II veterans) like Russell Baker of the *New York Times* and the late Mike Royko of the *Chicago Tribune,* normally bemused observers of the passing scene, were reduced to sputtering fury that anyone—especially anyone who did not actually fight in the war—could even hint that the atomic-bomb decision involved motives beyond those publicly proclaimed by Truman, one realizes the depths of the ideological and generational chasms exposed by this debate.

Even the Smithsonian's secretary, I. Michael Heyman, in a postmortem on the canceled *Enola Gay* exhibit, gave the back of his hand to the historians who had helped plan it, and ignored his institution's mandate to promote "the increase and diffusion of knowledge," as he abjectly capitulated to the exhibit's detractors: "In this important anniversary year, veterans and their families were expecting, and rightly so, that the nation would honor and commemorate their valor and sacrifice. They were not looking for analysis, and, frankly, we did not give enough thought to the intense feelings such an analysis would evoke." Whether the "intense feelings" aroused by thoughtful analysis and a broader diffusion of the relevant scholarship might in the long run have been therapeutic as Americans continue to struggle with the meaning of Hiroshima and Nagasaki, he did not consider. In the face of assumptions like this—that "analysis" and "feelings" are mutually exclusive, and that when passions run high, analysis must give way to feelings—it is understandable that historians, with their boring insistence on research and their readiness to question established interpretations and mythic versions of the past, should be viewed as a threat.

For all the rancor it generated, the *Enola Gay* controversy was only the latest manifestation of a half-century process by which the events of August 6 and 9, 1945, figured rhetorically in a variety of public discourses. For many, the obliteration of Hiroshima and Nagasaki brought victory in a just cause, spared countless American lives, repaid the treachery of Pearl Harbor, and demonstrated a powerful nation's scientific and technological mastery. For others, it was needless slaughter, symbolizing the utter collapse of all ethical restraints in modern warfare. Still others viewed it as a calculated move on a larger strategic chessboard. For antinuclear activists, it was the ultimate warning.

In the fiftieth-anniversary year, with the cultural mood both retrospective and ideologically charged, attention focused once again on the original events in all their jagged immediacy. In the process, many citizens grasped—perhaps for the first time—that for several decades, scholars had been questioning the official justifications originally advanced by President Truman and endlessly reiterated thereafter. The result was not thoughtful discussion and the search for a new, more historically defensible consensus, but recrimination and accusations of bad faith and disloyalty. The Smithsonian exhibition simply provided a context for this unfolding cultural psychodrama. The Smithsonian's location in the fishbowl of Washington guaranteed that the drama would be played out with shameless political posturing and the glare of media publicity. Though muted, the controversy will probably persist so long as politicians see capital in it and vast numbers of Americans—especially World War II veterans—remain convinced that the atomic bomb was an essential, wholly justifiable means to a righteous end. But historians, too, have their convictions and commitments, and one ought not underestimate the long-term power of critical historical inquiry, even on emotion-laden topics. Whatever the ultimate resolution of this divisive and unhappy national quarrel, Hiroshima and Nagasaki seem likely for the foreseeable future to remain the Banquo's ghost of World War II, perennially challenging comforting generalizations about the conflict and underscoring the disparity between the mythic past inscribed in popular memory and the past that is the raw material of historical scholarship.

INDEX